**FOR
ALISON**

*The Murder
of a Young
Journalist and
a Father's Fight
for Gun Safety*

FOR
ALISON

ANDY PARKER
WITH BEN R. WILLIAMS

FOREWORD BY
SENATOR TIM KAINE

APOLLO
PUBLISHERS

For Alison: The Murder of a Young Journalist and a Father's Fight for Gun Safety
Copyright © 2019 by Andy Parker

Apollo Publishers books may be purchased for educational, business, or sales
promotional use. Special editions may be made available upon request. For
details, contact Apollo Publishers at info@apollopublishers.com.

Visit our website at www.apollopublishers.com.

Library of Congress Cataloging-in-Publication Data is available on file.

Cover and interior design by Rain Saukas.

Print ISBN: 978-1-948062-32-9
Ebook ISBN: 978-1-948062-33-6

Printed in the United States of America.

CONTENTS

———

This book is for all the members of the club that no one wants to join.

FOREWORD BY

SENATOR TIM KAINE

I have known Andy Parker and his family for many years. I campaigned with him when he once ran for office and got to know his daughter, Alison, when she served as a dynamic television news reporter in Roanoke, Virginia. Her tragic death—shot along with her cameraman, Adam Ward, on live television by a disturbed former employee of their station—still haunts our state.

Andy has turned his boundless energy and passion to the important task of promoting meaningful steps to reduce gun violence. And he is doing this for Alison.

This is a painful story of loss and violence. It is also a story of indifference. Andy's frustration with legislative inaction and the empty words of leaders brims over in these pages, just as they do when you meet him in person. As a grieving dad with a powerful and earned sense of righteous indignation, he doesn't mince words. Sometimes he makes folks, even his own friends and family, uncomfortable with the way he expresses his outrage. But he is candid in acknowledging this personal challenge and affectionately points out how his wife,

Barbara, often pulls him back when he goes too far. And after all, who among us can fault a suffering father for candidly expressing the raw emotion that still wells up every morning when he awakens to find his daughter gone?

Of course, Andy's larger point—that gun violence is out of control and we have lacked the will to do simple things to reduce this scourge—is correct. We need his voice—and the voices of all survivors—pushing, encouraging, and even shaming us until we take appropriate steps to keep people safe.

Alison was a wonderful and talented young journalist. Her life continues to inspire Virginians, and her tragic death has helped change political will in the state where the NRA has its headquarters. In Virginia, the NRA rankings of candidates used to be all-powerful, and getting an "F" from the group was seen as ending any chance of electoral success. Now, an "F" ranking from the NRA is a badge of pride for many candidates and poses no challenge in winning a campaign.

We all know an Alison, a person whose life has been cut short by needless gun violence. Possibly it was in a high-profile crime like a mass shooting or Alison's own death on live television. Maybe it was in a crime in a nearby neighborhood, barely covered by any media. Or an accidental shooting, such as when a child finds an unsecured gun in a drawer or on a shelf. Or a suicide driven by momentary or chronic despair. Or a murder brought on by domestic violence. Each of these deaths is a tragedy, and each calls out to us to act.

Evil exists not just because of its perpetrators. It exists because of bystanders. Will we continue to be bystanders to gun violence? That is the question posed by Andy Parker. The question is a painful one, but it has to be asked, and it has to be answered.

PROLOGUE

On August 26, 2015, my daughter, Emmy Award–winning reporter Alison Parker, was murdered on live television.

She had gone to Bridgewater Plaza in Moneta, Virginia, with fellow WDBJ employee and cameraman Adam Ward. They had gotten up bright and early to interview Vicki Gardner, the head of the local chamber of commerce. This was going to be a feel-good piece about how many great things were coming to the Smith Mountain Lake area. It was something for folks to watch in the background as they ate their bagels, sipped their coffee, and checked Facebook on their phones before heading to work.

Instead, the home viewers saw horror. A disgruntled ex-reporter shot Alison, Adam, and Vicki in cold blood. He was a lunatic, hired at the station in spite of what should have been abundant red flags, and fired only after showing so many signs of mounting mental instability that it was impossible to forge a pretext for keeping him on.

He had planned the shooting for months, claiming to be inspired by instructions from God Himself, or whatever voice sounded most like God's within the howling storm of his diseased brain. He faxed a manifesto to ABC News on the morning of the murder, claiming inspiration from the Columbine shooters and the Virginia Tech gunman. He promised the Charleston church killer a "race war." His outlook on the world had been molded by killers, and thanks to the countless news programs that probed for insight into the minds of these worthless individuals, there was no shortage of grist for the mill.

That morning, he drove to Bridgewater Plaza, strapped a GoPro camera to his head, and using a legally purchased handgun, shot three people, killing Alison and Adam. Then he strolled back to his car and uploaded the video to Facebook.

He uploaded my daughter's murder to Facebook.

He then tweeted a link to the video to maximize his audience.

Nothing is ever lost on the internet, no matter how horrific or vicious. That video is still out there floating around, and it always will be. They may call it the Information Superhighway, but it runs above a toxic cesspool.

I haven't seen that video, and I never will. I am grateful to whatever higher powers may or may not exist that I wasn't watching WDBJ the morning of the murder.

Would you believe that people have tried to show me that video? It's happened more than once. People have even tried to describe it to me. Many of them have meant well and have been surprised when I lashed out at them.

I know how the fucking thing ends. I don't need to watch it to see how it happened.

Even though I have never seen it, it is hideous enough to know that it's out there, floating in the digital ether, just a few clicks away for any sick son of a bitch who wants to see an innocent young woman gunned down in cold blood.

Anyone who chooses to watch that video will not merely see my daughter die. They will also see the moment I died. The person that I used to be is gone, obliterated like a sandcastle in a windstorm.

My heart stopped on August 26, 2015. I still think, speak, and eat on occasion, but I'm a different person now, a dead thing made animate through some cruel miracle. To paraphrase Cormac McCarthy, for the rest of my life, the shadow of the axe will hang over every joy.

Every day since August 26, 2015, is one day further from Alison, another mile marker on the path leading away from my life's greatest treasure. One more day since the last time I saw her, since I heard her voice, since I told her how much I loved her, how much she meant to me. I would have taken her place without a moment's hesitation. I would have died without regret to spare her an ounce of pain. If I had the power to turn back time, I would do just that.

Well-intentioned people tell me that each day is not one day further from Alison; it's one day closer to "healing," to "getting over it." They offer their "thoughts and prayers." Is there anything more worthless than thoughts and prayers? More than three years have passed, and while I am gradually learning to cope, there is no miraculous healing on the horizon, no divine intervention that will make me somehow accept what happened to my daughter.

So, what is there?

There is righteous fury. And there is a desire to spend the rest of my life doing whatever it takes to prevent this from ever happening to another family.

Let me be perfectly clear: this is not a book about reaching out to the other side, those people who feel that the occasional mass shooting is the price that must be paid to ensure that an amendment drafted in the age of muskets should also apply to a Bushmaster rifle capable of killing people just as fast as you can pull the trigger—faster if you buy a bump stock. I've talked to these people. I live in southwest Virginia; I'm surrounded by these people. The opposition is interested in what I have to say only to the extent that they can glean tidbits with which to assassinate my character (and rest assured, plenty will buy this book for that exact purpose).

I have said, in countless interviews, that I don't want to take anyone's guns away. All I want is meaningful commonsense firearm legislation that will keep guns out of the hands of maniacs. Yet when I make the mistake of reading the comments at the end of those interview articles or videos, what do the gun nuts have to say?

"Andy Parker wants to take everyone's guns away."

Someone ought to study the correlation between reading comprehension and gun ownership. Maybe I can find a way to get through to the folks who sit where that X crosses on the line graph.

But rest assured, my ire isn't only reserved for the gun nuts. Since becoming a full-time activist, I've had plenty of experience with folks who, like me, want commonsense gun legislation. I was a spokesman for Everytown for Gun Safety, the biggest gun violence prevention nonprofit in America, until we parted ways. I felt too constrained by their timid message. And they thought I was a wild man.

The NRA and the politicians the NRA pays off paint organizations like Everytown and people who support them as rabid, gun-hating liberal lunatics. Perhaps in response to that, those who oppose gun violence have tried to scale back their message, to whisper rather than shout, to search for common ground in the middle of a raging battlefield.

This is the wrong approach.

This cause needs angry people. It needs people who have lost daughters and sons, wives and husbands, people who are not afraid to stand up and say, "I appreciate the fact that you want to buy ten guns per month and walk into McDonald's with a SIG Sauer hanging off your hip, but I lost the goddamn light of my life, and maybe, just this once, you should listen to what I have to say."

That, to a large extent, is what this book is all about. It's not about holding hands around the campfire and singing "Kumbaya." It's not about reaching across aisles and finding common ground between people who want every man, woman, and child armed to the teeth and people who want to feel safe in a grocery store. It's not about rattling off dry gun violence statistics to try and convince a militia member that they don't really need another AR15.

This is a book about an ordinary man who lost his daughter to gun violence and is mad as hell about it. This is a book about showing people, in painful detail, what it's like to receive the worst phone call of your life and feel your guts get ripped right out on the kitchen floor. This is a book about struggling to make something meaningful out of a meaningless death.

Along the way, some minds might be changed. That would be wonderful. But I'm not reaching out to the lunatic fringe with this book. This is a book for the average Joe, the massive majority of people in the middle who don't have strong feelings one way or the other. This book is designed to interest them, hook them, and then grab them by the collar and shake them until they realize the full magnitude of what we're dealing with in this country—until they realize that there's a damn good chance this could happen to them, too.

You might wonder why I'm the person to write this book, and that's a fair question. After all, there are other grieving parents out there, and their numbers increase by the day.

There are a few things that set me apart. The first is that the horrifically unique nature of my daughter's murder was without precedent in our nation's history, and if there is a just God, it will remain so.

The second is that, since Alison's death, I have devoted every day of my life to spreading a message of gun violence prevention. My name and number are in a lot of important phones. I've written countless articles for *Newsweek* and the *New York Daily News*, for CNN.com and *USA Today*, for the *Washington Post* and the *Huffington Post*. I've been featured in *People* magazine and *Cosmopolitan*. I've appeared on *Face the Nation*, *CBS Sunday Morning*, ABC, NBC, MSNBC, Fox, Fox News, CNN, and NPR. I've been on TV in Canada, Mexico, France, the United Kingdom, Australia, and Japan. I've been on CNN International, Al Jazeera, a regional network in Latin America, and a German program whose name I can't spell, much less pronounce. I've been to the White House, the West Coast, and states in between, just trying to prevent others from experiencing my living nightmare.

And that's why I've written this book.

1

ALISON

It was Monday, August 19, 1991, and the world was on edge. Communists from the old Soviet regime had orchestrated a coup against Boris Yeltsin and his fledgling democracy. If it succeeded, no one knew what the implications were for our country, but the prospects weren't promising.

Barbara was in labor with our daughter, Alison, and we watched the live CNN broadcast on the overhead television at Anne Arundel Medical Center in Annapolis, Maryland. It was a nice but unremarkable facility, made to feel as homey as possible while still being sterile. All hospitals look pretty much the same.

We were both shocked by the unfolding world events, but we had other things on our minds. *Just great*, I thought. *We're bringing a child into a very uncertain world.* The excitement of Alison's imminent arrival was tempered by what appeared to be a world on the brink of war.

Adding to my concern was the health of the coming child. A few months before, our first-born, three-year-old Drew, had been diagnosed with Asperger's syndrome. At that time, little was known about it; doctors knew it was somewhere on the autism spectrum, but it mostly remained a mystery. Now my wife was giving birth at age forty-one, an age where all kinds of problems can occur. The obstetrician who was supposed to deliver Alison was not on duty, so another from the practice was there instead. We had never met him previously, but this fortyish mustachioed doctor bore an uncanny resemblance to Barbara's brother-in-law, and thankfully he had a good sense of humor. His joking demeanor helped take our minds off the ominous events that were unfolding, but only a little.

Barbara's first delivery with Drew was via emergency C-section; I hated that I couldn't be in the room when he arrived. Sometimes after a C-section doctors discourage natural childbirth, but Barbara's doctor saw no reason for this. This time everything was going smoothly, except there was one spot on her abdomen that the epidural did not seem to help. Barbara was not thrilled by this development. Barbara's not exactly the natural childbirth/midwife/delivery in a kiddie pool type, so she was ready for Alison to make her debut as quickly as possible.

Fortunately, Alison cooperated, Barbara pushed like a champ, and before long, I saw my daughter emerge into the world.

There are no words to describe what it's like to witness the birth of your child. It's a wonder, a miracle, but even that doesn't go far enough. As with parents since the beginning of time, emotions ran the gamut from relief to joy and ultimately profound love for this life we had created.

At that moment, we didn't care about the rest of the world or what it would turn into. I just knew we had something special from the moment I laid eyes on her. Two days later, we were all home, the Russian Federation survived, and I knew the light that had come into the world on such a dark day was destined for great things.

I want to tell you what Alison was like. This is no easy task.

Imagine your own child, or if you don't have a child, imagine your wife, or your husband, or your mother or father. Now imagine describing that person—capturing everything that makes them special with crystal detail—in a single chapter of a few thousand words. Even if this entire book was solely devoted to describing how wonderful, unique, and talented Alison was, it would still fall short.

But my hope is that if I share a few stories—the little moments over the years that stick out—you'll get a glimpse, and hopefully that glimpse will be enough.

The first thing I'll tell you is that Alison was an easy baby. She was perfectly healthy, she slept through the night, and she was never colicky. About the only thing you could remotely call an issue was that she took a little while to get the hang of potty training, but once she mastered it, boy was she proud of herself.

On her first Halloween outing, Drew dressed as radio legend Dr. Demento and Alison dressed as a fairy princess, complete with a purple gown, a sparkling tiara, rosy cheeks, and a candy bucket that Barbara fashioned into the perfect gaudy accessory using tin foil and purple ribbon. I escorted them as they went door to door. We lived in a newly built subdivision in Bowie, Maryland, with lots of kids, nice sidewalks, and houses that were as close together as houses in new subdivisions tend to be. I would hang back on the sidewalk in front of each house while Drew took Alison's hand and escorted her to each front door.

Alison was a little over two years old at the time. I'm not sure the concept of Halloween registered with her as much as the excitement of it all. It's like the kids whose parents take them to Disney World at that age. They enjoy that excitement, but it doesn't have much more impact than going to the local Chuck E. Cheese's.

In Alison's case, it presented an opportunity to turn on the charm and engage the public. As I waited for them to trick or treat, to get their candy and return to meet me at the sidewalk, I began to notice a pattern. I was too far away to hear what was being said, but I saw parents in their doorways laugh, say something, and put more candy in Alison's sparkly princess bucket. This went on door after door, so I finally walked up behind them to get within earshot.

Then I heard what prompted the neighbors' responses. In unison, the kids would say "Trick or treat!" But then Alison would proudly proclaim, "I poo-poo in the potty!" to which the reaction was, "Well, that's very, very good. I'm going to give you some extra candy for that."

It was clear she understood marketing at an early age.

Middle and high school were an awkward time for Alison, though I suppose it's an awkward time for all of us. But in the days when girls go through puberty at a sometimes alarmingly early rate, Alison was the opposite. Barbara and I were late bloomers, and Alison was no different. It didn't help that, because her birthday was in August, she was effectively a year younger than many of her peers.

Middle school can be particularly rough on kids like Alison. Barbara had been relentless with her about skin damage from the sun, so her skin was snow white, and while it would give her a luminescence as a young woman, it was a subject of mockery among some of the crueler middle school boys. They nicknamed her "Casper," as in the ghost. She was a gawky little kid with too many teeth surrounded by boys and girls who were physically mature if not emotionally so.

As she entered high school, she was not cheerleader material, and most of those girls and boys just ignored her. She wasn't cool enough for them. It must've hurt in some ways, but Alison never seemed to let it get to her.

She embraced being a nerd through high school as she started to transform from the ugly duckling into the beautiful swan. She was proud to be a part of the Piedmont Governor's School's award-winning robotics team called the STAGS, and she put all of her other energy into academics, swim team, and dance classes. She also had rock-solid stability at home, and while many of the "cool" kids were out getting drunk, she spent her free time with a few good friends or with family. Her only dates in high school were to proms. It didn't bother her. And as so often happens, while many of those kids reached the zenith of their lives waving pompoms or playing football, Alison kept on going and didn't look back. Funny how just a few years later when she became a television personality, many of those kids wanted to be Alison's friend.

Summers were spent on our boat at Smith Mountain Lake, a place we all loved. It's a vicious irony to have such wonderful memories of a place and yet never be able to return.

Alison had a knack for doing a remarkable job at everything she tackled. She worked hard on academics, but athletics seemed to come naturally. During those Casper years, she won the respect of her peers by being down-to-earth, and also by demonstrating her athletic ability.

It all coalesced one field day. The sprinting competition was the main event. As Alison would laughingly tell the story, "As I was racing in my heat, I could hear one black classmate shrieking at the top of her lungs, 'Run little white girl, run!'" She led the field.

Her classmates respected her ability, and it was an example of Alison's underlying fierce competitiveness. Alison wasn't content to just compete at anything. Her goal was to win at everything. And she practically did, with extraordinary composure.

Barbara and I put Alison in gymnastics when she was around seven years old. After a couple of years of learning various skills, she was ready for her first competition. Like any sports dad, I vividly recall the first routine she did at her meet. It was the floor routine, and while my heart was pounding with excitement, she coolly nailed it. On the balance beam and vault she was fearless. I can't remember now how the meet turned out, but I know she placed in her very first event.

Through sixth grade, she competed around the state and took home her fair share of medals. All the while, she was taking dance classes, which she'd started when she was four years old. The wear and tear on her knees was taking its toll, so she decided to give up gymnastics and concentrate on dance. By then, she was also hitting her growth spurt. It's rare to see a 5′9″ gymnast, and it was clear that was the direction she was heading in.

Alison excelled in dance just as much as she excelled in gymnastics. At her dance studio's year-end recital, she performed the role of Dewdrop in *Waltz of the Flowers*. I will never forget it, just as I'll never forget the tears of pride that streamed down my face as I watched her. She was in sixth grade, the youngest dancer in the class to dance en pointe. Those strong gymnast ankles made all the difference. She was the graceful little angel upstage in the spotlight while all the older girls were downstage. She glided gracefully, effortlessly executing pirouettes. At the end of the performance, the crowd went nuts and I went to pieces. My heart was bursting with pride, but Alison was cool as a cucumber.

By the time Alison was a junior in high school, I was sure she had the talent and the looks to go to Broadway. That opinion wasn't just subjective. I had performed on Broadway in a past life and I knew what talent looks like. The mark of a great performer is performing effortlessly. She was fluid and graceful and she danced that way through high school. I'll always wonder what it would have been like to watch her in New York.

As a junior, Alison decided to try out for the swim team. She had reached her full height, and her strong dancer's body also turned out to be perfect for swimming. She was a competitive swimmer during her last two years of high school, swimming freestyle, medley, and her specialty, the butterfly. She won each event in every local meet. Some girls on the swim team were in it for the social aspect and merely wanted to participate; Alison wanted to beat every one of them—and she did. She received the Piedmont District Swimmer of the Year Award both her junior and senior years.

In cities the size of Richmond, Virginia, high school swimmers were in the pool practicing twenty hours a week, but our much-smaller hometown of Martinsville, about three hours west, didn't afford that opportunity. They could only practice at the YMCA for about six hours a week. As a result, when Alison competed regionally, she didn't win, but she was able to qualify for the state meet her junior and senior years. She did it on sheer ability. Had she been part of the team that produced our good friend Lori Haas's son Townley, I have no doubt she could have gone on to win an Olympic gold like him.

Soon enough, we discovered the wonders of white-water paddling, first on guided rafting trips on the New and Gauley Rivers. By the time we graduated to kayaking, Alison was intuitive and fearless on the water. Our first guide told us, "When you get to that big rapid, keep paddling. Don't stop or you'll get pulled back into the hole."

"Keep paddling" became our family slogan, though we didn't know at the time how much it would one day mean to us.

While Alison had a talent for nearly everything she touched, she didn't let it inflate her ego. She never lost the ability to laugh at herself. There was one story in particular that followed her for her whole life.

It began back in 1994 when we had had enough of Maryland's cold weather and high taxes. We sold the house, stored the furniture, and drove to Texas to spend Christmas with family. I had sold my golf shirt business and was about to start a new job as a partner in a new endeavor, but it fell through the day after Christmas. I had to get another job fast, and I ended up taking one with Cross Creek Apparel in Mount Airy, North Carolina. They also made golf shirts, and the president of Cross Creek liked my creativity and offered me a job to make licensed PGA Tour merchandise.

We were in Mount Airy for a year and then I was transferred to Columbus, Georgia, where they housed all their licensing projects. It was a miserable time for me and Barbara. The brutal heat and humidity in Georgia made us miss Mount Airy more than we did already, but Drew and Alison were quite resilient. They adapted well, and we did everything together. We were fortunate that our best friends just happened to be each other.

In Columbus, Alison was in kindergarten at Reese Road Elementary School. One day her teacher was reading a story to the class. All the students sat on the floor in a semicircle in front of her. What follows is an account in Alison's own words.

"When I was five years old, I started kindergarten at Reese Road School. My teacher Mrs. Enmond was full of encouragement and entertainment, and my classmates and I really enjoyed her class because she was kind, caring, and willing to help us whenever we needed her. Because she was so wonderful, we all wished she was our mother! On the day I discovered her flaw, I also learned an important lesson about myself.

"On that infamous day, Mrs. Enmond and the class were sitting in a circle for story time. Because she was reading [a story about] Marshmallow the bunny, I was in the front listening attentively to my favorite story. Suddenly, complete chaos invaded this peaceful story time, and everyone was shrieking and running around the room! Confused, I approached my friend Victoria and shouted, 'What's going on?' She exclaimed frantically, 'There's a cockroach on the floor!' At that very moment, I felt tiny little legs crawling up my arm and into my dress. I scrambled to find Mrs. Enmond, who was just as frenzied as the rest of us. 'Mrs. Enmond! I think there is a cockroach in my dress!' I screamed. She took one look at me, leaped onto her desk, and waved her arms in the air, screeching, 'I can't help you!' Because all of my classmates realized that the cockroach was not chasing them, but rather crawling on me, they all giggled while I just stood there. Finally, the teacher's aide grabbed me and shook my dress vigorously until the cockroach fell onto the floor. Calmly, she retrieved the fly swatter and flattened the bug."

Alison was embarrassed by the cockroach story, but as she demonstrated through her developing skills, a story like this could be helpful in learning how to find humor in situations. It could connect with an audience.

The cockroach story resurfaced five years later at a 4-H speech competition when Alison was in fifth grade. By that time, we had moved to Martinsville where I had a new job with Tultex Corporation. We didn't know it then, but Southside Virginia would become our permanent home.

The same confidence Alison had shown in her endeavors since the age of two was apparent in her speech competitions. She won the local competition and advanced to the district level. Some years later, she wrote about her 4-H experience:

"As embarrassing as the [cockroach] story may sound, I learned something from this and have been able to use it to my advantage. For example, I competed in the 4-H Public Speaking Competition. My classmates decided to write about cliché topics like 'the most influential person they know,' or 'what integrity meant to them.' This was the time for me to test the usefulness of this embarrassment. When I stood before my first audience and delivered this speech, people had puzzled looks on their faces. No audience member had ever heard something so 'unique.' I received my scorecard and had advanced to the next level! Finally, after a series of competitions, I reached the state level competition. I was extremely nervous because all of the other competitors had very intelligent speeches about the economy, social issues, and other serious matters that were over my head. Standing at the podium I took a deep breath and gave my speech. I won."

She wasn't through with the cockroach story. When Alison applied for early decision to James Madison University, she decided to use that story in her personal statement. The last paragraph sealed the deal:

"Having that ability to laugh at myself will benefit me. Who would have thought that a cockroach crawling up my dress in kindergarten earned me the 4-H Public Speaking trophy in my living room? Because I did not let my embarrassment overwhelm me, I was able to accomplish my goal. More importantly, learning to appreciate instances like this has helped me find humor in even the most unusual circumstances."

Later in Alison's high school career, she attended one of the best-kept secrets in Martinsville/Henry County: the Piedmont Governor's School for Mathematics, Science, and Technology. Rising high school juniors must apply to be accepted into the program, and if they're chosen, they begin the school day an hour before their peers. When Alison was in the program from 2007 through 2009, it was held in an old elementary school building in town. Before returning to their regularly scheduled high school programming at noon, she and her Governor's School classmates spent their mornings challenged with a college-level curriculum that helped turn them into creative thinkers.

Alison loved the demands placed on her, the inventive projects she completed, the teamwork the program fostered. Like many of the other successful students in the program, she graduated from high school with an associate's degree from our local community college without actually attending classes on the campus. It worked out to roughly sixty hours of transferable hours to James Madison University. She made good use of those hours, too. When she told me the courses she was taking her first year at JMU, most of which sounded like Underwater Basket Weaving 101, I asked her why she was bothering to take all that fluff. I'd placed out of some courses back when I went to college at the University of

Texas, but I still had to bust my hump taking tough freshman classes.

"Scooter," I asked her, "aren't you supposed to be taking a serious course load?"

"Dad, I got all that stuff out of the way at Governor's School. I have to get through my GMAD [General Education Media Arts] classes and be accepted to SMAD [School of Media Arts and Design] and then I can't take the other courses until I'm a junior."

"Uh, okay." She knew what she was doing, even if dear old dad did not.

During her entire first year of college, she mostly took electives. One of those electives was calculus. Most students wouldn't volunteer to take calculus even under penalty of torture, particularly if it wasn't their major, but Alison loved math, and she had already become an old hand at calculus during her stint at Governor's School. She aced every test.

One day, her professor took her aside and asked her, "Why are you in this class?" Alison told him she simply liked math and thought it would be a fun elective.

The following semester, the professor hired her as a tutor.

Governor's School is where Alison caught the journalism bug, which is the reason she chose JMU. Being on the Governor's School yearbook staff planted that seed, but a high school band trip to Atlanta (she played trumpet and French horn) made it sprout and grow.

During the band trip, Alison and her classmates had the opportunity to tour CNN. She was in awe. She had enjoyed the band trip to Disney World the previous year, but in her eyes, Disney had nothing on CNN. She saw her future in those halls. There is a picture of her beaming in front of the giant CNN block logo, arms outstretched over her head, palms out in a display that suggested, "This is where I'll be one day."

And she did appear on CNN, just a few years later. We'll return to that soon enough.

Once she knew that journalism was her calling, it was simply a matter of choosing a college. Barbara and I limited the search to Virginia schools to take advantage of in-state tuition, so there were only two schools that she ever really considered: James Madison University and the University of Virginia. When she discovered that UVA didn't have a journalism department, she didn't even bother to apply.

Alison sailed through her first two years at JMU before diving headfirst into her journalism courses. She honed her skills as a storyteller and soon became the news editor for the *Breeze*, JMU's award-winning student paper. She enjoyed mentoring her fellow students, and she liked writing so much that she nearly decided that was her calling. But that was before she took any on-air courses.

When she started in video production, it became clear to her professors that she had "it." Her beloved Professor Ryan Parkhurst, a trusted mentor even after she graduated, said, "I've never had a student with the talent, drive, and gift that Alison possessed."

I only saw one video of her from JMU. She was in the field, and got the "toss" from her student anchors. It was decent, but it wasn't prime time material. Hey, it was her first time, and she was still in school. Even in that brief clip, she did do something that was purely Alison; right before the live shot, a truck pulled up in the background, and she sprinted over to it in high heels to ask the driver to move out of the way, sprinting back just in time for the shot.

The next time I saw her on television, it was the real deal. It was the summer before her final semester at JMU, and she had an internship at WDBJ, a CBS-affiliated station in Roanoke.

"Scooter, are they going to let you go on-air?" I'd asked her.

"Oh Dad, they're probably just gonna make me go get coffee."

Clearly, she had no expectations. But the station did. They saw "it." She called me after she'd been there about ten days, bursting with excitement.

"Dad, I'm doing a package!" she said. "It's going to be on at the six! I just finished, and I think it's going to be really good!"

"What's a package?" I asked. "And what's the six? Does that mean you're going to be on TV?"

Indeed she was. In the months to come, she would playfully admonish me for confusing a "package" with a "stand up." (In broadcasting vernacular, a "package" is a report in which the correspondent narrates around video and interview excerpts, while a "stand up" is when a correspondent stands at a news location and talks directly to camera, live or taped.)

Barbara and I watched WDBJ that evening, breathless. There was Alison, doing a story about a camp for diabetic kids. She looked great, professional, like a veteran correspondent. Our hearts were bursting with pride. Barbara and I couldn't stop smiling, and we gave each other high-fives until our palms stung.

Proud Dad posted that clip on Facebook, and looking back, I think it was my all-time favorite. Watching our daughter take the first confident, practiced steps toward her dream was an experience like no other. I would give anything to relive it.

Alison went on to do five more packages until one of the reporters complained that an intern was doing all their work. I will always wonder if the complainer was the one who ended up killing her.

On her last day as an intern, we took a picture of her sitting at the anchor desk. Like the photo in front of CNN, it was another prescient "I'll be here one day" moment.

As her final semester at JMU wound down, Alison used the video from WDBJ for an audition reel to send to prospective employers in the TV news field. She graduated in December, a semester early, with genuine professional experience and an impressive list of accomplishments, but she had sent out her audition reel in November. She had a few criteria: The station had to be a top 100 market, it couldn't be anyplace cold, and it would preferably be close to home and/or family. She sent out just six packages. A couple of stations didn't reply, a couple said they needed someone with more experience, and two wanted to talk.

One was a station in College Station, Texas. It was farther away from me and Barbara, but close enough to the rest of the family in Texas. She had a phone interview with the news director who promised a follow-up in a week or two.

The other that wanted to talk was WCTI in New Bern, North Carolina. It was a top 100 station, reasonably close, and in a great area. The news director, Scott Nichols, received Alison's reel on a Tuesday and called her Friday. The interview went well. He asked her for references and said he'd be back in touch with her soon.

He called her references over the weekend and called her back on Monday, offering her a job as a reporter for the Greenville, North Carolina, viewing area. She would be working alongside another reporter, although that situation would change a week after she arrived.

After getting the news, she called me, breathless.

"Dad, he offered me the job! He even said I'd be making $24,000 a year!"

She had won the lottery.

"What did you tell him?" I asked.

"I said, 'Don't you need to see me in person?' He said, 'No, I see everything I need to see from your reel and your résumé. You don't have to decide right away, you can think about it for a few days, but we really want you.' I was so stunned I just said, 'OK, let me think about it.'"

"How do you feel about it?" I asked.

"I like it," she said.

"Then, Scooter, call him back and accept the job. It sounds like the perfect start for you."

And so she did. Alison had a job in television two weeks before she got her diploma. She graduated on December 15, 2012, started with WCTI the day after Christmas, and was immediately thrown into trial by fire, doing a stand up her very first day. I've heard from pros in the business that what she pulled off rarely happens, if ever. But Scott Nichols saw "it."

Scott wanted her to spend a month in New Bern learning the ropes at the station before heading to Greenville. The problem was, there was little to no temporary housing that she (or I) could really afford. I called around for her before finding a unique arrangement: she spent January in an assisted living community. She had a pretty nice apartment, and of course it was quiet. I joked with her that she should join the residents for dinner and enjoy those cooked-to-death green beans. She drew the line at that, but was grateful for a nice cheap place to live for a while.

Two weeks later, after several packages and stand ups, Scott said he wanted to meet with her.

"My original plan was to have you working alongside a reporter in Greenville," he told her, "and you can still do that if you want. But after watching your work, I've got another opportunity I'd like you to consider. Our bureau reporter in Jacksonville is leaving. How would you like to run your own show there?"

Alison jumped at the chance. Now she was a twenty-two-year-old bureau chief with her own veteran cameraman working for the number one station in the market. She covered hard news, but in Jacksonville it generally revolved around these kinds of stories:

"Marine Comes Home to Hero's Welcome," or

"Marine Shakes Baby to Death," or

"Big Meth Lab Bust."

A year in, recognizing her ability, Scott gave her an opportunity to be the fill-in anchor. Barbara and I watched the first episode at home, watched her sitting at an anchor desk for the first time. We were giddy with joy, and it marked the moment that Alison knew she wanted to be a full-time anchor.

When the noon anchor position became available, Alison lobbied hard, but the job went to another deserving candidate. She was disappointed, and she knew her options were limited. The other anchors at the station had been there for a long time and had established roots in the community. They weren't going anywhere. It was time to move up and move on.

As she was preparing her reel, Tim Saunders, a reporter from WDBJ, gave her a call. He said they had a couple of interesting prospects in the works and that Kelly Zuber, the news director, wanted to talk to her. Kelly told her they wanted to create a regional reporting position that was based in Martinsville. As always, Alison asked me what I thought.

"I could live at home and save a lot of money," she said.

"Yeah, Scooter, you could. But as much as we'd love to have you back home, and even if they paid you more money, this would be a step back for you."

Alison agreed. She thanked Kelly and declined the offer.

Kelly called her back a day later.

Melissa Gaona, the "Mornin'" reporter, had been promoted to anchor. Would Alison be interested in taking her old position? The job was mostly fluff reporting and spanned the station's entire viewing radius. She would work five days a week alongside a cameraman named Adam Ward, and she would get a $9,000 a year raise, a wardrobe, and a makeup allowance. Alison had won the lottery again.

Barbara and I got up at the crack of dawn, quite literally, to watch Alison's first "spot." It featured a climbing wall, and as would regularly happen, Alison was an active participant in the story. She was hooked up to the safety rope as she climbed the wall, a bundle of energy and enthusiasm. Unfortunately, that enthusiasm manifested itself in lots of wild arm gestures. In a Facebook comment on the segment, one viewer wondered aloud if she had some kind of neurological affliction.

Alison called me in tears.

"Dad, what am I going to do?" she sobbed. "This is terrible. They might fire me. What if I can't stop waving my arms?"

"Scooter, it's just one day," I said, marshaling all of my fatherly comfort. "You'll be fine. You did great."

That one Facebook comment was all it took. That's when she really became a pro. She didn't wave her arms anymore, and Alison and Adam became the Roanoke area's favorite news duo. She always had great story ideas and she often made Adam her foil, a role he cheerfully played.

Over time, she became a regular noontime fill-in anchor on WDBJ, and she was still working toward that anchor position. In the meantime, she became a celebrity in the New River Valley, and those viewers who watched her every morning fell in love. They knew she was electric. They knew she had "it."

I can tell you that Alison was smart, that she was naturally talented, that she was humble, but if there's only one trait about her that you want to commit to memory, make it this: she was, above all, kind.

So many parents these days want to be friends with their children, and as a result, their kids grow up with no boundaries, no manners, and a sense of entitlement. Alison was our friend, and we were hers—Drew is the same way—but we also raised them both with expectations. We held them to standards of achievement. The only thing we were going to force them to do was be good human beings, and we tried to teach them how to make the best possible choices in life.

I believe Barbara and I were pretty damn good at parenting. Alison never got into trouble. The only time I really yelled at her was when she was about ten. We were horsing around on our boat when she hit me in the ear. It obviously wasn't intentional, but that didn't make it hurt any less; I felt like my eardrum had ruptured. I screamed at her, saying to never do that again. She went to the bow of the boat, curled up in a ball, and started to cry. I apologized instantly, but the incident haunts me still. I suppose it always will.

Like all fathers, I was the smartest guy in the world until my daughter got into her teens, but even when she noticed my IQ had dropped substantially, we didn't butt heads all that often. She would, however, get ticked off at me for my wanting to fix things every time she had a problem, instead of just providing a listening ear and letting her solve it like an adult. That was the dad part in me coming out. I always wanted to fix her problems, to fight whatever injustices she encountered. She wasn't shy about being irritated by this; she inherited a great deal of my personality and could be just as stubborn and willful as I am.

But all kids are stubborn at some point; when she was, she was still able to listen. She was always polite, and she had an otherworldly kindness. It was easy being Alison's dad.

There was so much of me in Alison. Her fierce competitiveness and desire to win everything came from me. As an adult this desire bled into her career and that, plus her natural talent, allowed her to excel in journalism, just as she had excelled in athletics and academics. Alison always wanted to break the story, and the majority of the time she did. She was young for a TV news reporter, so very young, and already destined for an anchor's chair in her mid-twenties. There is no telling where she could have ended up. But while Alison was determined to be the best, she didn't step on other people in the process. She had a genuine grace and kindness.

They say that the light that burns brightest burns briefest, and there was always a part of me that feared, perhaps irrationally, that her light would burn so bright that it would flame out long before her time.

In the aftermath of her death, I've heard countless stories from her friends, teachers, coworkers, and perfect strangers about things she did for others, things I never would have known about had people not volunteered to share their Alison stories.

A typical example came from her time at WDBJ. It was just before Christmas and Alison, part of the skeleton crew still in the building, picked up the call. A desperate grandmother was on the other end of the line and spoke of a family with a struggling dad, a mom not in the picture, and children who were about to go without presents. All of the Christmas-assistance deadlines had passed and calls like these can sometimes be bogus—and bogus or not, they are generally met with a response of "I wish we could do something, but . . ."

Maybe Alison could tell the call was genuine, or maybe she was just willing to roll the dice, but she took a leap of faith. She made several calls and finally got in touch with an organization willing to help. Three children ended up with presents from Santa they wouldn't have received otherwise.

There were so many little acts of kindness that only she and the recipients knew about, so many stories she never shared with me. I'm so thankful her coworker Heather Butterworth shared that one.

Throughout her short life, Alison developed relationships and trust. There is no better example than the mutual trust she shared with the court clerks, judges, and law enforcement in Jacksonville, Onslow County, and the state police attached to the area. While they had to share appropriate press releases with all local media, Alison was clearly a favorite. Once while visiting her, she took Barbara and me to meet the previous Onslow County sheriff. He sang her praises and invited us to join him and his wife "for suppuh." I thought it quite unusual, but it clearly showed that Alison had left an impression on him. You don't invite someone over for suppuh unless you're fond of them.

She did once get "scooped" while she was working in New Bern, when she got an early tip from one of her police contacts that they were working on an active investigation. She was asked, however, not to break the story too early—the police wanted the media to keep it quiet until they wrapped up their investigation. The contact said this was because of its "sensitive nature." Alison was ethical and complied, but when her competition found out, they were not. They broke the story. Afterward, there were some people in her news department that criticized her for not reporting it. I remember her telling me how much that stung, but she never second-guessed her decision. She knew she had done the right thing, and she stood up for her ethics in subsequent staff meetings. Ultimately, prematurely breaking the story backfired on the other station and Alison was hailed by upper management at hers. The respect she already had was multiplied.

The immediate benefit came in the form of getting more news tips. When law enforcement had information to feed the press, they would send out a release to all media outlets at the same time. They often seemed to make a mistake, though, and Alison would get the releases an hour or two before anyone else. Funny how that happened.

All of this leads to my favorite story about Alison's news career. She was tipped off that there was going to be a major meth lab bust in the county. State as well as local police were involved, and the lead investigator assured Alison that they would be working long through the night at the crime scene. She requested the only live truck the station had for the entire area so she could lead the ten o'clock news with a live report. Before long, Alison and her crew were on the scene, raring to go.

At 9:45 p.m., the lead investigator called out to his team: "OK guys, that's it. Let's wrap it up."

Alison panicked. Her story was tanking before her eyes. She went to the lead investigator and asked if they could please just stick around for a few more minutes for her live shot.

A lot of law enforcement officers would have shaken their heads no, however politely. The lead investigator didn't.

"Sure, Alison, we've got you covered," he said. He then instructed his men to fire up the flashing light bars on all the squad cars. He positioned his team in the background of the shot and armed them with clipboards, which they furiously scribbled on as the cameras rolled. It was a dramatic scene and made a great backdrop for Alison's report. She nailed it.

Some readers will conclude, "Aha! Fake news!" But it wasn't. Law enforcement busted a meth lab. The outcome was the same either way. It was a benign recreation, the kind of harmless small-town courtesy that could have happened in Mayberry, North Carolina, as easily as Jacksonville. Would officers in a major metropolitan market have done this for Alison? Given the trust she'd garnered, I'd like to think so. Those officers did it for her because she was held in high esteem and they knew her ethics to be beyond reproach.

What was it like being Alison's dad? It was getting up each day with a heart bursting with pride. When I was running for Henry County's Board of Supervisors just before she was killed, I only halfway joked that my campaign slogan was "I'm Alison's dad." It's how I introduce myself still.

I worshipped my little Scooter. She will always be the best part of my life. I think she knew it, too.

2

THE DAY

I want to tell you what I was doing the day before the worst day of my life.

It was a good day, a great day even. Back when I served on the Henry County, Virginia, Board of Supervisors (I won by a single vote, so don't let anyone tell you voting doesn't matter), I worked to get weekend power generation at Philpott Dam, to allow kayakers to enjoy the Smith River on weekends.

I didn't achieve that goal during my time on the board, but seven years later, during the summer of 2015, all of the gears I'd carefully put into place finally meshed. Philpott Dam, an unassuming hydroelectric dam built along the Smith River during the New Deal era, would now have weekend generation.

I'm a paddler. One of my greatest joys, even now, is to gather together some friends and family, drop a few kayaks in a river, and enjoy nature's splendor. It's peaceful, relaxing, and when the speed picks up on that silvery ribbon of water and you're working to point the kayak's nose in the right direction, operating off of your instincts and your experience, it's exciting, too.

It's also great for tourism, which was my main goal. Henry County is a beautiful place, ripe for tourism, and paddlers are willing to travel miles and miles to find a good river. A good river is a fast river with just enough depth to keep a kayak from scraping the bottom, and until recently, the Smith was only a good river on weekdays, since that was when Philpott Dam was generating power and pumping a few million gallons of Philpott Lake through its twin turbines. I figured that if we could get at least one day of generation on weekends, it would be a boon to our river tourism industry.

On August 25, 2015, my labors finally bore fruit and weekend generation at Philpott Dam was made official. I drove out to the dam, parked in the narrow lot along the river, and then got out to greet a few folks. I saw Craig "Rocky" Rockwell, the project manager for the Army Corps of Engineers; he's a tall, good-natured older gentleman who always has a few sardonic quips at the ready should the need arise. We congratulated each other. He would end up retiring in a little more than a year, and I think he was glad to see at least one more positive mark on his record before he took his leave.

I saw Tola Adamson, a reporter from Channel 13, there to cover the big announcement. We said hello; she knew me because she knew Alison, a thread that continues to weave its way through my life.

I saw others, too, county officials, local politicians, American Electric Power employees, various local dignitaries of all stripes. It was a day of celebration, a day of speechifying, a day for people to line up at a podium and rattle off lists of all the folks who deserved a pat on the back for the good work that had been accomplished.

At this point, you might be thinking: that's all well and good, but what the hell does it have to do with this book?

The answer, in a real sense, is absolutely nothing, and that's exactly why I'm telling you about it.

When tragedy strikes—real tragedy, horrific tragedy—all the little things that you cared about prior to that moment are swept away as if by a blast from a neutron bomb, leaving only crumbling structures in its wake. Maybe you've got tickets to an upcoming concert you've been excited about, or you just bought a new designer handbag you had been scrimping and saving to afford, or you just got a promotion at work; whatever it is, when the black tidal wave of tragedy hits, everything else becomes meaningless, inert. You wonder why you cared at all.

August 25, 2015, was a day of celebration and personal victory. Less than twenty-four hours later, I would have barely been able to spell the words "weekend generation," let alone explain why anyone should care. And a little more than twenty-four hours later, I would find myself back at the dam, my former site of triumph, attempting to shout God Himself down from the Kingdom of Heaven.

———

I'm going to tell you about the worst day of my life.

The list of disagreeable things I'd rather do would make for a book at least twice the length of this one. I realize, however, that it's important for you to know what it was like. It's important for you to have a taste of what I went through on the day my daughter was killed.

Make no mistake, it will be just a taste. I don't know that a team of the finest living writers could record that day so that you would feel exactly what I felt. I can tell you about it; I can show you what happened; but I cannot truly put you in my shoes, and frankly, I wouldn't wish that on you if I could. If I can make you feel at least a fraction of what I felt that day, even 1/100th, I'll feel I've done my job.

Recalling the entire sequence of events precisely is as impossible as filling a jar with mist, but I will tell you what I remember, and I will tell you the most horrible parts I will never forget.

My wife, Barbara, woke me up a little before 7 a.m. on August 26, 2015, shortly after she received a phone call from Alison's live-in boyfriend, WDBJ anchor Chris Hurst. Chris says he didn't call until at least 7:15, but who can know? It was early, especially for me.

I was working from home in those days as a corporate headhunter, and I was accustomed to waking up about 8:00. I didn't usually watch Alison's early morning segments live; I would watch them on the internet over breakfast. I am eternally grateful that I'm not an early riser.

"There were shots fired at Alison's location," Barbara said, stirring me from sleep. "We don't know what's going on."

I stared at the gently whirring fan blades overhead, the fog of sleep still clinging to my brain. The words made little sense, but the uncharacteristic tremor in my wife's voice prodded me.

Shots fired? Alison was a morning news reporter an hour up the road. She wasn't a war journalist. Why would shots be fired?

"Huh?" I said.

"Just get up," Barbara said, leaving the room and padding down the hall toward the kitchen.

I watched the fan rotate against the backdrop of the white popcorn ceiling, watched as the blades stirred dust motes to life in the rays of sunlight streaming through the bedroom's wooden blinds. I crawled out of bed, grabbed the T-shirt and shorts I'd left on the floor the night before, and tried to sort out this new information.

A couple of months earlier, Alison had been covering a story on a meth lab bust in Jacksonville and someone had fired a warning shot to scare off the news crew. This was probably something similar, I thought; some story the locals didn't want covered.

But where was Alison, anyway? I rubbed the sleep from my eyes as I struggled to remember. The marina at Smith Mountain Lake? That seemed right. We'd spent a lot of summers at that marina when Alison was little, tubing and waterskiing behind the boat before retiring to the little Chinese restaurant nearby for some fried pork dumplings. The restaurant was gone, and I'd sold the boat, and since then, the marina had become a major tourist attraction replete with shopping and dining and minigolf for the kids. Why would someone at the marina fire off a warning shot? It didn't make any sense. It was an unlikely site for a meth lab, to say the least.

I figured the easiest way to get to the bottom of this mystery was to just text Alison. Hell, she'd probably already texted me. She was good about that. Ten minutes before her first live CNN report, she'd texted me to tell me to tune in. If she flubbed a word in the middle of a live broadcast, I'd hear about it by the first commercial break. There was little question that by the time I'd slipped on my flip-flops and shuffled into the kitchen to retrieve my phone, I'd have a text message waiting for me—probably two or three.

I walked into the kitchen to find Barbara sitting in her usual roost at the terra-cotta–topped island in our kitchen. The whole house has a Southwestern-style, uncommon for our little town in Henry County. It was one of the reasons we'd picked the place when we'd moved in two decades earlier. The turquoise walls and bleached-pine ceilings reminded us of Texas, which we called home until the late 1970s.

Barbara's coffee mug was in the sink; this was a bit of comforting normalcy. She usually woke up about 6:30 to make coffee, take a stroll in the nearby park, work through a Sudoku puzzle, and watch the videos from Alison's morning segments.

The Sudoku book lay ignored on the kitchen island; Barbara was hunched over her iPhone, her chin-length blonde hair pulled back, working the phone's digital keyboard with the speed and focus of a court stenographer. Her face was creased with concern behind her red-framed glasses.

She momentarily broke away from the phone's screen to glance at me over the glasses.

"Alison's last two hits never went up," she said, then returned her focus to the phone.

"Huh," I said.

When you spend half your life with someone, you learn all of their tells and cues, the subtle gestures that betray the workings of their mind. It might not surprise you to learn that of the two of us, my wife is the one more predisposed to holding her emotions close to the chest. Her eyes, however, never fail to tell the true story.

I've always called Barbara my "doe-eyed goddess." Her hazel eyes are large and expressive, easy to read, a window into her heart. They were one of the first things I loved about her. They've been my saving grace more than once, letting me know when I crossed a line without her saying a word. Alison had those same eyes, deep and rich as chocolate, far darker than you would usually find in someone so fair and blonde. They had that same power to draw you in, and I loved them every bit as much as Barbara's. Alison was my other doe-eyed goddess.

Barbara's eyes revealed her true feelings that morning, and for the first time that day, I felt my heart rate kick into a higher gear.

Alison was normally on the air each weekday morning for three segments ranging from three to five minutes each. The first of those segments ran at 5:45 a.m. After her first week at WDBJ, the sleep deprivation began to get to Barbara and me, and we told Alison that, proud as we were, we'd be watching her segments on the internet when we woke up instead of catching them live. She understood completely. Of course she did.

The fact that the last two segments hadn't dropped meant something was wrong. How wrong remained to be determined. It could be something minor, after all. The feed from the live truck had gone down a handful of times in the year and a half she'd been at WDBJ, which could delay videos for an hour or more. It was rare, but it happened.

I unplugged my phone from the wall charger and checked my messages. Alison hadn't texted me. That was rare, too. Alison always had her phone on her because the station needed to be able to reach her at the drop of a hat. She must be busy, unable to reach her phone. In the middle of an interview, perhaps, or maybe she left her phone in the car, or maybe she dropped it in a puddle and it gave up the ghost. There were a million reasons that she might not answer. There was no sense in jumping to conclusions . . . but then Chris had called, hadn't he? Barbara had mentioned that. And that was unusual, too, because at the time, we barely knew him. Alison and Chris had moved in together just three weeks earlier. It wasn't yet public knowledge, because Chris was an anchor at the station and Alison was next in line for an anchor position. When she got it, he didn't want anyone to think their relationship had been a factor.

Barbara and I knew that Alison loved Chris, and that was enough for us. We had all just celebrated her twenty-fourth birthday the previous weekend by kayaking through the Great Smoky Mountains, same as we did every year, staying in a rented cabin along the Nantahala River. He struck me as a good guy, but I didn't think I'd ever spoken to him without Alison present. I didn't even have his phone number, and I didn't know he had ours. If the situation was bad enough for Chris to call . . .

I pushed the thought from my mind. A man can drive himself crazy gathering up what-ifs. I'd just give Alison a call. As I tapped the icon to open up my recently dialed numbers (knowing hers would be at or near the top of my list), I imagined exactly how the call would go. I figured I'd probably be interrupting some important meeting, probably about how the live truck had lost its connection.

"Oops," I'd say. "Sorry, Scooter. Just your nervous dad. Heard someone was shooting, and I wanted to make sure it was just a camera."

"Oh, Dad," she'd reply with an exaggerated sigh, the smile and the comically rolled eyes somehow audible through the phone's speaker.

"Just wanted to hear your voice," I'd say.

"Don't worry," she'd say. "I'm busy on location. You won't believe what happened, but I've gotta go, so I'll tell you later. Loveyoubye."

Immersed in that reverie, I pressed the "call" button. The phone rang once; twice; three, four, and five times, each unanswered ring adding to the uneasy, tingling sensation working its way across my scalp.

"Hi, you've reached Alison Parker with WDBJ News," her familiar, cheery voice-mail greeting said in my ear. I ended the call.

Outside, I watched our nearly empty red plastic hummingbird feeder sway softly from the eave of the house. Beyond it, a bottle tree, an art project Barbara had assembled from some kit a while back, decorated with brightly colored wine bottles. When she bought the kit, she told me that the bottles were supposed to catch evil spirits and hold them at bay. Neither Barbara nor I are superstitious, but I sometimes wondered if those bottles ever needed to be emptied.

What the hell was going on? Alison always picked up the phone, *always,* even if just to tell me that she couldn't talk.

I read once that before a tsunami hits, the tide rolls out, farther and farther, exposing sand and rocks and scuttling creatures that never see the light of day except just prior to cataclysm. The tsunami needs to gather strength, you see, to marshal every ounce of its resources before flinging itself back at the shore in a towering wave of destruction.

Right then, I could feel the tide rolling away, exposing the dark, squirming creatures to the light of day.

Barbara gripped my hand. We said nothing, attempting to hide our worst fears, neither of us able to muster any bland pleasantries about how all was well and there was probably just some unusual incident, perhaps an exploded transformer or a solar flare or some other such nonsense that had brought down both the live truck and the cell towers around Smith Mountain Lake.

I sat down at the kitchen island and opened my laptop. Barbara moved behind me and placed a gentle hand on my shoulder. The laptop spun to life slowly (why do these damn things start slowing down the second you take them out of the box?) before creaking to life. I googled "Alison Parker." Plenty of old news clips popped up, but nothing new. Nothing that told me anything. I opened a tab and went to WDBJ's website. Nothing. Back to Google. Nothing. I opened another tab and typed in "Smith Mountain Lake." There were sketchy reports of shots fired, but nothing concrete, nothing useful, nothing that answered any questions. I navigated between the three tabs, compulsively clicking the reload button, the minutes ticking away.

My ringtone for Alison was Van Morrison's "Brown Eyed Girl." Surely the phone would ring any minute now, Van the Man's tinny voice echoing off the turquoise walls. I conjured an image in my mind of Alison picking up the phone, her eyes widening in mild surprise at the missed calls she had received, tapping the numbers to reply in order of importance. I knew I'd be the first one she called. I willed the phone to ring.

"I'm calling Lane," I said.

Lane Perry is Henry County's sheriff. I'd known him for years, back since I was elected to the Board of Supervisors in 2003. He's a good guy, a tall, plainspoken man with a crew cut so perpetually close-cropped that it probably requires daily maintenance. If Lane knew anything, I knew he would tell me.

Lane answered his cell immediately. He said he was sorry to report that he didn't know much more than I did. He had also heard that *something* happened up at the marina, and he was reaching out to his colleagues in Franklin County to see what he could learn. He promised to call me back as soon as he heard anything.

As I got off the phone with Lane, I heard the tail end of Barbara's phone conversation. She had been calling area hospitals, but no one named Alison Parker had been admitted, and they hadn't heard anything about a shooting.

Within minutes, my phone rang; not "Brown-Eyed Girl," but a generic ringtone. Lane Perry.

"They said there *has* been a shooting at the marina," Lane said, "but they think the news crew is OK. I'll let you know just as soon as I hear anything else."

"That's encouraging," I said weakly, and ended the call.

I thought about grabbing my keys and driving to the marina, but Smith Mountain Lake was at least an hour's drive away, better than half of it down a long, twisting two-lane road with intermittent cell service. What if Lane called back with news, or Alison called to tell me all was well, that she had just misplaced her phone about the same time a car had coincidentally backfired nearby? I was terrified to miss a phone call, so I stayed at the kitchen island with Barbara.

We sat there in silence for the most part, looking out the window at the hummingbird feeder, the bottle tree, the middle distance beyond. I'd occasionally refresh my tabs on the browser; there were no updates.

I couldn't tell you the exact minute that we began to lose hope, but it happened sometime after that second phone call with Lane.

Years ago I read a story—I can't remember where—about twin brothers in Kansas, or maybe Nebraska, one of those perfectly flat Midwestern states. They were both power company linemen, and one day one of the brothers touched the wrong wire and got zapped, dying instantly. Fifty miles away, his brother was in a work truck with a coworker. He pulled over and stopped the truck.

"Oh God," he said, sobbing, "my brother is dead."

As the story goes, they checked the times, and sure enough, he called it to the minute. He just knew.

Maybe that story is bullshit. It sure sounds like it. Or maybe there's something to it. Maybe close family—twin brothers, or parents and their children—have some sort of deeper connection, some quantum physics thing that science doesn't yet understand, an invisible umbilicus that connects us no matter how far apart we travel.

I don't know. But I do know that as Barbara and I sat at our kitchen island, the morning sun pouring through the windows, filtering different hues by those wildly ineffective evil-capturing glass bottles outside, we began to realize that our daughter was dead. It wasn't something we ever would have voiced. I don't know that we even realized it on a rational level. But on some subconscious wavelength, we knew it to be true.

We waited for the call.

———

I always had a premonition that Alison would die young.

Some would probably chalk that statement up to confirmation bias; the death of a child is every parent's greatest fear, after all.

Some might also blame it on intrusive thoughts. They say that a lot of new mothers end up going to psychologists for that, convinced they're psychotic. They tell the doctor that they were sitting in the lovingly assembled nursery bedecked with stuffed animals, stencils of the ABCs on the walls, their infant nursing peacefully at their breast, when they suddenly had a mad thought: *What if I took my tiny, fragile, defenseless child and threw it against the wall as hard as I could?*

That is an intrusive thought, perhaps the worst one. But the psychologists assure the new mothers that they wouldn't act on that impulse; it is simply human nature to imagine the worst things possible, the things that would utterly destroy us, and replay them in our minds like a looped filmstrip. The brain can be infinitely cruel.

For me, though, it never felt like an intrusive thought, and it never felt like confirmation bias. This was not standard-issue parental anxiety; it was disturbingly specific.

For one thing, Alison drove like a bat out of hell and it scared the living shit out of me. Barbara and I would white-knuckle our way through rides with Alison, instinctively pumping the imaginary passenger-side brake pedal as she streaked through curves.

I was afraid she would die in a car crash, but my imagination went far beyond that. I would imagine the scene of the crash, the twisted wreckage, the guttering flames on the asphalt from the spilled gasoline. I'd imagine having to identify her body. I'd imagine gruesome, unspeakable images of my child's death, and I wouldn't wish that on any other human being. To be clear, I wouldn't wish death on anyone, but I wouldn't even wish those mangled images my mind had conjured on another human being. For most of Alison's life, my imagination was a taped-off crime scene.

A car crash was the reigning fear, just because it seemed so eminently possible, plausible even. But my imagination wasn't limited to car crashes. I saw malevolent shadows at her periphery wherever she went.

I never imagined a shooting, though, not even in my wildest fears. Alison was in elementary school when the Columbine shooting occurred, in high school when the massacre at Virginia Tech took place, and then there had been Sandy Hook, Charleston, and all the others. So many others. For whatever reason, it had never even crossed my mind that Alison would die by someone's hand. Even as I compulsively imagined fiery car wrecks, maybe a shooting was just too terrible to even consider.

———

My phone rang a little before 8 a.m. It was Greg Baldwin, WDBJ's assistant news producer. I answered.

"Mr. Parker, I'm so sorry," he said. "I can't even imagine . . ."

I don't remember what else he said, or what I said, or even if I said anything at all. The last thing I remember is my vision narrowing to a point, blackness swallowing me up on all sides.

Barbara says that I gasped and crumpled to the floor, one hand stupidly clutching the handle on the oven door. I believe her, but I don't recall it.

I do remember sitting on the floor, Barbara holding me and me holding her, because of course she knew without a word passing between us. I remember blackness, the absence of light, the absence of everything. Whatever essence I had, whatever life force or soul, drained out of my body, from the crown of my head down the chest, gut, and limbs, down into some yawning abyss beneath me. Gone, never to be refilled.

I couldn't breathe. I looked at Barbara, my throat closed up, both our eyes pinched, mouths drawn as if to cry. But we couldn't, not then. That would come later. But in that moment, the shock was too great, like some horror so frightening that you can't even scream, you can only stand there mutely, waiting for the end.

I pinched myself at some point, because maybe this was a dream. Yes, *there* was something to latch onto, a dream, the worst I'd ever had to be sure, but a dream nonetheless, and now it was time to wake up, and when I finally did wake up I would tell everyone about it, what a hideous nightmare, the worst I'd ever had or ever hope to have. Maybe in time I would laugh about it, Alison would laugh about it too; we would laugh about it together because it was just so *crazy* and she would suggest that I probably shouldn't eat leftover pizza right before bed and I would say, You've got that right, lesson learned, Scooter; I'm just glad that wasn't real, thank Christ that wasn't real.

I would call Alison, that's what I would do, I would call her up and she would answer, just like always, because she's so good about that, and she'd tell us a wild story about that car backfiring or that transformer blowing up, and Barbara and I would hop in the car to drive to Roanoke, and there she would be, just like always, and Barbara and I would hug her. We would squeeze her so tight that she would joke that *she* was the one who couldn't breathe, and we would press our faces into her waves of shoulder-length blonde hair, and we'd smell that hairspray she loved that smelled like roses, and we would never let her go, never, and she would understand completely, she was always understanding, and everything would be normal again because nothing had happened at all, really, it was all just a bad dream.

I sucked in a ragged breath and held my wife, and she held me, and we sat there on the kitchen floor.

It didn't feel real then. It wouldn't feel real for days, weeks, months. Some mornings, when I first wake up and my brain is still winding itself up to full consciousness, it still doesn't feel real.

My daughter, my Scooter, was dead. My treasure was stolen. My world was obliterated; its carefully assembled parts, pieced together across a lifetime, picked up by the hand of a cruel, capricious God and dashed to the floor.

I was numb then, but that numbness would fade throughout the day, replaced by new emotions that made me yearn for the numbness to return.

I don't know how long Barbara and I held each other in the kitchen. I don't know how long we stared out at that hummingbird feeder. I don't know who spoke first or what was said. There's a lot about that day—*The* Day, as I've taken to calling it—that I'll probably never know. Some of it I don't want to know. Eventually, though, we decided we needed to tell our families. Part of me didn't want to. Part of me, I think, felt that it if we kept it to ourselves, it would be like it had never happened.

I knew we didn't have a choice, though. I'd gotten the call and I was fairly certain I wasn't asleep; I'd pinched myself, just to be sure. Barbara knew about it now, too, and I didn't think she was asleep. What were the odds that we'd both had the same dream at the same time and emerged into that state somewhere between dreaming and waking where you're not sure which is which and you don't know how much of what you remember has actually happened and how much of it was all in your head? I don't know if that even makes sense. Nothing made sense. It couldn't be real.

If it was real, we knew the shooting would soon hit the news and we wanted our families to hear it from us first. While Barbara called her sister in Sherman, an hour north of Dallas, I called Drew. As I mentioned, Drew has Asperger's, and he doesn't register emotion in the same way that you or I would. That call elicited as much shock and sorrow as I've ever heard from him.

I called my sister Jane Ann back in Austin, and I asked her to tell our mother, still living on her own at ninety-one. It felt strange to speak the words, to say something I knew was true—that Alison was dead—but still couldn't bring myself to believe. It was like I had found myself in the Twilight Zone, some parallel dimension where the sun didn't shine and water flowed uphill. I hadn't moved more than three feet from the kitchen island all morning.

As we were spreading the news, I got a call from someone telling me to meet at a staging area near the marina at 10:00 a.m. The words barely registered, but I made a mental note. Then the phone rang again. I didn't know the number, but I picked it up anyway. I would have answered it on any other day without a second thought. Maybe, I thought, if I answered like I usually would, things would finally return to normal.

"Hey, man," a voice said. It was Trey Weir, a client of mine from a bank in Charlotte. Nothing felt different yet, I thought, but give it time. "I need you to find me a new portfolio manager."

I said nothing. Still waiting. For what, I honestly didn't know.

"Andy?"

"Trey," I said, "I don't think I'll be able to help you. My daughter's just been killed."

It was probably unfair of me to dump that on him—he couldn't have known, but what was I supposed to say? What was he supposed to say? He managed to stammer, "Oh, my God, I'm so sorry. I can't even imagine."

I hung up. I might have thanked him first.

Looking back, I see a weird coincidence and wonder what to make of it. Just the year before, while working on a similar search, I sent a résumé to Trey and he passed on it. I emailed the candidate and told him the position was "not a good fit" but that I would keep an eye out for him for future opportunities. A few days later, Trey called to ask me if I'd heard the news about this banker. I hadn't. Apparently, he'd left a long, rambling message on Trey's voice mail and then shot himself. A forty-year-old with a wife and two young kids.

"Andy, you've got to start letting your candidates down a little easier," he said.

Of all of the phone calls I might have gotten at that particular moment, why was it Trey on the other end of the line? Was there some meaning in it, some cosmic message that was lost on me?

I might have thought that sharing our grief would somehow lighten our load, distribute the burden, but instead it seemed to multiply, the words landing with dull thuds, disbelief, then detonation. Every phone call made me feel worse. I'm sure it was no picnic to be on the receiving end either.

Soon it was time to go to the staging area. *Staging for what?* I wondered. I didn't know what we were supposed to do when we got there, but I never considered not going. Maybe I should have. With some effort I finally abandoned my post in the kitchen. It was much lighter in the bedroom now. The fan still whirred, the air purifier still hummed, the blinds were still drawn, but the window now lay in full sun.

This is where I was, I thought, *when she died. If I go back to bed, will she be alive again?*

My arms and legs felt heavy and numb as I went into the closet to change. I grabbed a polo shirt and khaki shorts, the first things I saw that looked reasonably presentable, feeling all the while like a condemned man preparing to walk down death row. In my mind I could clearly see the weather-beaten row of wooden planking at the marina leading down to the water, no doubt glistening in the late August sun. Death row, I thought.

It should have been me. Why her and not me? I'd have given anything to trade places with her. I imagined Alison lying on that planking. I didn't want to, but that's how intrusive thoughts work.

For weeks afterward, every time I stopped for even a moment, I found myself imagining her death. At the same time, I genuinely felt that if I saw it, if I ever saw the video I'd learned there was of it, I wouldn't be able to handle it. I wouldn't necessarily die. I would just end. I would cease to be.

They say that sharks swim even while they're asleep, because if they stop swimming, the water stops flowing over their gills and they drown. Like a shark, I couldn't stop. Even then, even on the day Alison was killed, I knew that I needed to channel all of the emotions coursing through my veins into something bigger than myself. I needed to pick a fight. It didn't really matter with whom. It was the only thing I could think to do, the only way I thought I'd be able to survive.

And I needed to survive. I needed to do it for Alison. If she was really gone, then her death had to mean something. Then and there, standing at the closet and picking out a polo shirt, I vowed I would make her death mean something.

Barbara must have been changing right alongside me, but I

don't remember it. The next thing I knew, we were sitting in our new charcoal-gray Honda CR-V heading north on Route 220 toward Roanoke, Barbara with her hair pulled back under a khaki Nantahala Outdoor Center ball cap the way she always did when she wanted to look presentable but didn't have the time or energy to make a big show of it.

The staging area was about forty-five minutes away. For the first half hour it was virtually silent inside the car. We didn't turn on the radio, didn't play any music, didn't say a word. There was no sound aside from the wind whipping past the windows and the tires on the road. Route 220 winds through the foothills of the Blue Ridge Mountains, the road surrounded on either side by a dense wall of evergreen trees. At the top of a hill we rounded a bend and the landscape opened up in front of us. From the crest of the ridge, the rolling wooded hills lay spread before us under a deep blue sky, the sun shining through fluffy white clouds. The scene was picture-perfect, like something off of a postcard. Scenes like that are the reason people move to Virginia, why the colonials settled here in the first place, why the Confederates fought and died over the land. Barbara and I had raised our family here because we loved this land too. As I stared out into that ethereal blue, I realized that that's where Alison was now. She was no longer on this earth. Her soul was out mingling somewhere in the vast expanse before me. And in that moment, the dam burst. Feeling finally returned to my body. I wept uncontrollably for the remainder of the drive.

For the first five minutes or so, Barbara reached over and held my right hand while I drove with my left. Then the tears picked up and I needed to wipe my eyes, so she moved her hand to my knee. All morning I had felt numb. Now as I felt pressed back into myself, I felt a heaviness settling over me like an astronaut might feel while being launched into a brave new world. Barbara asked a few times if she needed to drive, but I was not going to pull over. I couldn't stop.

Barbara has always been my rock. Even in the depths of her unfathomable sorrow, her incredible pain, she was stoic. She did not weep. In contrast, I was a wreck. All I could think about was how Alison was gone and I had failed her. I hadn't been there to protect her when she had needed me most. Certainly, there had been no God to protect her—as T. C. Boyle wrote: "We are powerless. We are bereft. And the gods—all the gods of all the ages combined—are nothing but a rumor."

I wondered what she had thought about at the end, whether she had thought of me, had wished for me, had called for me. I felt like I was going to throw up, simply erupt like a volcano, but I wasn't sure whether I was about to spew grief or sadness or stomach bile or red-hot molten rage or some combination. I wished again that I could have been there for her, that I could have gone in her place. Had any sort of supernatural being appeared to make the offer, "Devil and Daniel Webster"-style, I would have gone at a moment's notice.

I still would, if anyone's listening.

The staging area turned out to be a small church parking lot cordoned off and monitored by a middle-aged officer sporting a khaki sheriff's uniform and a crew cut, squinting behind aviator glasses in the glare of the late summer sun. He might have been a dad himself. He didn't know us, though, and when he asked who we were, it set me off.

"We're Alison's parents, goddammit!"

I regretted it as soon as the words left my mouth. He didn't know any better. He was just doing his job.

It was my first—but sure as hell not my last—angry outburst since it happened, even as I was still having a hard time saying what "it" was, even just to myself. It was only 10 a.m., but it was already oppressively hot. I could feel the heat rolling in through the open car window and rising into my face. I imagined one of those elementary school volcano diagrams, the lava merely a surface manifestation of deeper turmoil below the surface, turmoil touched off by a tectonic shift that threatened to topple all structures and all lives on this suddenly unstable terrain; lava that would rise and explode to incinerate everything it touched, buildings and bridges alike, leaving nothing but ash. Just like the diagrams, I felt the burning lava rise in my throat, molten anger that erupted from me in the form of vicious words I had little control over.

The officer winced, took a step back, put his hand to his mouth as if to protect his face. Chagrined, he apologized and waved us into the lot. We quickly spotted Mike Bell, the program, promotions, and operations director at WDBJ. I had met Mike the previous spring at the Franklin County Moonshine Festival. Barbara and I had met Alison and Chris there and they'd introduced us to Mike. His wife, Nancy, worked in the Henry County school system and Barbara knew her quite well. Mike was a kindly, professorial man with a salt-and-pepper vandyke beard, a shock of unruly hair more heavily salted than peppered, and dark-tinted glasses. He had a dry wit and habitually carried his mouth in a slight downturn while still managing to be warm and welcoming. What I noticed first, though, was his cane: he had just had his knee replaced. I was walking with a cane, too, and would soon be heading in for surgery of my own. We became fast friends and remain close to this day.

There were no smiles that morning in the church parking lot, the sun beating down on the blacktop, heat rising up beneath our feet. I had tried to wipe away my tears before exiting the car, but when Mike and I embraced, I lost it again. He was crying too. To tell the truth, it looked like he had just been to hell and back. I found out later that Mike, a former firefighter, had been asked to identify Alison and Adam's bodies. He later told me it was one of the hardest things he's ever had to do. I know it will haunt him for the rest of his life.

Mike lost a foster daughter to gun violence. He knew what we were going through. Because he knew our pain so well, he still has post-traumatic flashbacks to that miserable morning, episodes that contributed to the dissolution of his marriage. Despite all of the morbid images that had been flooding my mind, I hadn't even thought about identifying Alison's body. I don't think I could have done it. I don't ever want to know what Mike saw that day, and I'm grateful he was there to do it for me.

Mike told us that the third victim, the interviewee—a woman named Vicki Gardner, the executive director of the local chamber of commerce—had survived the shooting and was in emergency surgery. Then he dropped the bombshell.

"We think we know who the shooter was," he said.

The suspected shooter was a former reporter at the station, he said, a man by the name of Bryce Williams who had been fired almost two years earlier. That didn't make sense to me. A former employee of the station? Everyone loved Alison and Alison loved everyone. What brought this on? Why would he shoot his old coworkers? Why Alison?

Mike shrugged, wiping the sweat from his brow with the back of his hand. "We really don't know," he said.

"Mike," I said, my arm wrapped around Barbara's shoulder to support myself as much as her, "I just have to know if she suffered. Please tell me she didn't suffer."

He assured me she did not.

For a long moment none of us said anything; we just stood taking in the horror and the heartbreak in one another's faces. Cars went whizzing by on the road in front of the church, off to who knows where, the people inside minding their own business as usual. Couldn't they feel it? Didn't they know what had happened here, down by the water just over that rise? How could they carry on as if nothing had happened?

The chief deputy of the Franklin County Sheriff's Office, a barrel-chested, no-nonsense sort of man, snapped me back to attention. I hadn't even noticed his approach until he was right in front of me. He stood at least six-foot-four, and in a commanding voice, he confirmed that they had a suspect and were working on tracking him down. I asked what we needed to do next, and he said we should go home and wait for further information.

"When you catch this guy," I said, struggling ineffectually to contain the rage in my voice, "I want a few minutes alone with him."

"I understand, Mr. Parker," the deputy said. "I wish I could."

I have no doubt he meant it.

In that moment, all of my anger was directed toward the shooter, about whom I knew almost nothing. *If the police take him alive*, I thought to myself, *I'll kill him. I will find a way to get to him and then I'll make him watch home movies of the lives he stole. I'll make him live the moment when my little Scooter, all of six years old, wearing pigtails and overalls and missing a front tooth, got so scared by the special effects at Universal Studios's brand-new Twister attraction that she jumped straight up into my arms and buried her head in my chest, eyes wide as saucers.* It was always one of my favorite memories of her. It still is, actually, and even as I write these words, the page is swimming and I can feel the old familiar lump rising up in my throat. I used to tell that story over and over again and Alison would always put up a pro forma protest, but secretly she loved it. That was the moment I became her protector, and it was a lifetime appointment. If she ever needed me, she knew that all she had to do was say the word and I'd come running.

Except when I didn't. I wasn't there for her this morning. I didn't know she needed me until it was too late. I didn't know how I could possibly live with the shame, the incredible gut-wrenching guilt that wracked my insides, the barely contained rage bubbling just beneath it.

When I got my hands on the shooter, I decided, I would show him the pictures of that family vacation and then I would end him. An eye for an eye. At that moment, I didn't care if the whole world ended up blind. There was nothing left I wanted to see. I was so focused on catching the shooter and bringing him to justice that I never imagined what we would ultimately learn about him, or the heartache it would bring.

I was the same sobbing mess on the way home. Somehow we made it back in one piece, and at home we found our friends Lynn and Noel Ward waiting for us (no relation to Adam). I don't know if Lynn called Barbara or Barbara called Lynn. Maybe the Wards just heard the news and came right over, no questions asked. Barbara and Lynn had worked together for years at Piedmont Arts, the center of the social scene in small-town Martinsville, and they had been our best friends for most of the nearly twenty years we'd lived in town. Lynn looks like a made-to-order grandmother straight out of a holiday catalog. She's almost always smiling a big warm smile, and she has a cute button nose in the middle of a round face framed by wavy gray hair. Noel, with his square jaw, asymmetrical nose, and short, wavy gray hair, may have looked like an aging prizefighter but was actually an accountant who had done well enough with a local manufactured-home company that he had already retired. Barbara and I had spent quite a few enjoyable weekends with the Wards at their beach house.

That day wasn't a social visit—it was one of the first times I had ever seen Lynn without a smile—but I don't know what we would have done without them. The house felt stale, sterile. The weight of our grief slowly filled each room like a water balloon, pressing harder and harder against us the more it inflated. Lynn had brought over a card table that she set up in the center of the tiled living room floor while Noel went out for coolers, ice, drinks, cups, paper plates, plastic utensils, a guest book, and all the other items that you inexplicably need when a life ends. He lined the items up on the kitchen island as soon as he returned, while Lynn started answering the phone and receiving the visitors who showed up at the front door unannounced. She directed traffic with quiet efficiency and organized meal deliveries for the coming days. According to the guest book, that first afternoon there was chicken salad and pimento cheese, followed in the next few days by barbeque and baked spaghetti and banana pudding, all manner of casseroles, and at some point, a whole tray of tacos and enchiladas donated by the local Mexican restaurant.

I don't remember any of it. I don't remember eating anything that entire day—perhaps a spoonful here and there, but I certainly never sat down with a plate. I wasn't hungry. For almost a week, the very idea of food made me ill. I lost five pounds before September 1 rolled around. The Lose-a-Daughter Diet Plan is damned effective, but the sales numbers are abysmal.

Lynn and Noel took care of many of the immediate practical concerns, which freed us up to do other things. Barbara, meanwhile, had totally bought into Barbara Kingsolver's theory of grief, supporting the importance of staying busy: she moved fluidly from one task to the next without ever stopping long enough to let herself feel the pain I could see in her eyes. She sat down at the island—the same spot where we'd held vigil just hours earlier, to no avail—and called the funeral home to arrange a venue for Alison's memorial service. I still don't know how she made that call. The very idea of "Alison's memorial service" would have been blasphemous if spoken aloud not even eight hours earlier. Barbara did it, though, and the moment she ended the call with the funeral home, she was back on the phone, this time with Alison's alma mater, JMU, to set up a scholarship fund in her honor.

I look back now on everything Barbara did that afternoon and I can't help but shake my head in amazement. She tells me that she did those things simply because they had to be done. Women are stronger, she says, and that was her job. Maybe she's right. I once asked her if she resented me for not helping. Of course not, she said. She knew I wasn't ready. We have different strengths, she said, and we divided the labor of our grief between us in the same way we split the housework: she does the dusting, I mop the floors.

It was comforting to see how many people felt compelled to come by, how many people loved Alison, but I was in no way up to entertaining them. They mostly left me alone. No one really knew what to say, other than "I can't even imagine." My part would come later.

On that first afternoon, unsure what else to do, I sat down in the kitchen, mostly oblivious to the chaos bustling around me, and I looked out at the bird feeder. It was getting low. I thought about going out to refill it, just to have something to do, when my phone buzzed in my pocket. I pulled it out and read the CNN update:

POLICE: VESTER FLANAGAN KILLS SELF AFTER ON-AIR SLAYINGS

Vester Flanagan? I thought his name was Bryce Williams? Who the fuck is Vester Flanagan? My pulse racing, I skimmed the story: just before 11:30 a.m., Virginia State Police spotted the shooter's car heading east on I-66, almost 170 miles away from the marina, and attempted to pull him over. Instead of stopping, he sped up and led police on a high-speed chase down the freeway until he crashed into an embankment along the side of the road. When officers approached the vehicle, they found him dead from a self-inflicted gunshot.

It's difficult to explain what I felt in that moment. I certainly didn't mourn him. I obviously wasn't sad that the world had lost him, but I also didn't take any pleasure in his death. Mostly I felt the loss of a sense of purpose: he had killed himself before being brought to justice. There would be no arraignments, no trials, no tear-filled testimony, the shooter in handcuffs and an orange jumpsuit at a solid oak table, Barbara and I sitting day after day with our arms around each other in the front row of the gallery, staring daggers into the shooter and choking back tears. To be clear, I didn't want any of those things, but at least they would have given me a reason to get up in the morning. I felt, if anything, somehow emptier than before. I didn't mourn the shooter, but I did mourn my loss of purpose.

As I stared at my phone, my head throbbing, my stomach in free fall, I flailed about for a new cause, a new reason to keep on living. There had to be justice for Alison. She was too special and meant far too much to me for her to fall victim to a senseless tragedy, to be just another statistic. Her life had meant something. I vowed that her death would mean something too. There would be justice for Alison yet.

Thumbing quickly through the rest of the story, I felt my stomach lurch before the words mentally registered: my daughter's killing was recorded on video. Not just the interrupted news footage, which I knew existed but had no intention of ever seeing. The killer himself had taped the whole thing. He'd worn a GoPro camera mounted on his forehead. He'd shot three people in cold blood and then unloaded six or seven bullets into two lifeless bodies. Then he'd calmly walked back to his car and uploaded the footage to Facebook. On Twitter he added, "I filmed the shooting see Facebook."

As if it wasn't bad enough that my daughter, my vivacious, beautiful, award-winning daughter, had been murdered this morning.

Live footage of my daughter's murder was on fucking Facebook.

No, this couldn't be a nightmare. This was far, far worse than anything I ever could have imagined, because I didn't *have* to imagine it. It was right there in front of my face, the little gray triangle pointing directly toward the moment at which Alison's life was snuffed out.

This time I felt sure I was going to throw up. I stood up abruptly, my chair skittering across the linoleum, and quick-stepped my way to the bedroom.

I've been asked about that moment more times than I can begin to count. Yes, I was sickened, and yes, I was saddened, but those words aren't strong enough. No words are strong enough. This was a whole new level of violation. It was like some medieval execution, having your beating heart torn out and shown to you as you die.

As every parent knows, having a child is the best and the worst thing that can ever happen to you, the source of your highest highs and lowest lows, your greatest joys and your deepest sorrows. When you have a kid, you're no longer just wearing your heart on your sleeve. You're wiping her nose and tying her shoes and walking her to the school bus in the morning. Alison was my beating heart, and this son of a bitch wanted me to watch it stop beating in real time.

Never.

I have never seen that video, and I will never see that video. More than once I have exploded at people who tried to show it to me. Why? Why would anyone assume I had seen it, and more than that, why would anyone assume I want to see it? Isn't it enough that my daughter died? Do I really need to watch it happen on live TV? Isn't it enough for me to know that it's floating around out there on the internet for any sick fuck who wants to watch it? Who would want to, anyway? What kind of cruel, ghoulish rubbernecker would want to watch my daughter die?

I slammed the bedroom door and collapsed onto our unmade bed. The room began to spin. My daughter, murdered on live TV, the video available for all the world to see. It truly was worse than my worst nightmare, the perfect tragedy for the digital age. Shakespeare couldn't make this up. Already I felt wounded by all the unseen eyes gawking at the electric spectacle of her death, and I lay there listening to the muffled conversations in the kitchen, staring at the motes of dust aloft in the long shafts of sunlight, wondering if I could just go to sleep forever.

Why had this happened?

I had so many questions. I had to finish reading the article. Still flat on my back, the thin green blanket rumpled beneath me where I had thrown it off to get dressed earlier that morning, seemingly a lifetime ago, I curled one hand toward my face and unlocked my phone. Details were still coming in, the article said, and they would for days afterward. The biggest bombshells were yet to come, but what was known already was plenty explosive. Not two hours after the shooting, ABC News had received a twenty-three-page fax: "Suicide Note For Friends & Family By Bryce Williams (legal name: Vester Lee Flanagan II)." He'd gotten the fax number a few weeks earlier when he called the network wanting to "pitch a story." He never said what the story was.

I was wracked with a new wave of agony roiling in my gut, but still I couldn't stop reading. According to the article, the shooter alleged that he had been fired from WDBJ because of racial discrimination and sexual harassment, which he said had steadily fueled his anger. The final straw, however, came when he claimed that Jehovah appeared to him two months earlier, right after the Charleston church shooting, and told him to act. He put down a deposit on a gun two days later.

The murder weapon.

This guy's fucking nuts, I thought, *and he purchased his gun legally.*

In his fax he professed admiration for the Columbine shooters and the Virginia Tech gunman. But he wrote such vitriol about the Charleston shooter that CNN felt compelled to redact every other word: "As for Dylann Roof? You [deleted]! You want a race war [deleted]? BRING IT THEN YOU WHITE [deleted]!!!"

I shook my head. This guy was seriously messed up. He had needed real help. Part of the crime, I thought, was that instead of help, he was given a gun. This was the obvious outcome of handing a gun to a lunatic like him. The fault didn't lie with gun owners, by and large, and it didn't lie with gun sellers or gun manufacturers. The fault was with those who wanted to make guns available to anyone with as few restrictions as possible. The fault was with the gun lobby and their paid-for politicians.

How many shootings do we have to witness before we finally do something substantial to stop them? I had seen the president cry on national television, for God's sake, and I knew those tears were real. I knew how President Obama felt about Charleston and Sandy Hook, and as I lay in bed, clutching my phone, my world spinning, I wondered why more people didn't stand up, didn't pressure their legislators to finally do something about the endless shootings, didn't push to keep guns out of the hands of crazy people, to provide at least some half-hearted funding for mental health. I feared it was simply because they don't know what it feels like to lose a child. They're right; they can't even imagine. I felt another eruption building.

My phone rang.

"Mr. Parker, this is Terry McAuliffe." The governor of Virginia. In spite of my anger, I couldn't help but be impressed. "I'm so sorry to hear about your daughter. I can't even imagine what you and your family must be going through right now."

Governor McAuliffe is a consummate politician with a perfect politician's voice: smooth, confident, genuine, forceful enough to get what he wants, but polished enough that you wouldn't want to resist anyway. We talked for about five minutes, me pacing in the half-light of the bedroom, the purifier humming, the fan blowing cool air across my face, until he asked what he could do to help. I told him I was not going to let my daughter die in vain. I told him I was coming after the NRA, any politicians who wouldn't budge on gun control, and anyone who stood in my way.

"Andy, I'm right there with you," he said. And he was.

When I hung up with the governor it was almost 2:00 p.m. and the emails from the news networks were rolling in. Just the day before, when I wanted to trumpet my success at the dam, none of the national shows would have given me the time of day. Today everyone wanted me. They were all clamoring for me to be on their show, to tell my story—Alison's story—on their air.

And the funny thing is, I didn't really want to talk to anyone. What was I supposed to do? Go on a press tour because my daughter is dead? The first email came from Sean Hannity. *You've got to be kidding me*, I thought. Then Greta Van Susteren. Nope. I wasn't sure I wanted to do any interviews, but I sure as shit wasn't going to start off with Fox News, where I knew I'd have to tangle with some Second Amendment apologist who'd want to wipe away Alison's shooting like so many others before it. *Why don't you wipe up the fucking blood at the marina?* I thought. The image of her lying there on the wooden planking, eyes closed, haunted me. I imagine it always will.

Then my sister Jane Ann called back. Ian Shapira with the *Washington Post* had managed to get hold of her, hoping that she could put him in touch with me. I'll say this much for journalists, they're a resourceful lot. "He seems like a genuinely nice guy," she said. "I really think you should talk to him."

I sighed. So it begins. This is my Bull Run. I took down his information, hung up with Jane Ann, and punched in the number.

To his credit, Ian was every bit as kind and decent as Jane Ann had said. He really wanted to understand what kind of person Alison was, how devastated I was.

"Pretty damn devastated," I said.

We talked for close to thirty minutes. I paced the whole time. It still didn't feel real. He thanked me for my time and promised to email me a link to the story as soon as it was posted.

That was the first one, but it wouldn't be the last.

After getting off the phone with Ian, I knew had to get out of the house. I needed air.

"I'm taking the dog out," I told Barbara without breaking stride. Jack, our ten-year-old Chow-golden retriever mix, knew the drill. We often went out in the early afternoon, but that fluffball could sniff out a walk a mile away. We got in the car, Jack beside me in the passenger seat, and I started driving without really knowing where I was going.

I drove straight to the Philpott Dam kayak put-in. The icy, crystal clear water was rushing out of the lake, over the dam, and down the river, thin wisps of fog hanging just a few feet above the frothing surface of the downstream rapids. Jack and I crunched down the gravel path toward the water. Tall evergreens lined the banks on both sides, the scent of pine strong in the air. Jack lapped at the stream as it burbled by.

Of course I would come to the dam, just as a compass needle is drawn toward magnetic North. I'd told Barbara that I needed to be alone, but that wasn't true.

I needed to be with Alison. This was where she'd be.

We'd been coming here together for years. Alison and Chris and Barbara and I had launched our kayaks at this very spot just last month, on the Fourth of July. It's where I was the day before. The day before. What I wouldn't give to go back. Just twenty-four hours earlier, I'd been so proud of my success, the centerpiece of my bid for reelection to the Henry County Board of Supervisors. Just twenty-four hours earlier, Alison had been alive. Now she wasn't. And now nothing else mattered.

I gazed downriver and for a split second I saw her paddling around the bend, a big smile on her face. How could it be that I'd never see that smile again, except in memory? I ached to hold her in my arms again. I stood there, bitterness and resentment and anger rising within me, rage and vitriol and bile, and then I erupted with all the force of Etna, Pompeii, and Mount St. Helens put together.

This time it was directed toward God. I've never been particularly religious, but I gave that bastard an earful. People always tell me that it was Alison's time to go, that God called her home. What a stupid fucking thing to say. What kind of comfort is that? What kind of God would do something like that? Not any God I want to know, that's for damn sure.

When I ran out of expletives to hurl skyward, I collapsed onto the closest boulder, totally spent. Jack sat faithfully at my feet. There was no one else around, no sound but the soft murmur of the stream. I let the river wash away my anger.

One of our family's favorite movies has always been *Galaxy Quest*, a *Star Trek* send-up from the late nineties that now seems to be a staple of late-night cable TV. The aliens' motto in that movie is "Never give up. Never surrender." Over time it became something of a mantra for our entire family. With Alison's imitation of the aliens' comically stilted cadence echoing in my head, I knew I had to listen. I couldn't give up, no matter how much I wanted to. I had to keep her memory alive. I also knew that if I was going to make it through the night, I was going to need some help. Still propped up on the boulder, with Jack sniffing idly around the water's edge, I dug into the pocket of my shorts for my phone.

Our family doctor had already heard the news by the time I got hold of him. "I can't imagine," he said. He called in a prescription for Xanax to help Barbara and me get to sleep and said to take care and call him back if there was anything else he could do. I thanked him and hung up and sat staring off over the rushing water, into the lush greenery and the flowering mountain laurels, and I thought, *This is where she'll be. I'll always be able to find her here.* I felt a great sense of calm in that idea. I have no idea how long I sat on the boulder, Jack at my feet, before I finally rose and we trudged back up the hill toward the car.

On my way back home from the river something compelled me to stop at Town Gun, our friendly local firearms store. Part of me thought I might need to buy a gun for protection. There was no reason to do so because the truthers had not yet descended. Another part of me wanted to know how fast a person could buy a gun. Looking back, I expect those reasons were a pretext for a different, darker reason.

The guy behind the counter didn't know who I was and was quite eager to show me a Smith & Wesson .38 Special. According to him, it was the perfect self-defense weapon. "Is there a waiting period?" I asked, assuming there surely must be.

"Oh, no," he cheerfully replied. "You just fill out this paperwork, and we'll have the background check done in minutes. No waiting at all!"

What the fuck are you doing here? I thought to myself. Are you so deep in shock that you're actually thinking of buying a gun? For what? Do you really think she wants you to join her?

I returned to my senses, such as they were, and told the clerk I'd think about it and come back later. I realized later that the visit to the gun shop was my subconscious taking control, directing me to peer into the abyss as I stood precariously at the precipice. I wondered how many others had paid a gun shop that same visit, hiding their misery as I had, and bought that .38 that would only be fired once. As I would later discover, it happens daily.

The moment I managed to step back from the brink, I realized I had to fight. I had to come out swinging hard.

When we got back to the house, Alison's boyfriend, Chris, had arrived and Lynn had managed to clear out most of the other guests. Barbara's family and mine would come up in the next couple of days, but they hadn't arrived yet. It was Barbara, Lynn, Noel, Chris, and me, sitting around the island in the kitchen quaffing the finest Trader Joe's boxed wine we had available. We were drinking because we didn't know what else to do. It felt surreal, sitting there in the fading light of evening, the bottle tree backlit against the setting sun, the empty bird feeder aglow.

Was Alison still alive when Barbara and I sat in these very same seats not twelve hours ago? Or was it a lifetime ago? It was definitely a life ago. Maybe if we sat here long enough, I thought, this awful day would end and we'd wake up and she'd still be alive and we could try it again. Maybe it would come out better if we had a day to practice, like Bill Murray in *Groundhog Day*.

Of all the days in my life to live over, this would be the worst hands down. There was no competition. I was tired of it already and the day wasn't even over yet. I certainly didn't want to live it over and over again. But at the same time, every day that passed would take me one day further away from her—one more day since I'd seen her, since I'd heard her voice and held her in my arms and told her how much I loved her, how much she meant to me. I would have happily died to spare her even an ounce of pain.

I've been told that each day is a day closer to "healing," but I knew that day that I'd never be healed, never be whole again. There is no getting over it, there is no getting past it, there is only getting through it. Each day a constant struggle not to be overwhelmed by all the little things that remind me of her, of what I've lost, of what she's lost.

Wherever I am and whatever I'm doing, I stop to think where Alison would have been, what she would have been doing, what she would have done in the interim between August 26, 2015, and that moment. And then I'm left with the miserable math, all too familiar to those who have lost loved ones: how old would she be now? How many days have gone by?

It never gets easier. It just gets more familiar. The pain doesn't go away, you just learn to live with it.

Chris was in pain too, it was easy to see. Chris has always reminded me of Opie from *The Andy Griffith Show*. He's got the ginger hair, the big bright eyes, the cherubic smile. That he would show up at a time like this, I thought, even just to sit and drink boxed wine with us . . . well, that made him a stand-up guy in my book. We knew that Alison admired his character, his demeanor, his intellect, his compassion. But this—this was why she loved him. I don't remember what anyone talked about. It wasn't much, just idle chitchat in fits and starts, small talk whenever the silence started to weigh on us too heavily. I just remember sitting there next to Chris and staring out the window and watching the sun set on a whole new world. I put my arm around him and gripped his shoulder and we traded one of those clenched-jaw, tough-guy smiles even though we were both falling apart inside.

My phone buzzed again. In truth, it had been buzzing more or less all afternoon and into the evening, but since I'd returned from the dam I'd mostly ignored it. It was Ian Shapira, following up just as he'd promised. He'd posted the article. I read it. He nailed it. I lost it. Ian's article was thoughtful and compassionate and it was exactly the balm I needed to face this new world.

The rest of my in-box was filled with an avalanche of media requests. One name stood out: Megyn Kelly. Ordinarily I disdained Fox News and everything they stood for, but this was right after her public dust-up with Donald Trump at the first Republican presidential debate and she'd gained some credibility in my eyes. Of the invitations I'd received, her program was certainly the highest-profile. If I wanted to send a message, her pulpit would carry it a long way. And as the enemy of my enemy . . .

"What do you guys think of this?" I asked the room.

"Fox News?" Barbara scoffed. "Are you sure?"

I explained my reasoning. "Chris, what do you think? I think we should do it. Both of us."

If I was going to survive this, what was going to get me through it was channeling all of my grief, all of my frustration, all of my anger into something productive. Even lava doesn't stay red-hot forever. It cools, it hardens, and if you haven't shaped it into something useful before it does, then it's just a dumb inert rock. I had to channel my rage, I told them, shape it into something useful. This was the start of what would become my life's work, or at least, the work of the rest of my life. I'd found my fight and I was going to fight it for Alison.

Chris took a big swig of his wine. "Fuck it," he said, "let's do it."

I wrote back to accept Megyn Kelly's invitation. As a producer was texting me the address in Franklin County where we were supposed to meet, I got another text from a CBS producer. I don't know how they got my number, but I was already drained, too tired to be surprised by anything at that point. Since CBS was "our" network, the WDBJ affiliate, I texted back to say that Chris and I would be available after our Fox News appearance and asked where we should meet him. He said he'd find us. I wasn't sure how he planned to accomplish that, but I didn't push him. I didn't even pull up the address on Google. I figured it was going to be right off Route 220 in Rocky Mount, so I plugged it into my phone and off we went.

3

THE NIGHT

It was dark by the time we set off toward the interview with Megyn Kelly. I hadn't eaten anything all day and I'd been drinking for hours. I had no business being behind the wheel of a car, but that thought never crossed my mind at that moment. I even had a "to-go" kit: a red Solo cup full of wine.

Chris and I didn't say two words to each other the whole way, just stared ahead into the black as the road twisted and turned through the mountains. It was the same road Barbara and I had driven earlier, but we were going much farther (or so we thought), and somehow it felt much more desolate. I sped the whole way. Chris told me later that I crossed the double yellow line a handful of times and almost hit a semi head-on. He said he was thinking, *Well, if I die, at this point I don't give a shit.* At that point, I obviously didn't either.

The map showed that we were approaching our destination, but I still didn't know exactly where we were going. It was pitch black. Then we rounded a bend and everything was lit up like Times Square.

I instantly knew where we were.

We were right across from the marina. Every major network was there; their trucks parked hither and yon, thick cables snaking across asphalt parking lots, satellite dishes mushrooming upward toward a thin sliver of moon. The media had set up a tent city, each network with its own little enclave. The whole surreal scene was set ablaze by every watt they could find in Southwestern Virginia and probably more trucked in from miles away.

I couldn't believe we were at the marina.

I couldn't believe they had brought us to the marina and that no one thought to tell us where we were going. I wouldn't have come if I'd known.

I was furious.

Across the street, the marina was deserted. Once upon a time I had loved that marina. Less than twenty-four hours earlier I had loved that marina. I had so many happy memories there, and for a split-second I saw her, the TV trucks and the news crews fading away and my darling pigtailed little Scooter skipping her way toward the boat we no longer had.

Now I didn't have her either. I had nothing. I had nothing, emptiness, a void, a hole, a hole in my heart, my heart that was somehow still beating even though a big piece of it was gone, irretrievably gone, gone forever, but I also had Chris and Chris understood because Chris had suffered the same loss; our losses were one and the same, and now Chris had the same aching hole in his heart and in both of our hearts the hole was shaped like Alison, the one thing we didn't have, either of us, and would never have again, the one thing that could have filled the hole and made our lives complete once more.

As long as I had that hole, I knew I would never come back to the marina. I was a leaky vessel and I knew I would sink under the weight of my grief.

In the darkness, the marina looked sinister, downright evil, a terrible place where my brilliant, beautiful daughter had lain dead on the planking for hours until she'd been photographed and fingerprinted and identified, until she'd been searched and tagged and bagged, until she'd become not a she but an it, not a person but a body, not Alison but evidence. She had lain there for hours, her precious blood soaking into the decking, until at last someone came to take her away.

Did they cover her? Did someone think to cover her face when the hot summer sun was beating down on her perfect porcelain skin? Did they shield her from the eyes of the crowds that inevitably gathered when they heard the shots, when they saw the news? The eyes that probed and profaned even as she lay stiffening like the splintered wood underneath her?

This was the last place she had ever been. Something here was the last thing she had ever seen. Somewhere around us was the last breath she'd ever drawn, her last exhalation, thrumming in the air around us. I took a breath, maybe sharing some of the same molecules, and then I turned my back on the marina. I have never looked at it again.

Chris and I were met by law enforcement and escorted through the mad bustle of media frenzy, everyone chasing the same story. En route to the Fox News camp, the CBS producers caught up with us—now I understood how they'd planned to find us—and were brushed off by the Fox handlers before we could say a word to them. It was like watching seagulls fighting over a chicken bone, and we were the chicken bone.

Fox's field studio was a large collapsible tent in the middle of the grassy field across the street from the marina. They intended to put us on air with the marina at our backs. That was fine with me, just so long as I didn't have to look at it. The producers miked us and fussed with our shirt collars. Chris was wearing a black-and-white striped dress shirt; I'd apparently changed into a solid black button-up at some point, though I couldn't tell you when that had happened. They fitted us with earpieces so we could listen to the audio before we went on. Rick Leventhal, the Fox correspondent, was describing the shooter's "manifesto": he'd had a list of targets at the station, Leventhal claimed, and he'd used hollow-point bullets with his victims' initials Sharpied onto the tips.

Hollow-point bullets? I looked around in shock. Did he say hollow-point bullets? Surely he didn't. Chris's grim face was ashen and I could tell that he had already heard this detail. It was news to me, though, and I was furious. I had never been angrier in my entire life. I was ready to pick a fight with the next son of a bitch who crossed my path.

How could they let the father of a shooting victim, on the day his daughter was murdered, hear a reporter speculate on live TV about how much damage the goddamn bullet did as it ripped its way through her body? Hollow-point bullets are so brutal that most of the world agreed to stop using them even in international warfare as far back as 1899. And this fucker was in here talking about my daughter's initials being written on the tip of the hollow-point bullet that blew her brains out. I didn't give a fuck if he wrote a goddamn poem on it. What were they thinking letting me hear something like that? What kind of fucked-up news outlet thinks that's newsworthy in the first place?

What's worse, I found out later, is that it wasn't even true. He didn't use any hollow-point bullets. But who has time to check your facts when there are ratings to be won?

Most of that interview is a blur for me. I remember Megyn's voice, that soft vocal posture of deep concern. I remember that she tried to speculate about whether Adam, the cameraman, had tried to use his camera to capture the image of his killer as he fell. Chris immediately chastened her for asking us that question, a question we couldn't possibly have known the answer to, and she apologized twice, once live on the air and again the next day in a voice mail. The apology wasn't specific, so she may have meant for it to cover the correspondent's on-air speculation as well. I don't know for sure, but I remember being impressed that she reached out.

I've been told that one of the most gut-wrenching parts of the interview for viewers came when I was talking about Alison and corrected myself, referring to her in the past tense for the first time. I don't remember doing that. It certainly wasn't planned. I'm sure it would wreck me to see it. From that day forward, I vowed never to watch the replays of any interview I did. I was there, so what was the point?

What I remember most is the end of the interview, when Megyn asked if there was anything we wanted to say. That was the moment I'd been waiting for.

"We've got to do something about crazy people getting guns," I said. "Next week, it isn't even going to be a story anymore and everybody's going to forget it. But mark my words, my mission in life . . . I am going to do something, whatever it takes, to get gun legislation, to shame people, to shame legislators into doing something about closing loopholes and background checks and making sure crazy people don't get guns. This is not the last you've heard of me."

"Andy and I have been trying to be strong today," Chris picked up, "because we felt that it was our duty to Alison because she was a journalist and this is what she would have wanted us to do, to share her story . . . to make sure that her life was not in vain."

I told Megyn, "This is Alison's legacy."

I ended with a challenge to her and to the rest of the media, one I would reiterate many times in the days to come: "She was one of you. Don't let this go. Don't let this slide."

The rest of the evening is a blur. I know that Chris and I did another interview, with CBS. I know that his parents came to pick him up. I know that we embraced in silence. There were no words and no tears left. I know that I drove back in silence, my red Solo cup beside me, as I stared off into the void, still struggling to come to grips with the idea that my daughter was dead. I wasn't thinking. I could barely feel anything. I was just fighting through my grief and my exhaustion and my bottomless sadness, trying to get back home even though I knew I'd never be home again.

Most of all, I was angry. I had picked a fight because I didn't know what else to do, and I'd committed to it on live television. I had to follow through. I hoped I had some of Alison's strength inside me, because if anyone was strong enough to conquer this problem, to end gun violence once and for all, it was Alison.

———

I can't tell you how many people have offered me that well-intentioned platitude: "I can't even imagine." Perhaps you feel the same way.

You're right. You can't even imagine. So let me help you.

Imagine your daughter has been killed on live TV. Imagine that her killer planned it and filmed it and posted the bloody rant-filled video for anyone to see. Imagine that you spent the whole day talking to the police and the press, cursing at God and trying to drink away the pain, and then you come home from a national interview during which the network speculated about all the gruesome details you've spent the whole day expressly trying and failing not to imagine. An interview into which you poured what little was left of your heart and soul, most of which you'd poured into your daughter long ago and which the shooter then spilled onto the deck at the marina some twenty hours before—your heart and hers, not just intermingling but one and the same, running down the deck and soaking into the earth.

You come home from the interview and you find your wife sitting alone in a silent house that suddenly feels far too big, far too empty, your wife sitting alone in your daughter's room, exactly as she left it, the way it will stay for months and months after, both of you feeling guilty if you so much as bump the knickknacks on the nightstand, feeling that you've lost a little something of her all over again. As your wife sits there alone, cross-legged on the rug next to the neatly made bed, a single lamp ablaze against the blackness pressing inward, she leafs through the scrapbooks and photo albums that she made for your daughter. The photos show the two of them laughing, side by side, your beautiful doe-eyed goddesses and their musical, life-giving laughter captured in photos like butterflies sealed in amber.

As your wife sits flipping through photos, she looks up at you with a pain so deep it seems permanently etched into her face and you worry you'll drown in the sorrow in her eyes and then there will be no one left to save her. You look sadly back at her, not knowing what to say, what to do, until without a word she sets them aside and stands up and hugs you tighter and tighter and you hug her back tighter and tighter because the force of the hug is all that feels real, the two of you standing together alone in the room that once was your daughter's and now belongs to no one at all.

You take your wife's hand and she takes your hand and together you switch off the light and walk down the hall and enter your room, washing as always, undressing as always, still moving to keep ahead of the grief, even though nothing feels real, nothing feels right. The two of you climb into bed, the fan still whirring above you, the air purifier still humming below, and you scratch her head and she scratches your chest, just like you've always done on each night before, except this night is different, this night is like no other, this is the darkest night of your lives. For a long time you both lie awake and silent, together but terribly alone, and you stare up at the ceiling through the blades of the fan and you wonder where your daughter is now, what's up there beyond. Can this be happening? Can this be real? Then you toss and turn and finally take a pill and, teetering on the edge of the nightmare world you now find yourself living in, you flip off the light and succumb to the black.

———

I want this book to hurt you. I want you to understand my hurt. If we hurt together, then maybe you can help me save others from ever feeling that pain.

This is not a grief memoir. This is an anger memoir. We tend to think of anger as a destructive force, and it is, to be sure. But so is fire. So is a volcano. Volcanoes represent one of the most destructive forces of nature, but they also may have created the land underneath your feet right now. Anger, like lava, can be productive. You don't have to run from either one. If you channel it without being consumed by it, then anger, like lava, can be a good thing. You can use it. You can shape it. You can build on it.

I hope this book points the way forward for those of you who are angry. I hope it helps you find a purpose for your anger. And I hope that it allows you to channel your anger into something productive before it cools into something misshapen, twisted, and dysfunctional.

4

THE WHIRLWIND

In the immediate aftermath of Alison's death, the truthers began crawling out from beneath their rocks.

If you don't know about the truthers, consider yourself fortunate. They are well-known to those who have suffered gun violence tragedies. Shortly after Chris and I were interviewed by Megyn Kelly on the night of the shooting, these conspiracy theorists began contacting me and Barbara, claiming that our daughter's death was just a big hoax. Alison was living under an assumed name somewhere, they said, and I was a crisis actor brought on to shill for the anti-gun lobby.

Most of the public responses we received after the shooting were and continue to be deeply compassionate, deeply moving. But the trolls have been such a vocal and thoroughly vile minority that they threaten to overwhelm the majority. Before they started spewing their hate and idiocy at us, I never would have believed they really existed. I firmly believe that the truthers and the deniers personify the very worst parts of human nature, and I wouldn't have wanted to believe that about anyone.

If I asked you to imagine what it would be like to lose a child, you might think of identifying the body and planning the funeral and sorting through her things. You would never imagine the truthers, though, and the venom they spew at total strangers under the guise of getting to the truth. I know I didn't.

One of the pieces of "evidence" they most frequently point to while developing their half-baked theories is that Chris and I didn't look "convincing" on the air with Megyn Kelly. They said that, because I used to be an actor way back in the 1970s, I couldn't be trusted. They criticized my performance and said I was a bad actor in search of the spotlight. That actually made me laugh. Don't you have to pick a side? I'm either a good actor or a bad actor, but nobody's good enough to be both at the same time.

Just as I could never have imagined these trolls, so too are they apparently unable to imagine themselves in our shoes. They think Chris and I weren't convincing enough? We were barely standing. We were punch-drunk and wine-drunk, shocked and grief-stricken and utterly drained. And then we were live on Fox News with Megyn Kelly shortly after 9:00 p.m., right across the street from the marina where my daughter, my treasure, the love of Chris's life, had lost her life some fourteen hours earlier. It wasn't an audition for us. We weren't trying to impress anyone. We didn't care if we offended anyone. We didn't care about anything. You can see for yourself—it's not hard to find the video.

As the truthers began their harassment campaign, I knew that if I was to survive the coming days, weeks, months, and years, I had to keep my exercise regimen intact. I was an emotional wreck, but if I allowed myself to become a physical one as well, it wouldn't be long before I would suffer dire consequences. I had to keep going, and the only way to do it was to continue working out while bandaging my psychological wounds by whatever means necessary. I took my steadfast companion Jack and hit the trails.

Southside Virginia has a number of nice trails with densely wooded switchbacks along the water. I loved them because I would never encounter a soul, which meant Jack could run off-leash. One of my favorite trails was at Patrick Henry, our local community college. The trailhead started at the end of a parking lot that was always deserted.

As I drove up the hill and made the turn into the parking lot, I saw something that made my heart race and my blood boil. There in the lot was a lone truck complete with two giant Confederate flags rising from either side of the bed. I'd been coming to the trailhead for three years, and it was the first time I'd ever seen a vehicle in the lot. And now, only days after Alison was killed and the truthers started coming out of the woodwork, evil had mysteriously dropped into my path. I was scared, infuriated, and unhinged. As I got closer I saw there was a driver inside. I pulled up next to him on the passenger side. A young kid in a dirty cap was sitting in the driver's seat.

"Are you stalking me?" I yelled. "What the hell are you doing here?"

He looked startled and said "No." I didn't wait for any other explanation. If he was a real threat he could have easily shot me right then and there, but at that moment I didn't care about my safety.

"I've never seen you out here before, and you need to get your ass outta here right now," I said. He got the message and started backing up. I paralleled his move and stayed on his tail. He pulled up outside the campus police headquarters and I watched him get out and go in. I drove back to the trailhead and Jack and I started down the path.

Even then, I wondered if this kid was really stalking me or if I was manifesting symptoms of post-traumatic stress disorder. In retrospect, I think he was simply in the wrong place at the wrong time, and his toxic Confederate display caused him to be accosted by an emotionally charged man who was responding to the cruelty that had been unleashed upon him by monstrous truthers, who—wonder of wonders—also tend to like their Confederate flags.

I was traumatized by what had just transpired. The internal volcano had erupted for the first time. It would be the first of many outbursts of rage that would dog me for some time, something I mostly stifle but can't completely shake.

The sanctuary of the lush trail beckoned. In moments, Jack and I were immersed in the solitude we were accustomed to enjoying, just the two of us in the woods like so many times before. It was a typical late August afternoon in Southside Virginia, hot and muggy. There were no clouds and nothing to suggest the temperature was about to change.

But it did. We had only traveled about fifty yards when a cool breeze suddenly swept through the woods. It was intense, lasting several minutes. I knew instantly what it was. It was Scooter's angel breath offering solace to her miserable dad. My arms stretched out to embrace this balm.

"I know it's you, Scooter," I yelled, tears streaming down my cheeks. And then I broke into another bout of raspy crying; I was like a drowning man gasping for air. Heartbreak would be my lifelong companion, but mysterious comfort would be too.

A week later, we got a call from Kris Landrum, the public relations manager at the community college. She said she'd like to come over and talk with us. I knew what it was about.

Kris got to our house twenty minutes later and gave us a big hug. She said she was worried that we'd seen some vile Facebook posts coming from the kid I had confronted and his parents. Apparently the kid's parents had gone to her office and complained that I'd harassed their son. Kris said the mother had done all the talking and rambled on and on about racism and how they were the real victims. The dad just sat there glowering. Kris said the father was wearing a Confederate cap and looked like a Civil War reenactor. She said the kid was a decent student who seemed to be caught in the middle of his parents' intolerance.

Kris said she had politely told the parents that after reviewing the surveillance video, she had seen no evidence of a threat on my part. You have to understand, she told them, that when you choose to bedeck your vehicle with giant Confederate flags, there is a good chance it will elicit a response.

The parents sulked out of her office after the conversation, and we later found out that they tried to pitch the story of their poor little boy's plight to the *Martinsville Bulletin* and the *Roanoke Times*. Neither would touch it.

Thankfully, I've never seen the truck there again, but I have seen more and more of those "proud" flags waving from pickup trucks ever since Donald Trump was elected president.

———

The kid in the pickup, or maybe his parents, had certainly recognized me. What I soon realized in the days following The Day was that our gut-wrenching interview with Megyn Kelly had turned me overnight into an advocate. I was about to enter a whirlwind of interviews with media from across the country and around the world. Like the fulfillment of a malevolent genie's wish, I had become a celebrity for the worst possible reason.

It began just hours after the Megyn Kelly interview, the very next day in fact. That Wednesday, I awoke at 7:00 a.m. to the sound of our doorbell. It's an old crank style that sounds like a ringer on a child's bicycle, but it's loud and it works. I opened the door to find a young woman in her early thirties with a pleading look in her eyes standing on the stoop. As I looked past her and up the hill, there was the large live truck parked at the curb on the street in front of our house.

"Mr. Parker, I'm Jennifer Henderson with CNN. I'm so terribly sorry for your loss, and I was hoping you would be willing to talk to our viewers. We had Chris on this morning and we wanted you too."

My initial thought was, *How the hell did you find my house?* After the events of the previous day, though, I realized that the press has the resources to find anyone anywhere.

I told her to come inside and we'd talk.

"Your niece Regina and I worked together at *Entertainment Tonight,*" she said. "I called her to see if she would reach out to you for me, but she was very protective of you. She said I had to do it on my own."

I smiled internally, appreciating Regina's ethical grounding. And then the odd coincidence that this earnest young woman had a connection to my family hit me like a ton of bricks. The wave came crashing over me, and I embraced her and cried on her shoulder. Unlike the previous night with Fox News, I felt I was in the hands of someone I could trust. She assured me that CNN wouldn't cause me to hear any audio from the shooting, as I'd heard in the run-up to the Megyn Kelly interview.

"I hope you'll go on," she said. "We saw you last night, and you've got a powerful message to share."

"Well, I guess I started something, so I might as well keep going. What's the program?"

"You'll be on *New Day* with Chris Cuomo, and we'd like to do it in the next hour."

Despite being a news junkie, I really hadn't watched much television news other than Alison's work since she became a journalist. I gathered my news online, primarily from the Google News page or Flipboard where I could get a wide range of stories from multiple sources and watch video clips of interest. As a result, there were only a handful of programs and news anchors I recognized. *New Day* and Chris Cuomo didn't register, although I had some recollection that he might be Mario's son. Since it was CNN, a national platform, I agreed to the interview.

One of the reasons we bought our home was its character both inside and out. We loved the southwestern-style interior, but we also loved the exterior. For one, there is no grass to mow. The first owner cleared only enough foliage for a driveway and the house. It sits below street level and is completely canopied with maples, oaks, and pines that in season form a lush green barrier and natural screen from the rest of the neighborhood. The adjacent lot is also on a severe slope, and for that reason it has never been developed. It creates another barrier, giving us the feeling of pleasant isolation in the middle of a small development. Our deck out back runs the length of the house, and we look out into a dense stand of trees and a dry creek bed that masks the houses on the other side. It's such a private setting that I can walk out in the buff and climb into the hot tub without exposing myself to the neighbors.

Jennifer and I agreed that the deck and its perfect backdrop would be a great remote studio. We didn't have enough time to set it up for the interview with Chris Cuomo, so I did that one on the driveway across from my garage. I felt respected during the interview and I was touched by Jennifer's compassion and professionalism, so I accepted her request to do another. I wanted the world to hear my message of Never Again—and, in truth, having a mission and staying busy helped me keep it together.

Pretty quickly, Peter Morris, a photojournalist at CNN, started running cables. They snaked their way from the truck down the driveway, through the kitchen and dining area, and ended up on the deck next to the camera. Field engineer Scott Garber started raising the mast holding the big satellite dish and aiming it through the trees at the right spot. Once the cables were hooked up and the satellite found, I was seated with the woods behind me and was "miked up." This involved running a wireless microphone cable under my shirt and getting an earpiece, or IFB (interruptible feedback), to hear questions from the interviewer. As was the case the previous night, there was no monitor on which I could see the studio anchor. I had no complaints there. I didn't need the distraction and I needed to stay focused on the black iris of the camera lens staring back at me. This would soon become a familiar routine.

With perfect natural lighting filtering through the trees and finches and chickadees chirping away in the background, my subsequent CNN interviews that day went as follows: Ashleigh Banfield at noon, Anderson Cooper around 8:00 that evening, Don Lemon at 10:00 p.m.

In between, I must've done more with NBC and/or MSNBC, because Alan Cohen, a big old teddy bear of a man, also showed up at the house that morning. Like Jennifer, he was kind and respectful. Before he left on Sunday, he warned me about becoming overexposed. Jennifer was the first to let me feed the monster, and the more interviews I did, the more they wanted. She told me, only half-jokingly, that she could put me on the air every hour. I was quite conscious of the pitfalls of overexposure and felt I was walking the tightrope between getting the message out as much as I could and looking like I was using my daughter's death as a vehicle for self-promotion.

I would soon discover that there were plenty of truthers who thought the latter.

By the afternoon, the house was abuzz with friends and television crews. Lynn and Noel had made sure the fridge was stocked with soft drinks, beer, and wine. People were bringing food trays and home cooking. I was able to grab and graze on occasion, but when I wasn't doing an interview, I was on the phone or responding to what had become an avalanche of email condolences from friends and a pile of media requests from all over the world. Focusing on these responses kept me from becoming a complete nonfunctioning mess, but the distraction could only go so far. I broke down a lot. And while I tried to keep my composure on camera, I couldn't always maintain it. I was fine when I was advocating for gun safety, but I lost it whenever I spoke of Alison.

Even today, I still can't talk about her without breaking down. Jennifer later said to me, "You just kept going. You were in constant motion, and you broke down a lot. It broke my heart."

Somewhere in that maelstrom, I got a call from a Houston area code.

"Andy, this is Mark Kelly," the voice on the other end said.

Damn. The badass astronaut and the husband of Gabby Giffords, the Arizonan former member of the House of Representatives who narrowly survived a shooting in 2011. I was kind of awestruck that he had found me, and that he was so gracious. He told me he wanted to reach out and give me an attaboy for taking a stand, and that he would be back in touch with me soon and hoped we could meet.

As darkness fell on the first full day of my new life, my outdoor studio "work lights" were our citronella-filled tiki torches that lined the deck railing to keep the mosquitos away. By the time I went on Anderson Cooper's show, I was running on fumes. My brain was fried, but this was a guy I'd heard of and respected and I wanted to get it right. I sat down, was miked up, watched Peter fire up the camera lights, and the routine began once more. After it was over, we had an hour break until I was up again for Don Lemon.

During that hour, the studio space reverted to the quiet sanctuary it had been just a day earlier. It was time to come up for air, albeit briefly. Peter shut down the lights and Barbara, Jennifer, and I sat there watching the dancing flames from the torches that momentarily created an atmosphere of normalcy. The four of us talked about normal stuff, chitchat, never touching on the horror of the previous day. The deck and the tiki torches made me feel as though I was on a pier on some remote island, far removed from any pain. After spending the day inside a media circus, Barbara and I found an odd comfort in the company of our benevolent ringmasters. For an hour or so, we talked shop. I think we even shared a rare laugh.

As 10:00 p.m. approached, it was time for me to give it one more go. By then I was truly gassed, just running on pure adrenaline. I went back to my deck chair, re-miked, and Peter fired up the lights again. In what had become routine, I listened to the lead-up, and then I was on the air with Don Lemon.

For this interview, I was joined by two strangers whom I would soon come to know as good friends. I was the newest member of "the club nobody wants to join." Lonnie Phillips had already been in it for three years and Richard Martinez for one. They didn't know me, but they knew exactly what I was going through. Richard's son Chris had been gunned down in a mass shooter's rampage in Isla Vista, California. Lonnie and his wife Sandy's daughter, Jessi, was a victim in the movie theater massacre in Aurora, Colorado. Both became advocates in the aftermath of losing their children. I became fast friends with them, bonding over our shared experience.

Friday morning, August 28, I was back on the studio deck with another news crew, this time from ABC's *20/20*. After I finished that interview, Barbara and I got ready to go to Roanoke. WDBJ had asked if we would do an interview, and we felt it was time to appear together. We had to go to WDBJ anyway since we needed to meet with the human resources manager to go over some paperwork, a situation I'm sure that HR manager never anticipated when taking the job.

It was our first time heading back up Route 220 since The Day, and this time Barbara drove. I was too busy fielding calls from friends and the press.

We arrived at the station to find a towering wall of flowers, balloons, and posters adorning the big oak tree next to the chain-link fence at the station's entrance. People were milling around and taking pictures of this makeshift memorial. It was like a vigil for a fallen rock star. We pulled into a parking space and were met and ushered into the building by Mike Bell. He buzzed us in through the glass security doors, which I later learned had been installed two years' before in the aftermath of the shooter's dismissal.

The wide corridors encircled a square courtyard. The walls on one side were filled with large posters of various CBS programs; pictures of current and past on-air talent were on the other side. The opposite glass walls looked out onto a bland, uninviting courtyard, the sun beating down on a couple of lonely plants. The courtyard looked as if it had never been used.

We rounded the next corridor and entered the newsroom. There were multiple round workstations brimming with computer screens, stations accommodating three or four people at a time. Behind us was the news director's desk and overhead was an array of television monitors showing news feeds from every conceivable outlet. Past the workstations were the news set and the anchor desk, facing away from the newsroom, which provided the "working background" for the telecast. It's the same desk where Alison, Barbara, and I sat on Alison's last day as an intern two years before. Sitting at that news desk, I told Alison, "You'll be delivering the news here one day." And it came to pass.

Being in the building was tough enough, but seeing the empty chair she had occupied as a fill-in anchor just a few weeks before was yet another twist of the knife in my heart.

We embraced Kimberly McBroom. A blonde with big features and a warm smile, Kim was Alison's morning anchor and called Alison her "little news sister." They were close. Kim had been at the station for more than twenty years and had become a fixture in the community. This was her home. She knew Alison was going places and had become a mentor and friend to her.

Like everyone else in the newsroom, Kim was in tears. The WDBJ staff milled about like zombies, functioning but dazed. Alison's friend Heather Butterworth, a producer who joined the station at the same time as Alison, was particularly distraught. Unbeknownst to me at the time, Heather, like Adam Ward's fiancée, Melissa Ott, had watched them both die from the control room that day.

Melissa wasn't in the newsroom when we were there. August 26, the day Alison and Adam were killed, was Melissa's last day at the station, though not because of the shooting. Weeks earlier, she had accepted another job in Charlotte, North Carolina, and Adam had been in the process of finding a job there as well. They were to be married. A big farewell party had been planned for Wednesday. In a cruel twist of fate, her farewell was watching the horror of her fiancé's murder.

Heather shouldn't have been there either. Nobody should have been there. It shouldn't have happened, but it did, and they all had to soldier on because the news never stops. As was already becoming a routine, we hugged, we cried, we tried to hold one another up. I think our presence there was as comforting as it was disturbing. We all needed those embraces, but being there reinforced what we'd all lost. Our seeing the WDBJ staff, and them seeing us, poured salt into our open wounds.

After we let everyone get back to work, we were led to large conference room where we were met by Governor McAuliffe and his wife, Dorothy. He had seen my interviews, and true to his word, he was ready to engage.

We spoke with the governor and his wife, then we headed out to the corridor and were met by Adam Ward's brother, Jay, who had flown in from Seattle. Jay told us that his parents, who were in Roanoke, were too devastated to come.

"Jay, I understand," I said. "It's hard for us too, but we just feel like we have to. Please tell your folks we're thinking of them."

Barbara and I were then led to another conference room where Nadia Singh was waiting for us. Nadia, with jet-black hair and exotic features, was the weekend anchor. Only a few weeks before, she had informed the station she was leaving. Alison had been in line for her job and was actively lobbying for it.

For whatever reason, Kelly Zuber, the news director, decided to have Alison and two other reporters rotate anchoring throughout July. It made no sense to me. The other two reporters were good, but Alison had the star quality, the ability, and the viewers' hearts. Alison hadn't been pleased, either. You'll remember that competitive streak. She had made it clear to her bosses that she wanted to anchor, and they had made assurances that she would, but when it came time to deliver they dawdled.

It makes me bitter to this day. I find myself playing the "what if" game. What if Alison had gotten the anchor job she deserved when it first opened? Would she still be alive today, or would the shooter have ambushed her somewhere else?

The interview with Nadia was emotionally tough for us, Nadia included. We were playing on the home field. When the interview hit the internet, the accompanying thumbnail photo of Barbara and me told the whole story. We both looked like ten miles of bad road. No surprise there, but still startling to see.

After the interview, we saw the governor again, said our goodbyes, and were shown to the human resources manager's office. Monica Taylor was the typical HR person I had come to know during my years as a headhunter. Paperwork was her specialty—hiring, not so much.

We soon found out that Alison's killer had been hired without what we regarded as sufficient due diligence. Chris did a little research and discovered that before the shooter came to WDBJ, he had been fired three times for exhibiting the same anger that prompted police to escort him from the WDBJ premises, and at least one station installed a security system after he was fired. How a ticking time bomb like him could keep getting chances is a testament to what I consider lazy background work on the part of Monica, the news director Greg Baldwin, and ultimately the general manager, Jeff Marks. Jeff claims that the shooter's references all spoke highly of him, and maybe they did, and maybe Monica accepted that at face value. Because of the privacy laws in place, it's likely that many employers couldn't say anything substantial without risking a lawsuit.

However, any hiring manager with a lick of sense knows there are ways to get around that. Over the course of my fifteen years as a headhunter, I regularly called the people a prospective candidate had worked with and asked, "Would you hire this person?" I never once had an issue. What angered me even more was finding out from the governor that the shooter had been pitched to the station by John Derr, the owner of a talent agency called LornaDave—one I consider pretty sketchy. The first thing Derr should have asked, and probably did, was "Why do you not have a job?" I contend that he knowingly foisted damaged goods on the station without regard to ethics or reputation. I believe he was only out for the commission.

I'm sure the thought that his candidate would be a killer never crossed his mind or anyone else's, but I consider representing someone with that many red flags to be completely unconscionable. If Chris and I were able to find the red flags in the days after Alison was killed—the threats, intimidation, and madness directed at former employers and coworkers—then John Derr should have been able to do his due diligence and find them too. I hate the notion of frivolous litigation, but as soon as I found out John Derr's connection, I looked to pursue legal action, to put him out of business, if nothing else. My attorney said that while there was clearly an ethical violation, proving intent would be difficult.

With no legal recourse and no response to a voice mail I left for Derr, I sent him the following email:

> John, I left you a voice mail, but I really didn't care to talk to you. As I
> reflect on what I wish to do vs. what I can do, it would take more time

and energy than I care to spend. I will leave you with this narrative that I considered publishing in the trades and on HuffPost but decided against. It will never see the light of day, but I think it accurately describes a bottom feeder like you.

For 15 years prior to Alison's murder, I was a headhunter. I acquired executive level talent for clients first in telecom, then in banking. I held myself to the highest ethical standards and because of the reputation for integrity I achieved, I was able to keep my business in banking afloat even after the financial meltdown of 2008. There were lean years, but my clients knew that I was never going to waste their time with a candidate that didn't fit their need or had red flags in their background. It happens in business, but particularly in recruiting, there are some bad apples that give the entire industry a dubious reputation. They are the ones that only care about one-offs, not building relationships.

The first question any reputable recruiter asks a prospect candidate is 'Why do you want to leave your job?' or 'Why did you leave your job and what were the circumstances?' I had to know what type of character I was dealing with and if I saw job hopping on a résumé combined with a poor response to the question, I wished that person luck and told them I could not present them to my clients. Through minimal detective work I could also easily find out without violating any law if the person had been fired. I gleaned background information that my clients couldn't. When they engaged my services, they knew any candidate I put in front of them had no skeletons in the closet.

Media talent agencies operate differently from search firms, but at the core, they should function the same way relating to background discovery. One would think the first question asked by the agent to the talent would be the same one mentioned above. And that brings me to the agent who represented Vester Flanagan, Alison's killer. Flanagan had been fired from his previous two stations prior to his hiring at WDBJ7. Chris did a little more research, and we found out that as with WDBJ7, he had to be escorted from the premises. So how did this ticking time bomb get the job in Roanoke? He had a talent agency, LornaDave, that pitched him. Even though he exhibited extreme behavior, Flanagan was never arrested, so he had no criminal background. But either LornaDave didn't know (hardly likely) or concealed (likely) his past that had so many red flags it looked like a communist May Day parade.

If you visit their website, you may notice the claim that "LDA [LornaDave Agency] is very picky about who we represent, we want quality over quantity." I would argue the opposite. Pitching Flanagan to any television station was the equivalent of throwing shit on a wall to see what sticks.

A few months after sending the email, I heard from a network person that the word on the street was that LornaDave wasn't sufficiently vetting its candidates. As of this writing the company is still in business, but I'm sure it has taken a big hit, as it should have.

Monica went through death and workers' comp benefits. I discovered later that once I had accepted the workers' comp settlement, the station was held harmless for any of the blunders I described. The more I heard, the more I wanted to punish WDBJ in court, but I was advised that I had little recourse there, either.

After we concluded our meeting, we headed out. Under a large oak tree just inside the station entrance, I saw a throng of reporters behind multiple mikes sprouting from a stand. I didn't know I had a press conference coming, but there it was. Mike Bell took my arm and said, "Do you want to do this?"

"Yep," I said. "Let's go."

The most memorable question came from a reporter at my immediate left, crouching down and holding a mike with a big foam windscreen toward me. She asked me if I thought Alison and Adam would still be alive today if they had been armed when the killer attacked.

I turned directly toward her and pointed out that in that moment, as she was asking me the question, all of her attention was focused on me. All of her cameraman's attention was focused on me. Even if she was interviewing me with an AK-47 strapped to her back, it wouldn't matter; she would never see the killer come up behind her.

I've received a lot of mileage out of that explanation while I've been debunking the constant nonsense from the gun crowd over the last few years.

The presser lasted maybe fifteen minutes and then I was done. On the way back to the Honda, we looked over at the employee parking lot.

Alison's Kia Sportage was still parked where she had left it on Wednesday morning, waiting for her to drive it home. We opened the door; it smelled like Alison. Even though she would grab fast food on occasion and eat it on the road, her car never smelled like anything other than her. Sweet and fresh. I asked Barbara if she wanted to drive it back or if she wanted me to. "I'll drive," she said.

I was relieved; I had suspected Barbara would want to, and we both knew I would have been a total mess if I'd taken the job. She followed me back home, and as we were cresting a hill on Route 220, I called her.

"How are you doing?"

"Just spending time with her," Barbara said. "I want to sell the Honda and keep her car. I'm going to keep it till the wheels fall off."

Even though the Honda CR-V had a better ride than the Sportage, I knew we would be keeping Alison's car.

That evening, for the first time, I got to talk with Harry Hurst, Chris's father. Harry's career has been in public relations; after seeing his work, I know where Chris gets his considerable writing talent.

Over the phone, Harry's voice had a slightly gravelly but warm, thoughtful tone. He had been watching my national political assault over the last two days.

"You've been doing great," he said. "Would you like me to help you with some national op-eds?"

Until that moment, I'd never even considered that option.

"I'd love to Harry, but I just don't know if I'm up to it right now."

"I've got ins with *Washington Post*, *New York Times*, and *USA Today*," he said. "Just give me a few names you want to light up and I'll take it from there. They all want exclusives, so we'll have to tailor each one a bit."

I gave him my short list of politicians I wanted to target—Virginia Senator Bill Stanley, Congressman Bob Goodlatte, and the Democratic Virginia Senator John Edwards. Harry went to work. To me, they were the unholy trinity representing everything wrong with NRA politics (although John Edwards later found redemption).

Within hours, Harry had taken a handful of my interview comments and crafted them into terrific, hard-hitting op-eds. Most included the paddling metaphor, which quickly became my signature message. It went like this:

The weekend before Alison died, she was rafting on the Nantahala River in North Carolina with her mother; her boyfriend, Chris; her close friend Katy; and me. It was her favorite place on earth. She was a brilliant kayaker and it was a family tradition that she relished. We often told one another the mantra all paddlers must keep in mind while fighting the force of the rapid water: Never stop paddling. You just have to paddle through the rapids. You just have to paddle through.

"Never stop paddling" became the soul at the core of my message.

The op-eds appeared in major publications across the country that Sunday. I was all in, and I was coming out swinging just like I had promised myself I would.

I was also still doing interviews, and the more interviews I did, the more interview requests I received. It was clear I had to feed the monster. On Saturday, I did the first of many interviews with Ben Williams, a reporter at our local newspaper, and it's possible that I also did an interview with a Canadian television program via FaceTime.

On Sunday morning I was back on the deck with Jennifer and Peter from CNN, preparing to do *State of the Union* with Jake Tapper. It was going to be a long day. After Tapper, I was scheduled to be interviewed by Poppy Harlow in the early afternoon. Up to that point I'd been going solo, but Barbara was going to join me and make her CNN debut with Poppy. We had a monitor for this one so we could actually see Poppy on the other end. I'd never heard of Poppy (or Jake Tapper for that matter), but I could see she was an attractive blond in her early thirties. She asked good questions.

As we were winding down the interview, I said to her, "Poppy, she was going to be you. She was going to be you." Tears began to stream down her face. I'm not sure what words followed, if any. I'm sure there have been other network anchors overcome with emotion on-air, but I've personally never seen it. She was touched, and I received a warm, handwritten note from her the following week.

We went back inside to a busy, bustling house, only to find a message from Alan Cohen asking if I would do the *Today* show on Monday.

I decided it was time for a media break. I wanted to keep driving home the message, but I also didn't want to be overexposed to the point where people across the country would click on their televisions and say, "Oh, there's that guy again. He needs to give it a rest."

And so I did give it a rest.

At least in the US.

Even as I was trying to take a break from the media whirlwind, there were other whirlwinds to contend with. That same Sunday, a nondenominational memorial service was taking place in Roanoke for our family and Adam Ward's family.

We were back on that painful stretch of 220, but this time we noticed the business marquees along the way. Every bank, restaurant, gas station, and retailer that had a sign along the route had an "Alison and Adam" reference. It was astounding and touching. Those messages were all over Southwest Virginia in the weeks and months following The Day, a clear outpouring of love for them both. Sixty thousand people had awakened each day and watched them. They were part of their lives, members of their family, and now those family members were gone.

The memorial service was at the Jefferson Center, an arts venue in a neighborhood of old commercial warehouses. The Jefferson Center is one of Roanoke's oldest and stateliest spaces. The building began life as a school in the 1920s, and had recently been remodeled. We met Chris out front and made our way to the Shaftman Performance Hall where we were escorted to the front row. The mayor of Roanoke, David Bowers, came over and introduced himself, telling us that he couldn't express how sorry he was. Jeff Marks was also there. There was no sign of Buddy or Mary Ward, Adam's parents, but we didn't really expect to see them. They were grieving differently than we were.

As we waited for the program to begin, Barbara pulled something out of her purse and slipped it into Chris's hand. It was the black onyx David Yurman ring that he had given Alison the week before. A promise ring. Chris smiled and squeezed her hand. Alison had been wearing the ring the day she died, and Barbara found it in the personal effects the sheriff's deputy delivered to our house on Saturday. Barbara hadn't mentioned to me that the deputy stopped by; I suppose she knew how hard it would have been for me to see those last tokens from Alison. Barbara simply put the bag in her closet, opening only a small box that contained the jewelry Alison was wearing that day.

I looked at the program and I immediately knew it was going to be a long one. It was a nondenominational ceremony, but it could have been billed as a pan-denominational ceremony, as nearly every faith seemed to be represented by a pastor, priest, or rabbi.

The rabbi entered first, and she was accompanied by two boys who looked to be about twelve. They were each carrying what looked like long animal horns. The rabbi stepped to the podium, the two boys flanking her on either side, and without a word, they raised the horns to their lips and blew. The blast sounded like a trumpet hunting for the right note. They paused, and then blew again.

Touched though I was by this outpouring of kindness, I also thought I was in sitting in on some kind of Vulcan *pon farr* ceremony and Mr. Spock was going to appear at any moment. Barbara was sitting between me and Chris, and we all glanced at one another at the same time. I leaned over to Barbara and whispered, "Alison would be going, WTF?" She passed the message along to Chris, and we all smiled and inwardly chuckled, a much-needed moment of levity.

I could just imagine Alison's reaction if she had been sitting there with us. I know her spirit was there, and this was the first of many "winks" she would give us. I have a lot of Jewish friends, but they never clued me in about the shofar, typically made from a ram's horn, that these boys were blowing. I later found out that blowing the shofar is a tradition that dates back to biblical times. I guess I wasn't on Vulcan after all.

The service moved on, and I know I nodded off a couple of times. I could only hope that people in the audience thought my closed eyes and expressionless countenance was that of someone in deep reflection rather than a dog-tired dad.

Barbara and I returned home after the service ended, both of us exhausted beyond measure. Just when I thought I was done for the day, I received a voice mail from a producer for *Good Morning Britain*.

Kathryn Milofsky had reached out to me days before, wanting me to appear on the program on Friday morning—2:30 a.m. my time. I told her there was no way. Now, on Sunday evening, she called and pleaded with me to do *Good Morning Britain*'s Monday show, which she said they could record in the WDBJ studio.

"Kathryn, I just got back from Roanoke," I said. "I'm not driving back up there. Sorry. Maybe one day."

"Andy, you're just amazing and we want you to be on the show. It's the biggest show in the UK. Please. I'll send a car for you. Will that work?"

It would, and if it was going to be in Roanoke, it might provide another good opportunity to tag team an interview with Chris. I told Kathryn I'd do it, but I wanted Chris to join me if he was willing.

"Oh, that's fabulous," Kathryn said. "You're amaaaaaazing." I would hear that same closer every time I spoke with Kathryn.

All weekend long, my house had been full of family, both mine and Barbara's. I told my twenty-year-old nephew, Jonas, my sister's son, that I was going to do *Good Morning Britain* live at 2:30 a.m. and asked if he wanted to ride up with me. They were sending a car, after all, and it might be a neat experience.

"Sure," Jonas said, "that would be cool."

Kathryn somehow managed to find a car that would pick us up in Collinsville at midnight, drive us to Roanoke, wait, then drive us back home. That was no small task; at the time, we didn't even have Uber in our part of Virginia. She was understandably nervous that the driver might not show up, and she texted me nonstop until he arrived.

He got there around 12:45 a.m., in a massive stretch limo with LED running lights, a real prom night special. It pulled up to the curb and Jonas and I climbed in, only to discover that it was as pimped out on the inside as it was on the outside. It even had a minibar and cocktail glasses in a glass case. Under different circumstances, I might have sampled the luxurious amenities on offer, but my desire for a nap on the way to Roanoke far outweighed my desire for a fancy cocktail in a limo.

"You ever been in something like this?" I asked Jonas.

"Nope."

"Me either."

We rode the rest of the way in silence, and I might have even taken that nap.

We arrived at the station with only ten minutes to spare and the limo was quickly directed to the employee entrance. We walked into the studio, and after Chris and I exchanged a weary hug, we sat together at the anchor desk. Alison's anchor desk. I was about to do an international interview in her chair. There weren't many things I wanted to do less.

I noticed Chris had his TV makeup on. "I need some of that stuff too," I told him, "but I'm not sure it's going to help much." Once again, the thumbnails accompanying the internet link to the interview would show two people who looked drawn and haggard.

Chris and I debated how much we should pull our punches when we answered questions about gun laws. Lynn, the chief photographer running the camera, listened to us through an earpiece and nodded as we discussed it. Just before we went on air, Jonas unexpectedly weighed in.

"Fuck decorum," he said. "Just say whatever it is you need to say. What happened is complete bullshit, and you need to tell the world."

I knew Jonas to be a thoughtful young man, but his comment still surprised me. I was glad he decided to come along.

Looking back, there was nothing particularly earthshaking about that interview; what I mainly remember is the exhaustion. The earth-shaking part came shortly after. As the three of us headed back to the parking lot and the waiting limo, Chris stopped me.

"You know, as we were doing the interview, I realized what I need to do going forward," he said. "Alison and I talked about the future, and at one point she told me, 'I'd love to be a senator's wife.' I laughed and told her I'd love to be a senator's husband. What she said was meaningful, though. I think I have to run for office. I've gotta do it. It's what she would want me to do. It's how I can honor her and do something to affect change."

The tears began to pour down my cheeks. I put my arms around him.

"Oh my God, son," I said. "I love it. I love you, and she does too."

And sure enough, he did run.

Jonas and I got into the limo and headed home. The long day was over, and for the first time since The Day, it ended with a glimmer of hope.

———

Wednesday, September 2, 2015, the one-week anniversary, was bittersweet. Jennifer Henderson scheduled my last CNN interview for the immediate future, an interview with Carol Costello. I knew her name; a little less than a year earlier, she had been the CNN anchor who talked with Alison on live TV.

As travelers prepared to head out of town for Thanksgiving the previous year, a snowstorm had descended on the Roanoke area. Instead of her usual morning piece, Alison was out in the field covering the blizzard for WDBJ. At 9:15 that morning, she sent me a text: "OMG, I'm doing a live hit for CNN in 10 minutes!" It was pure Scooter. She barely had time to collect her wits, but she made sure Dad knew what was about to happen. Her excitement was tangible, even through the screen of my phone.

"Wow!" I texted.

"I'm so nervous."

"You'll be fine. You do the same thing for 60,000 people every day. You're just doing it for about a million more. ☺"

Barbara and I tuned in and watched. It was incredible, just like the first time we saw her live on air. We were so transfixed that the thought of taking a screenshot never even occurred to us. Thankfully, it did occur to someone at WDBJ. Alison nailed it, as if there was ever any doubt. With her usual panache, she showed off her houndstooth scarf and matching boots as she demonstrated how much snow had fallen, cheerfully walking the viewers through the storm's progress, and then, with the timing of a pro, she tossed it back to Carol Costello.

Our hearts were bursting with pride, and when Alison finished, Barbara and I whooped and jumped up and down like we had just witnessed Texas beat the University of Southern California for the national championship. Ten minutes later Alison called, excited and relieved.

"You were awesome, Scooter," I said.

"Did you really think so? I was *so* nervous."

"If you were, it didn't show. You were so smooth."

Later in the day, she sent me a picture of the WDBJ morning news team watching her hit from the control room. They were glued like we were, leaning into the monitor and cheering like the family of a baseball player who hits a home run in his first major league at bat.

Less than a year later, I was about to do the first of many interviews with the same person who had introduced Alison to a national audience for the first and only time.

Alison was the one destined for fame. Not me. But I was the one who got caught in the whirlwind, the one who had achieved celebrity, a horrible kind of celebrity I never desired.

5

CELEBRATING A LIFE

I slept in the following Monday. There was no media that day, as best I can recall. But Monday evening was Alison's Celebration of Life. We didn't want to have a traditional funeral; everyone grieves differently, and it just wasn't for us. It wasn't the way to remember Alison.

When asked by the funeral home if we wanted to see Alison before she was cremated, we said no. There was part of me that wanted to, a part that wanted to hold her in my arms one last time. Thankfully, there was a louder part of me that knew it would be ghastly. That would have been the last image I had of Alison for the rest of my life, indelibly etched into my soul. It would have destroyed me, annihilated me. I opted to remember her alive and happy, and that's the image I'll carry forever.

Barbara knew exactly how we should commemorate Alison. It was going to be a party, a celebration of her short, incredible life. We wanted as many friends and family there as possible. Barbara and I had talked about our own arrangements, and we knew that was how we would want to go out. We never thought we'd have to consider it for our daughter, but we knew she would have been right there on the same page.

Putting the party together was going to be tricky, but Lynn Ward, our steadfast caretaker, picked up the ball and ran with it. She gathered every mover and shaker in town and organized the event in a flash.

The venue was New College Institute (NCI), a college in Martinsville that was supposed to have been the answer to our community's economic woes in the aftermath of the furniture and textile manufacturing exodus at the turn of the century. As in *Field of Dreams*, the idea was build it and they will come. NCI started modestly in 2005, in a couple of renovated buildings in uptown Martinsville. Sadly, they didn't come, but a dazzling new facility was completed in the summer of 2014. The vision of a real college hasn't materialized, but they created a beautiful event space with high ceilings and state-of-the-art sound and lighting.

The space was simply given to us. Barbara's old boss at Piedmont Arts, Toy Cobbe, bought all the food and beverages, including beer and wine. The only thing Barbara did in preparation was to create a PowerPoint slideshow from the hundreds of pictures she had of Alison. Beyond that, all we had to do was show up at 6:00 that evening.

But who to invite? As much as we wanted to open the party to the public, we knew it wouldn't go well. Doing so could have drawn a thousand people, probably more. We had also received a warning from the Henry County Sheriff's Office about the possibility of the craven lunatics from Westboro Baptist Church showing up to protest. In Alison's obituary, we simply said that we were having a private ceremony and we relied on Lynn to quietly spread the word.

The criteria for invitees was that they had to be someone we knew, Alison had known, or was simply a good person. Barbara barred one person, a former school superintendent, for not meeting this latter requirement. He was steered away.

We arrived shortly before 6:00 p.m. and the parking lot was already starting to fill. We were greeted by several friends before we made our way inside, and thankfully, there was no sign of the Westboro crowd. Inside, Barbara and I were separated almost immediately, our attention pulled by the different currents of friends eager to offer condolences one-on-one. I was in the lobby for several minutes before I could even make my way into the banquet hall. By then, the room was filling up and a brass quartet from the Roanoke Symphony Orchestra (RSO) was playing beautifully. No dirges, just uplifting music. I was touched that the RSO thought so much of us to send them down.

Barbara's slideshow of photographs of Alison from childhood through her recent WDBJ days was sizably projected just below the ceiling on every wall. It was visually spectacular, but I could only take in a few seconds of it. I was not emotionally prepared to revisit her life in pictures. As of this writing, I'm OK seeing photos of her, but I still can't bring myself to watch a multitude of videos of her, especially from her days on television.

It's a bottomlessly cruel situation. When Alison was alive, I relished seeing every stand-up, every anchor opportunity. Now I can't bear the thought of watching those videos. I would see her alive again. I would look at my phone and wait for her to text me, seeking guidance or just letting me know about her latest triumph. I'm content for now to look at photographs. One day, maybe I'll be able to watch her on television again, but not today.

I kept my eyes level, concentrating on the person in front of me, and I didn't look up again throughout the celebration of life.

In the hall I saw a long table with a bartender behind it and I headed over to grab a beer. As I turned around, in walked Governor McAuliffe accompanied by Brian Moran, Virginia's secretary of public safety and homeland security. Although we'd never met in person, Brian donated to my campaign for the House of Delegates eight years before, back when he was the chair of the Democratic Party of Virginia. He's a tall, good-looking man with angular features and sandy hair, with a quick, winning smile, a lighter version of John Kennedy. "Glad to see you, Brian," I said. "Thanks for coming down."

"I wish I didn't have to see you under these circumstances, but I wanted to be here," he replied. I gave him a big hug and then turned to Governor McAuliffe.

"Thanks for coming, Governor," I said. "We've got some adult beverages I hope you'll take advantage of."

"Hey, we're Irish," he said, grinning and gesturing toward Moran. "Don't worry." And with that, he was lost in the crowd.

Barbara and I had long since been engulfed in different groups of the crowd, people pushing us in different directions. I was carried toward the center of the room by a stream of people, one after another, offering whatever solace they could muster. "No words" was the prominent sentiment. Most were in tears, and all I could do was give them a hug. We allowed our friend Ben Williams from the *Martinsville Bulletin* to come, but he was the only one from the press that was officially "working." The photograph he took of me hugging Delane Heath, a paddling buddy of mine, captured it all: the tears, yes, but beneath that, the friendship and camaraderie.

In addition to state and local dignitaries, there were paddlers and golfers. Most were somber, but one golfing friend of mine, Mark Hawks, was especially shaken. Mark is a dead ringer for Larry Culpepper, the character in a series of Dr. Pepper commercials. He was crying in jerks and gasps. I knew those sobs well, because I cry the same way; it's the grief of a man who isn't accustomed to expressing it. Mark probably hasn't cried like that since, but for me, it became routine.

As I made my way through the crowd, I briefly spoke with people who had traveled a long way to be there. I felt bad that I couldn't talk with them more, but the current kept moving me along with no eddy in sight. Finally, I saw my dear friend Don Bernhardt, who drove eight hours from Indiana, and Mimi Bessette, who flew in from New York. They were both in the national tour and Broadway production of *The Best Little Whorehouse in Texas* with me forty years earlier, and we'd remained friends ever since. I was touched and moved that they made such an effort to be with me. It was the first time I'd seen Don in ten years.

Several men in suits who appeared to be part of an entourage came up to me. The first to introduce himself was Jon Alger, the president of James Madison University. Alison had interviewed him at Rutgers immediately after he was named as JMU's new president. He brought members of the administration with him.

Almost every on-air talent from WDBJ was there, and I wondered how they were doing the news that evening. I later found out that an anchor who had retired from the station had volunteered to do the news that night so they could all be in Martinsville.

I saw Jennifer Henderson from CNN at the event; by that point, she was a member of the family. I then bumped into Katie Fulp and Mike Hennessey, reporters from Jacksonville, North Carolina, who had worked with Alison before she started at WDBJ, Katie at the same station as Alison, and Mike for a different station. The three were competitors but friends, part of the journalism family. Alison had played matchmaker and introduced Katie and Mike, and now they were engaged. They wanted to be in Martinsville to let me know how much she meant to them. This was the first of many stories about the little acts of kindness and compassion that Alison had spread throughout her network of friends. She was loved.

It was then that I saw George Lester.

Earlier in the day, I walked up the driveway and checked the mail in a vain attempt to find a moment of normalcy. In the mail was an invitation from George Lester, the biggest landowner in Martinsville and Henry County, and likely in Virginia. He was hosting a fundraiser for Senator Bill Stanley.

I had known George for years. He had even grudgingly and quietly contributed to my House of Delegates run. He and Stanley had been pushing for the completion of the mythical Interstate 73 project, a project that had been in the works for decades with virtually nothing to show for it, at least in Virginia. George was certain that I-73 would bring jobs to the area, but the Virginia stretch of it is never going to come to fruition, at least not this century. While the concept was noble, the reality was that there was no funding for it, and there probably never will be, at least not in our lifetimes.

That didn't stop George, and, unfortunately, his enthusiasm didn't seem entirely altruistic. The proposed route would pass through many of his properties and he clearly stood to gain if the road was built. For Senator Stanley, it was typical snake oil sales. I suspect he knew I-73 was never going to happen, but it made for good political hay, particularly with George.

I stood in front of the mailbox, holding the invitation in my hands, seething. Out of all our local Republican politicians who raked in NRA money and quietly killed life-saving legislation, Stanley was the most craven. I'd had run-ins with Stanley in the past; on one occasion, he promised he would support a bill that I was in favor of, then he turned around and argued against it. He was the personification of everything wrong with politics. That I would receive an invitation to a Stanley fundraiser in the wake of my daughter's shooting death was disgusting, an affront.

But then a thought crossed my mind. I figured every mover and shaker in Martinsville would be at Alison's celebration, and I had to think George would be there too.

My suspicion was correct. I was standing in the middle of the room when George and his wife, Lee, made their way over to me.

George is a big man, easily six feet, two inches, with a noticeable toupee that somehow belies his wealth. I knew what was coming and the adrenaline kicked in.

"We're so sorry," Lee said, then passed the baton to George.

"Terrible, just terrible," he said. "If there's anything I can do . . ."

There it was. A fat pitch in the middle of the strike zone, ready to be slugged out of the park.

With all the quiet venom I could muster and convey, I looked him straight in the eye.

"Well, George, there is one thing, actually. I got an invitation from you today to attend your fundraiser for Bill Stanley. I'm not going to be able to make it. But please tell that little bastard I'm going to be his worst fucking nightmare, and I'm sorry you have to associate with him. Enjoy the rest of the evening."

George looked like I'd hit him across the solar plexus with a two-by-four. His mouth dropped and he was flummoxed, struggling to find words. He never saw it coming. I turned and walked away.

I don't know if that was the best outlet for my rage, but damn if it didn't feel good.

After that pleasant exchange, I found myself alone near one of the doorways. A stranger with a graying, neatly trimmed beard approached me, wearing a suit.

"Andy, I'm Steve Capus, executive producer of *CBS Evening News*," he said. "I just want you to know that she would have been with us one day."

I was floored, not only that he made the trip, not only that he said those words, but that I knew it wasn't hyperbole. She *would* have been there, and sooner rather than later. In the TV news business, there are "pass-through" stations, like her first job in Jacksonville, where you get some experience and move on to a bigger market. WDBJ wasn't quite a pass-through; it was ranked number one in the market, and many members of its on-air talent had decided that Roanoke was a great place to put down roots and stay awhile. There's certainly nothing wrong with that, but it wouldn't have worked for Alison. She wouldn't have stopped until she went national. Or international. Or intergalactic.

I saw Steve Capus again months later on a trip to New York. As we were making small talk, I brought up his comment about Alison. I told him it got me to my core.

"Do you remember what else I told you that night?" Steve asked.

"No clue," I said.

"I asked how you have the strength to do what you're doing so soon after her death. You know what your answer was?"

It was a blur. I told him I had no idea.

"You said, 'Steve, what else can I do?' And that really hit me. It was incredibly brave."

Back at the celebration of life, the RSO brass quartet had been replaced by Delirious, a cover band made up of local doctors, all friends of ours. One of its members, Tom Berry, had recently retired. At heart, Tom was an old hippie, and his ponytail was part of a look he'd cultivated even while he was practicing medicine. The casual observer would conclude that this guy was right at home on the keyboard of his Hammond B3, but they might not have guessed that he left medicine with a reputation for being one of the best surgeons in town.

Tom knew that "Brown Eyed Girl," a song the band played at all their gigs, was my ringtone for Alison, and I told him I'd like him to play it that evening. He was surprised. Earlier in the evening Barbara had told him not to play it. It's a hard thing to explain; I needed to hear the song, needed that connection to Alison, but I knew it would be brutal.

As the party drew to a close, hundreds still in attendance, Tom took the mike and asked if I was ready for them to play "Alison's song." I gave him the thumbs up.

I fell to pieces just a few notes in, and Barbara found me in the throes of my grief. I hadn't seen Chris all evening, but he came over too, and so did Drew. We clung to each other as the band played.

"Sha-la-la-la-la-la-la-la-la-la-la-ti-da" echoed through the room as the band drew out that final a cappella riff, the crowd raising their arms and swaying. We gamely tried to wave along with the crowd, but it was a sad effort that seemed to go on forever.

The evening wound down, and eventually it seemed that only me, Chris, Barbara, Don, his wife, and Mimi were left, but then our dear old friend Randy Brooks found us. Barbara and I had known Randy for forty years, going all the way back to our days in Texas.

Randy, who looks like an older version of Conan O'Brien and was also an alum of the Country Dinner Playhouse, is one of the cleverest guys I've ever met. This trait must run in his family. He's the nephew of Foster Brooks, the comedian who made a living playing a drunk, most notably as a regular on *The Dean Martin Show*. Randy gained celebrity in his own right many years ago when he penned everybody's favorite Christmas song: "Grandma Got Run Over by a Reindeer." Randy has always had a jovial demeanor, and I've never heard him say a cross word about anyone. He met Alison two years earlier when Barbara arranged for him to come up and play Grandma for the annual Roanoke Symphony Orchestra Christmas Show in Martinsville. Somehow, I'd known he would be at the celebration of life.

We sat for a little while and caught up, and then decided it was time to take the party home to our deck. We fired up the tiki torches, grabbed every available chair, and gathered on the deck. Family wandered in and out, beer and wine flowed freely, and I found myself surrounded by my oldest and dearest friends. We traded war stories from our acting days, most coming from me and Don. The two of us had spent three years together in *Whorehouse* and were roommates both before and after Barbara and I got married. Don was family.

The theater world is a small one, and if you stay in it long enough, you work with a good chunk of its members. John Wolfe, still in the business with his wife, Brenna, at his side, recounted one show he did about ten years earlier. I can't recall the story, but I do remember Mimi saying, "You know, John, I was also in that show."

"You were?" John asked. He clearly didn't remember. He tried to graciously extricate himself from the situation, but I don't think it worked. Barbara and I exchanged a quick glance and a smile. It was kind of funny, like all the stories we shared that night. It was as if we were transported back in time, back before the horror of the previous week. For a few all-too-brief hours, right up until we said our good-byes at 2:00 a.m., I could laugh and take comfort in the oasis of old friendships.

At long last, I laid my head on my pillow.

"I know you were there tonight, Scooter," I whispered. "I hope you liked it."

———

The following weekend was the opening game of the football season for Alison's alma mater. We were invited to sit in the JMU president's box to see a pregame presentation honoring Alison; around the same time, we also received word that Virginia Tech, where Adam graduated from, was going to honor Alison and Adam two days later at their Labor Day opener against Ohio State.

Aside from Alison's graduation in December 2012, the last time we were on the JMU campus was for a tailgate party Alison's senior year. Arriving on the campus brought back those memories. Tailgating didn't really exist when I was at the University of Texas at Austin, and I'd never had the occasion to participate in a tailgate party, much less throw one. Alison was an old hand, however, and she convinced me early in the football season of her last semester to host one for her and her friends, some she had made while working at the JMU student newspaper, the *Breeze*, some from her sorority, Alpha Phi.

I took on the assignment with great relish, no pun intended, and bought a little portable gas grill for the occasion (charcoal grilling, my preferred method, wasn't allowed). We arrived in the designated parking lot late that morning and had a perfect day, nothing but friends, sunshine, and pleasantly warm weather. We got everything set up and I started cooking my famous beer brats and hamburgers as Alison held court with her friends, who filtered in and out. A cooler full of beer was the perfect complement to the occasion, and I had the occasional tipple as I cooked and greeted her friends.

Alison suggested that I tippled a bit too much, as I had such a wonderful time impressing her friends with my delicious food and my sparkling wit. I know I succeeded on the first account, and although she protested, I knew she was happy with our showing. She must have been, because she eagerly accepted my suggestion that we host another tailgate party before the football season ended.

Barbara couldn't go to the next tailgate, so Drew and I met Alison in the parking lot, the warmth and sunshine replaced by a cold drizzle. In contrast to the first tailgate, where people showed up early and often, we huddled by ourselves like refugees in a winter relocation camp. Alison fretted that no one was going to show up, and she started to get peeved since we had put so much work into it. It was just like her. She expected people to honor their commitments.

Finally, the weather broke and all her friends who had decided to sleep in started showing up in waves. This time we'd brought Jack the dog with us, and as always, he was a hit. In spite of the weather, it ended up being a great time, dear old dad coming through for his girl once again. I looked forward to the chance to do it all again when she was an alum.

Instead, Barbara and I arrived at the campus for a very different reason. It was about an hour before the kickoff for the game honoring Alison, and we were lost in our own thoughts. We had wanted Chris and Drew to be there, but they were tied up with family and work commitments.

We had been instructed to park in front of JMU Director of Communications Bill Wyatt's house. He has a kind, unassuming manner and was the perfect escort. He met us with a warm smile and led us through the newly remodeled and upgraded stadium and into the president's suite. The only thing I could compare it to was Martinsville Speedway owner Clay Campbell's box at the racetrack, lush and fancy with comfortable seating and all the amenities you could ask for. The room was huge, and so was the spread of food. We were enthusiastically greeted by JMU's president, Jon Alger, and Nick Langridge, its vice president for university advancement. We had asked that Ryan Parkhurst and Roger Soenksen, two of Alison's professors whom she deeply admired, be there for the game. I used to joke with Alison, "Does Parkhurst have a first name?" She valued my opinion on career options, but her go-to was WWPD: What Would Parkhurst Do? He was one of those rare, caring professors who stayed in touch with his students. Of course, it didn't hurt that she was his one-in-a-million, an example he held other students up to both before and after her death.

When we saw Parkhurst, Barbara pulled out Alison's graduation cap and presented it to him, telling him that Alison would have wanted him to have it. He fell to pieces.

Roger, for his part, had delivered an incredible eulogy earlier in the week at an early morning memorial service at JMU, which was attended by hundreds of students. If nothing else, it was remarkable that college kids would get up that early.

We mingled and ate. As I headed to the bar for another beer, a young black man sidled up next to me. He introduced himself as

Levar Stoney, and said he remembered me from when I ran for the House of Delegates. He told me he'd been the director of the Virginia Democratic Party and we'd talked several times.

It was nice to suddenly have a pleasant reminder of my past life. "Oh wow, I remember you, Levar," I told him. "We never met, but I remember talking over the phone. Geez, I didn't realize at the time that I was going to be cannon fodder."

Obviously, I hadn't served in the House. Levar broke into a guffaw, his big, genuine smile reminding me of a young Eddie Murphy.

When I asked what he was doing now, he said he was secretary of the commonwealth for the McAuliffe administration. I asked him what brought him to the game.

"I'm also a JMU grad," he said, "and I am proud of your daughter."

I thanked him and told him it was good to see him. It really was. Next, Barbara and I were introduced to Ron Devine, a JMU grad who owned a chain of Burger King franchises and made enough money to field a NASCAR racing team. He was a big bear of a man who greeted us with a great outpouring of affection. He showed us a model of his JMU race car and proudly announced that at the race in Richmond the following weekend, Alison's name and photo would be on his JMU car. He invited me and Barbara to go to the race.

I was deeply touched. I'd never cared for racing, but suddenly, I was an overnight fan of racing and the JMU/Alison #83 car.

"Ron, we'd be honored to come to Richmond next week. It is so cool of you to do this for her."

"The honor is mine," he said.

We then headed to another suite, one belonging to the Showkers, a couple who were such major donors that the school named its football field in their honor. After Alison's death, they challenged the JMU community to contribute to Alison's scholarship, which Barbara had set up at JMU just days after Alison died; if contributions reached

$25,000, the Showkers would match it. That match happened in a matter of days. It was an incredible honor to meet these generous people who understood what Alison meant to the JMU community.

The big moment was almost at hand. The band was on the field and the crowd was on its feet as the national anthem drew to a close. And then there was my Scooter's picture on the giant scoreboard, looking out over the crowd as the PA announcer addressed the stadium.

I don't remember what he said. I could barely see through my tears. All I remember is that when he finished his eulogy, the crowd erupted in prolonged applause. I later learned that the coach asked his football team if they preferred to come onto the field during his remarks or if they would rather wait until afterward. Their answer was unanimous; they wanted to be on the field. I didn't see it at the time, but they all raised their helmets in Alison's honor during the ceremony. The outpouring of love was overwhelming, simultaneously wonderful and agonizing.

After the ceremony, we talked to Kelly Zuber, WDBJ's news director, and her husband, Tim, for bit. They are also JMU alums, and there's little question that Alison's JMU connection with Kelly helped cement her getting the job at WDBJ. We chatted pleasantly about how skilled JMU's marching band was, but underneath, I still had a lingering resentment eating at me. Kelly had dragged her feet on Alison's supposed promotion to anchor.

Of course, Kelly couldn't be blamed for Alison's death. She couldn't possibly have predicted what would happen.

But for Christ's sake, if she'd only made the correct decision in a timely fashion, then maybe . . .

We made it through halftime and then decided it was time to head home. Barbara and I were in for another episode just like this one in another two days.

The day before the Virginia Tech game, I received tickets via FedEx from Larry Hinker, Virginia Tech's associate VP for university relations who was retiring at the end of the season, after a twenty-seven-year career there. We'd spoken on the phone that week, and in another escapist moment, our talk centered on football.

"Larry," I joked, "you know that if it weren't for my alma mater, Virginia Tech wouldn't be on the map," referring to the famous Texas-VT Sugar Bowl game of 1995. I was living in Mount Airy, North Carolina, at the time, and I told Larry that when the match-up was revealed, I went around the office saying, "What the hell is Virginia Tech and why are we playing such a lower tier school?" There were quite a few VT grads in the office, and since I'd only recently moved to the area, they quickly brought me up to speed.

"The UT Horns got schooled, and VT went on to fame," I said to Larry, smiling.

He laughed and agreed with my assessment. "I look forward to seeing you Monday," he said. "Call me if the tickets don't get there." He gave me his cell number, which turned out to be a very good thing.

On game day, Chris met us at the designated parking spot at Lane Stadium. As with the JMU game, we arrived about an hour prior to kickoff. Even though we were close to the stadium, we were about to discover that we'd need all of that time to get to where we were supposed to go.

As we made our way to one of the entrance gates, we were stopped by several people along the way who offered condolences and encouraged us to keep fighting. It was my first experience being recognized by strangers, and it was an odd feeling. Chris was a local celebrity, but I sure didn't consider myself to be a celebrity of any kind. Now, though, I realized that had all changed. People had seen my interviews, and maybe, I hoped, my message had struck a chord after all.

We got to the gate and encountered our first ticket checker, an elderly woman who took her job seriously. She eyeballed the tickets, and while she let us in, she couldn't tell us where to go. I never thought to look at the tickets until just then, and I noticed there weren't any seat numbers printed, only a general section. After I explained that we were supposed to be in the president's box, she sent us to an elevator tower, and as we stepped out of the elevator, we were met by another senior sentry. She took her job just as seriously as the last one and suggested that our seats were in a different section, not in the president's suite.

Down we went and continued our misguided journey. "Can you believe this?" I steamed at Chris. "First we're in the president's box at JMU, and here we're in the end zone." We finally ended up in a section that appeared to be correct, but we still had the problem of no assigned seat numbers. As we stood lost in the aisle, I remembered I had Larry Hinker's cell number. The call went to voice mail, but thankfully, he called me back almost immediately and said he'd have someone come get us. At last, we were rescued and escorted to the president's suite. (We did go through one more layer of senior gatekeepers, but our escort was able to pull rank and get us in.)

Larry found us and apologized profusely. "We've got a new ticket system and a whole new usher staff," he said. "Things are screwed up."

"Well, I can tell you your staff takes their job very seriously," I joked. "I've had an easier time getting through airport security. Rest assured, no one will get in that isn't supposed to."

The VT president's suite was almost twice the size of JMU's, as you would expect, and the spread of food was just as impressive. To my surprise, I ran into a familiar face: Levar Stoney.

"Damn, Levar," I said. "I want your job. You get to go hang out in the luxury boxes at football games. Pretty sweet gig." It was one of those few times I could escape for a moment of normal, everyday humor, however fleeting.

He flashed his big grin and said it was a tough job, but somebody had to do it.

"You know, the governor seems like the kind of guy you just want to have a beer and hang out with," I said.

"He's exactly that kind of guy," Levar said. "And the next time you're in Richmond, call me and we'll make it happen."

Yeah right, I thought.

"We're in Richmond this Saturday for the race," I said. "How's that?"

"OK, just call me and let me know when you'll be around."

When the PA announcer paid tribute to Alison and Adam, their faces were displayed on the stadium's giant scoreboard. As soon as the photos went up, sixty-six thousand people erupted in a deafening cheer. Barbara, Chris, and I soaked it in from the suite balcony. I'd never been to a Tech game, but I'd heard how loud it could be; now I got to experience it firsthand. It was electric, and the thunderous roar continued as the Hokies took the field.

With the game underway, I retreated inside and was greeted by well-wishers. I soon discovered that among them was the rogue's gallery of politicians I'd been calling out over the last week. Congressman Morgan Griffith, whom I'd worked with only a few weeks before on the Philpott Dam weekend generation project, came over and humbly shook my hand, offering the familiar "no words" commentary. At that point, I still held out some hope that somewhere down the road, I'd be able to persuade him to come around on gun legislation.

Then came my first encounter with Congressman Bob Goodlatte. I stared him down as I shook his hand. "We'll be talking," I told him, and I said the same thing to Senator John Edwards. I don't know if they were able to read my contempt from my body language or comments, but just seeing them made me seethe with rage. They had been Alison's representatives, and they lined their pockets with NRA dollars. I despised them for it. But as much as I wished to confront them right then and there, I think Alison was looking out for me, whispering in my ear, "Dad, don't make a scene." It was her favorite admonishment;

she had witnessed a few of my "scenes" in her lifetime, attempts to correct bad behavior and right everyday wrongs.

I found Chris deep in conversation with a bookish man in his early thirties, sporting round glasses and a vaguely hipster appearance. Chris introduced the man as Joseph Yost, the state delegate from the Blacksburg area. We talked for quite a while about the mental health aspect of gun violence. He struck me as being reasonable and open to my contention that gun legislation was the necessary path forward. Yost is a Republican, but he seemed to have more progressive ideas than his counterparts. There was none of the usual pomposity I'd encountered in my dealings with many of his colleagues. I sort of liked him, and in another reality, I might have supported him.

Occasionally I could hear a roar from the crowd as the Hokies made a play to stay in the game. I'd go the balcony, catch a few plays, then head back inside. I caught up with Chris and Barbara and we plopped down on an overstuffed couch away from the milling VIPs and politicians. We sat for a bit, chatting amiably, before Barbara and I decided to head back home and leave Chris to rub elbows with the VIPs. We had an hour-and-a-half drive ahead of us, and it was getting late.

Barbara and I drove down Interstate 81 without much conversation, if any. I was going over the speed limit, as usual, and in my desire to get home as fast as possible, I'm sure I exceeded the unofficial policy of the Virginia State Police: "Nine you're fine, ten you're mine." Suddenly, I saw bright headlights quickly bearing down on my tail. I knew it was a state trooper; I had just seen a patrol car parked in the median a few miles back.

"Shit," I muttered, braking down to the speed limit. The trooper just sat there, camped on my tail.

What was he doing? I expected the blue lights to flash at any moment, but they never came. The trooper tailgated me for what felt like an eternity before suddenly breaking away and speeding down the interstate at blistering speed.

I freaked out. Why had he tailgated me? What was he trying to do? Did he know who I am? Was he sending some kind of message? I called #77, the number for the state police, and described what happened.

"I'm going to find out who this is," I said to the dispatcher. "It's bullshit and it scared the hell out of me." I sped up, driving like a crazy man. At that point it was barely a metaphor.

"You've got to stop this," Barbara pleaded. "You're losing it. *Stop it!*"

I was hell-bent on catching the mystery trooper and reporting him. Driving recklessly, erratically, I finally caught up to him and read the plates to the dispatcher, and I was told they would be in contact with the patrol car. Shaken, I ended the call, finally slowing down. My stewing emotions and frayed nerves had gotten the best of me, and I knew it.

"You can't be an asshole to people if you want them to be on your side," Barbara said, a voice of reason in stark contrast to my own display. "And you were just a giant asshole. And you sounded like a crazy asshole, which is worse. You just have to stop."

I drove the rest of the way in silence, reflecting on what I'd done.

It was a late Saturday night on a dangerous stretch of I-81. A state trooper saw a vehicle flying by him. He did what he was supposed to do. He pursued me and got close enough to run my tags before he flipped on his blue lights. When the driver came back as Andy Parker, he let me go, a small gesture of kindness, only to get a radio call from dispatch saying I had just called to berate him.

I don't know if that's exactly the way it went down, but I suspect it was. I was ashamed of myself. The man who screamed at the kid in the Confederate truck had returned.

6

THE CLUB NO ONE WANTS TO JOIN

I was standing at the beginning of a road I never thought I'd walk, inducted into a club that no one wants to join: the families and survivors of gun violence. Since Alison's death, there have been thousands of new members. We all share a common bond, and we hate it. I was about to get a crash course on my new membership.

Two weeks after Alison's murder, we dove headlong into the social and political quagmire of guns in America. Even labeling the issue inflames both sides. Gun control or gun violence prevention? Do assault weapons bans work? How many rounds should a magazine hold? And of course, should we institute universal background checks?

"Yeah, but no law is going to stop a crazy man with a gun. If it hadn't been a gun, he'd have used a machete."

I can't tell you how many people said that about Alison's killer, their heads so deeply buried in the sand that the words are muffled.

You can't swing a machete at one thousand feet per second. You can't kill multiple people with a machete within the blink of an eye. Ten people armed with machetes couldn't have replicated the horror that one gun-toting madman wrought at a Jason Aldean concert in Las Vegas. And you can outrun a machete, but you can't outrun a bullet.

"Thoughts and prayers." "Thoughts and prayers." "You're always in our thoughts and prayers."

Fuck your thoughts and prayers, I thought. I prayed that the thoughts and prayers crowd might be delivered from their own stupidity.

Our course had already been decided. The next few months found me and Barbara deep in the weeds, and no one told us the devil grass would leave so many scratches.

After spending a week as a virtual prisoner in my own home, an ever-present CNN satellite truck parked out front, I went to Washington, DC, to continue the media tour. Barbara stayed behind to deal with Alison's affairs.

Because Barbara was absent from the spotlight, it gave some people the impression that she preferred to stay out of the media glare. That was hardly the case. Barbara does much better in front of a camera than I do. The reality was that someone had to take care of the house, the dog, and all the awful shit that comes with an unexpected tragedy.

Barbara learned how many copies of your daughter's death certificate you need to close bank accounts, 401(k) plans, and insurance policies. We were both a mess, but Barbara held it together much better than I ever could.

My first trip to Washington made me the new face of gun violence prevention. It also became a source of friction in our marriage, because Barbara felt left out, and justifiably so.

Chris, Drew, and I hopped into the truck and started the drive to Washington, a five-hour slog at daybreak to make it there in time to start lunches, meetings, and public appearances set up for us by Lori Haas and Chris Kocher.

Lori had come to our house the week before, and I found her compassionate and insightful. When her daughter was wounded in the

Virginia Tech massacre, she quickly took up the mantle of gun violence prevention. Her organization, the Coalition to Stop Gun Violence, is the main voice of the movement in Virginia. Her family is one of the oldest in the commonwealth, she likes to point out; her voice is authoritative but has an undulating lilt that offers comfort and reassurance. She had clearly counseled bereaved family members before, but here we were, a great ball of white-hot rage ready to follow her lead.

Kocher was more aloof and distant. He is a lawyer who followed New York Mayor Michael Bloomberg from Mayors Against Illegal Guns to Everytown for Gun Safety. In 2014, Everytown offered a pivot away from the old group of largely white politicians making pleas for gun safety legislation. The pivot intended to show that brothers, sisters, sons, daughters, and especially moms and dads were also urging Congress to do something, anything, about the growing rates of gun homicides and suicides in the country.

It was Harry Hurst, Chris's dad, who connected us with Lori, who in turn put us in touch with Kocher. Alison's death was, in a grim public relations view, great timing for a CNN town hall event and gun reform rally outside the U.S. Capitol in mid-September. The CNN event and rally had both been previously scheduled, and then came August 26. Lo and behold, the Alison Parker family is pissed off and wants to shout!

Lori was our liaison to Everytown, and she pitched the event to us, now called "Whatever It Takes."

I asked Lori, "What is 'Whatever It Takes?'"

"Your words," she said. "You said them during the interview with Megyn Kelly."

I didn't remember saying that at all. I was still in a fog.

The drive to DC was silent, each of us listening with separate headphones to our own podcasts, books on tape, or movies. I listened to an audiobook through my new Bluetooth-enabled hearing aids. It was probably for the best that, outside of our own entertainment, the Honda Ridgeline was quiet. It was hard not to drift back to just a few weeks ago when we were all packed in the same pickup for our trip to the Nantahala River to celebrate Alison's birthday. The neoprene seats smelled of stagnant water and were speckled with sand and small fragments of leaves. Our minds were elsewhere, and we chatted only when it was time to pull over and take a leak. That time came on Interstate 81 as we came into Harrisonburg and stopped at JMU.

The semester had just started and mobs of students covered the streets as they walked to and from fraternity and sorority rush meetings, intramural sports sign-ups, and perhaps least of all, classes. With an almost hive-mind uniformity, the young women wore black yoga pants and white tennis shoes. They all looked happy, walking up-tempo and focused on what they had coming up in their next lecture or dormitory social. They lived in the present, but they reminded me of the past, of moving Alison into JMU, where she went from "my Scooter" to "Alison the wunderkind."

We pulled into a gas station in the middle of campus on Port Republic Road to fill up the gas tank and trash our empty coffee cups. Considering the warm sun and mild September breeze, we must have looked odd in our coats and ties.

Our heads were down as we shuffled in and out of the convenience store. To navigate grief is to go through it, not around it, not that I was cognizant of that at the time. I was simply treading water as best I could. The hypotheticals were flowing through my mind, and here, so close to JMU, I couldn't help but examine the bitter dichotomy.

Could I ever have thought five years ago, when hauling up Alison's fluorescent bedspread and buying my "JMU Dad" cap, that I'd be here now on my way to Washington as a gun violence prevention activist?

I hurried us back onto the interstate and up to DC. Soon enough, the zigzag network of people and cars changed their look, becoming gradually more professional. Men in tailored suits and women in formfitting dresses walked with purpose up and down the sidewalks of our nation's capital. We pulled up to the Capitol Holiday Inn on C Street where we checked in and dropped our bags in our rooms before heading to the hotel restaurant, where we were supposed to meet Lori Haas. We found her tucked away in a back corner table, facing away from us, and could tell from a distance that her phone was lit up. If multitasking is a young person's game, then Lori had found some kind of fountain of youth. She was texting with her folks at the coalition, coordinating legislative meetings, scrolling through her Facebook feed, and reading Google's latest headlines, all at the same time. When we joined her, she showed an immediate warmth despite her attention to her iPhone, and she graciously balanced her need to stay in touch with making a human connection with her three new recruits.

"It's nice to finally put a face to the voice," Chris said.

"What's the plan?" I asked.

Lori and Chris Kocher had earlier provided a detailed itinerary, but I hardly remembered any of it. I knew we'd be meeting with the Virginia members of Congress, Senators Tim Kaine and Mark Warner, and our local congressmen Morgan Griffith and Robert Hurt. All were most likely perfunctory, but the one who wouldn't commit was Bob Goodlatte. I figured his team was smart enough to know that it was a good idea to grant us an audience, if for no other reason than the optics.

"Anything from Goodlatte's people?" I asked Lori.

"Not yet," she said. "They keep saying maybe a half-hour tomorrow morning, but nothing firm." At a previous time, Lori had been an attractive socialite, graduating from a prestigious Catholic preparatory school outside Richmond. She had been a successful real estate agent, but once her daughter Emily was shot twice on a chilly morning in April 2007 at Virginia Tech, her life began anew. She was battle-tested after years in the trenches, legislative fights to get guns out of the hands of men with temporary restraining orders, to get guns off college campuses, and to create a system in Virginia for universal background checks. Her face and posture didn't show the battle scars as much as you might think. Her eyes locked on me as she asked how we had been holding up over the last few days.

As we were getting to know one another, Kocher found us at our corner table. A hugger by nature, he gave each of us an embrace and then pulled up a chair. Lori, Drew, Chris, and I were already devouring the lunch buffet, but Kocher was ready to get on with the schedule.

"So how we doing?" he asked.

I shrugged and waited for him to continue.

"Andy, first off, I can't believe you, Chris, and Drew found the strength to come up here," he said.

The son of working-class parents in Long Island, Kocher had a slight upspeak at the end of his phrases. His next words were kind, remarking on how talented and bubbly Alison seemed and how horrified he was when he heard about how she was killed. He complimented me for speaking out right away, and his words didn't sound hollow. Kocher was the director of the Everytown Survivor Network, a new support system for the families of those shot and killed. Like Lori, he too had consoled people like us before, and he tried not to come off as rehearsed.

But in terms of the launch of Whatever It Takes, an empowered group made up of a network of grieving loved ones, what more could he want than a timely face and a high-profile story like Alison's?

Some might consider it opportunistic, but it didn't bother me one bit. I just wanted to get the message out.

We finished the last of our buffet of mashed potatoes and unsweetened tea, and we waited for our marching orders.

"So we need to hurry downstairs to meet with some other folks from the media team and go over a few things before we go to the

Newseum," Kocher said. The Newseum, like it sounds, is a museum dedicated to journalism. Dozens of survivors were to gather there and appear on CNN for a town hall called the "Loneliest Club." The name was cringeworthy, but I didn't have the capacity to care.

At the basement conference level of the hotel, we met the rest of Kocher's team, a collection of young, vivacious men and women, all well versed in the academic strategies of publicity.

At the entrance of the room was Colin Goddard; built like a tight end, with a confident posture and handsome features, he was a leading voice for changing gun laws. I vaguely remembered seeing him over the years as he became an activist, but I didn't recall his story until he introduced himself. Then it clicked. He was a survivor of the massacre at Virginia Tech. Goddard had been in French class when he heard intermittent pops of gunfire; then the shooter entered his classroom and killed his professor and twelve of his fellow students. (In total, thirty-two people were killed and dozens injured before the shooter took his own life.) Colin was shot four times; three of those bullets are still inside him. He said he was proud of us for being there and wanted to talk more, but there was no time at the moment; the pregame debrief was about to start.

The morbid realizations continued as we walked into the small conference room, a sea of vaguely familiar faces and names. We all sat down at a table and took turns introducing ourselves, sharing the basics of our stories.

Lucy McBath introduced herself. "My son Jordan Davis was killed because he was playing loud music in a gas station parking lot." *Oh God*, I thought, *I remember that.*

"My son, Alex, was shot and killed during the Aurora theater shooting," Tom Sullivan said, wristbands covering both arms. I found out later that each mass shooting or public murder carries with it a wristband in remembrance. Many in this "club" exchange and wear the bracelets of others they meet along the way. The Aurora families we've met have embraced this more than others, a compelling showing of solidarity.

Diane Sellgren lost a husband and daughter to gun suicides. She wore that anguish on her face as she quietly explained what brought her to this place, what brought her to join all of us. I'm sure Chris and I wore similar expressions as we stood in the back of the room. Drew didn't want to be a part of the publicity portion of our trip, so he'd set off on his own to tour DC and take photographs, one of his true passions and talents.

Next, the team Kocher had assembled introduced themselves. Everytown Chief Communications Officer Erika Soto Lamb gave us a rundown of what to expect with CNN. There would be private interviews with members of some families, she said, including Chris and me. The rest would sit in an auditorium and wait for the taping to begin. Each family member was asked to bring a picture of their loved one to hold up for the cameras. In the fog, I forgot to bring one, but Chris had thought to bring Alison's iPad and had a picture of her ready to go.

Stacey Radnor and Lizzie Ulmer were Erika's deputies. They gave us the rundown on how to provide effective answers to the questions. They passed around folders, each marked with our names and the hashtag #WhateverItTakes. Inside the folders were a handful of talking points:

- Every day, 88 Americans are killed with firearms and hundreds more are injured because of the easy access dangerous people have to guns.

- We can prevent gun violence with commonsense measures like background checks to keep guns away from dangerous people in the first place.

- In short, we will do #WhateverItTakes to ensure Not One More mother, father, child, boyfriend, girlfriend, brother, or sister has to bury a loved one after yet another shooting.

It was pointed out that the gun lobby's usual response after these shootings is to say, "If only the victims had been armed . . ." There were two suggested responses in my folder, the first tailored to me specifically. They stung as I read them over.

The first was:

- That's an insane proposition. What was the cameraman supposed to do exactly? Gun in one hand, camera in the other?

Okay, I thought. *They're going all-in on Alison and Adam's murders.* That was followed by:

- That's why today we are echoing Andy Parker—Alison Parker's father—in his pledge to do "whatever it takes" to get commonsense gun legislation passed, because lives can be saved from gun violence.

Well, I guess I have to perform now. I'm playing the lead role in this choreographed dog and pony show.

The rest of the handouts were filled with infographics and statistics I knew I wouldn't commit to memory. It was too much work for me anyway. I knew I had to get down in the weeds at some point, learn all of those terrible statistics, but I wasn't ready that day. I was there to praise Alison and shame some politicians.

By mid-afternoon we were on our way to the Newseum. It was a place Alison visited in college, and going there, of all places, seemed like both a wink from her and a tortuous exercise. We were moved to a meeting space in the back, with hanging black curtains creating multiple partitions. Camera shutters and flashes were going off in staccato bursts of blinding white light. CNN wanted portrait photos of each of us, staged in a way that showed our grief and determination.

"Head a little to the right and angle your body away from me," the photographer said.

I did my best, and the camera fired off a burst of high-speed shots. I felt disoriented. It was bizarre and a bit perverse to line up all these still-grieving families and ask them to mug for an online photo gallery. Again, I understood the purpose, the importance of it, but the process left me off-kilter.

The photos completed, we were whisked away to another part of the production maze, a camera's bland black eye recording us. The producer was struggling to repeat the same prompt to each member of the club.

"Okay," she said, "so, please state your name and your situation and end with, 'and I'm going to do whatever it takes to stop gun violence because . . .' And then just finish however you'd like."

The same words I used in previous interviews reemerged: I'm Alison's dad. Murdered on live television. Pissed off. Coward politicians who won't stand up to the NRA.

I was barely into the performance and I felt oddly disengaged, like I wanted to phone it in. The producer didn't seem to notice, as she hit the stop button on the camera.

"Thank you and so sorry for your loss," she said. It was the same thing she said to everyone. Maybe she should have just prerecorded the message on a tape player and punched "play" for each grieving family member.

Next, Chris and I went up into the Newseum auditorium where dozens of people were already seated. The CNN remote crew fine-tuned the camera angles, microphones, and lighting. We were ushered past them and into a greenroom nearby. Chris immediately went to get a cup of coffee and some fruit; the hotel buffet hadn't been enough to stem the pervasive fatigue. We waited a few minutes and then another young woman, with a headset, badge, and lanyard, came in. She introduced herself as a producer for Brooke Baldwin, the CNN anchor hosting the town hall.

"Brooke is almost ready for you," she said. "We're going to take you up to the roof for your interview."

As we continued through the Newseum, we walked past the studio for Al Jazeera America and down several long corridors lined with massive black storage cases for television production equipment, and then onto a service elevator. As we walked onto the rooftop patio, the sun was just beginning to set; the perfect "golden hour," as they say in TV. Even with construction on the rotunda of the Capitol, the skyline of Washington was breathtaking. The ample clouds looked like swipes from an artist's brush, streaks of pink, violet, and crimson. Brooke got up from the director's chair where makeup artists were painting her like a canvas and walked confidently toward us in a tight green dress and heels that made a tall woman such as herself all the more imposing.

"Andy, Chris, I don't even know what to say," she said, a hand extended. I can't remember how I responded, other than to sing Alison's praises and potential, to tell Brooke how Alison was robbed of the inevitable opportunity to be the one interviewing people for the national news. It was my same refrain whenever I appeared on a national show, from CNN to the *Today* show to *CBS Evening News*.

"She was one of you guys," I said. "Don't forget about this. It could have been you."

Brooke admitted it was the talk of the industry and among her friends in the business. Were more journalists going to be targeted?

She said it had shaken her up, and I don't think she said that just to placate me and Chris. A brutal murder had been broadcast on live television, the ante had been raised, and the prospect seemed to truly disturb Brooke.

The interview was so much like the others, despite her best attempts to ask revealing questions. Her most prodding queries were for Chris, who was repeatedly asked how he could balance being a journalist with appearing at a partisan event. He dodged it like he had so many other times, but he was truthful. He was here to be with me and Drew. He wanted to be around others who had lost the most important person in their lives. He, like me, had no idea if this could be survived. The chance to meet others in this "Loneliest Club" was something he simply needed.

After it was over and the union production crew helped take off our microphones and tear down the lights, each member of the club came over, one by one, and in a hundred different ways told us to keep going.

The actual town hall came next, and it felt a bit contrived. Chris and I were so worn out from the media appearances of the past two weeks that we had no problem shutting up and letting the three-dozen other club members speak. We heard stories of children accidentally shot and killed by friends. We heard the story of a young boy in Indianapolis who was paralyzed by a stray bullet at a birthday party. There were also the families from the major mass shootings that ignited the gun violence debate, including Erica Smegielski, the daughter of the principal killed at Sandy Hook Elementary School, and our new friends Lonnie and Sandy Phillips, whose daughter, Jessi, was murdered in Aurora. Then we heard from Sharon Risher, whose mother and two cousins were among those slaughtered at the church in Charleston, South Carolina.

Suddenly, my anguish had context. It wasn't lessened at all by my knowing there were others out there like me. If anything, it was amplified.

I wanted to quit this goddamn club. I didn't want to be a member. But these were my fellow soldiers, and there was a war we all wanted to fight. They had already been through the boot camp of trauma, while I was still figuring out how to get my bunk to pass inspection. I thought I wouldn't have anything to say at the town hall, but Rich Martinez, whose son, Chris, was killed in the mass shooting at UC Santa Barbara the year before, teed me up. He told Brooke that "We would do whatever it takes, like Andy said."

Brooke asked me the last question: "How do you fight the NRA?"

I said the only thing I could think of: "The NRA spends a ton of money to protect their interests, so we need to outspend them."

After about forty minutes of taping, Chris and I were briefly introduced to our fellow club members, a quick procession of short hellos and I-can't-wait-to-see-you-agains, and then we met up with Kocher and Lori for dinner at a little Asian restaurant right next door. Minutes later, we were seated at a small table with large menus and equally large prices for meals and drinks.

"I got it," Kocher said. "Whatever you want."

He didn't have to tell me twice. The dim sum and *shumai* came out for us to share, and we also shared a few drinks.

We sat at the table lamenting Washington's political gridlock, the reluctance to institute policy changes that were so clearly logical and necessary. Kocher told us how he had grown up in New York, coming from relatively nothing. His father was a janitor who encouraged him to study hard in school, and he was the first in his family to graduate from college, followed by the Duke University School of Law. His humble upbringing, he said, didn't expose him to the esoteric vernacular he encountered in Durham.

"I remember having to read a passage aloud in class and I came to the word 'paradigm,'" he told us. "You know, like 'paradigm shift?' Well, I had only read that in books before. I'd never said it aloud. So I said it like I thought it was pronounced: 'para-dig-em shift.'"

We all laughed—with him, not at him—at the thought of Kocher in class at one of the country's most elite law schools, at a loss on the pronunciation of a basic SAT word. But his determination and work ethic allowed him to rise quickly in the progressive movement, working as a policy advisor on political campaigns and eventually as special counsel to New York City Mayor Michael Bloomberg. The laughter and storytelling continued well into the evening, until Drew was ready to meet us back at the hotel. It had already been an exhausting day, and I knew the next day would be yet another marathon.

The following morning we joined the Everytown team for breakfast, including key members like Rich Martinez and Shannon Watts, the founder of Moms Demand Action for Gun Sense in America. I was also asked to mike up for a documentary that Katie Couric was producing. I'd have to keep a tight lid on my proclivity for dropping f-bombs.

After breakfast, we headed to a church next to the rally point to go over the final details and speaking order. Soon after, I was on a platform with Governor McAuliffe, Senators Warner and Kaine, Rich, Shannon, Chris, Drew, and other members of the club we had met the day before. Before us was a vocal crowd of like-minded souls holding signs and wearing red T-shirts, all of them emblazoned with my spur-of-the-moment slogan: Whatever It Takes.

The day was hot. I was perspiring profusely and it wasn't from nervousness. As I watched Warner, Kaine, and McAuliffe deliver their terrific remarks without referring to their notes, I was struck by how cool and collected they looked. How could they be so smooth while I was standing there sweating buckets and looking like a pile of wet rumpled clothes? I'm sure the world would have given me a pass, but I didn't want my pathetic appearance to reflect on Alison. Thankfully,

Erika was standing behind the platform and I was able to get her attention. She found some tissues for me to at least mop my face, although a beach towel would have been more useful.

Soon enough, it was my turn to speak, and the sweat spigot at the top of my forehead mercifully decided to shut itself off. In my speech, I worked in a reference to Congressman Goodlatte whose office had reached out that very morning to ask if I could meet with him at the exact time I was speaking at the rally. The attendees picked up the irony and the sarcasm in my voice.

"I would much rather be with you here today than with him," I said to the crowd.

I'm told it was a stirring speech, and I delivered it with as much conviction as I will ever be able to muster. It felt good. I was back in the game, albeit for the wrong reason, and the venting provided a desperately needed pressure release and a distraction from my inevitable daily emotional meltdown.

After the rally, Erika led us to the first cluster of reporters. Chris and I went on a rotation from one group to another. They were national and international with some local press sprinkled in, including all the Roanoke affiliates, except, noticeably, WDBJ. Maybe they were trying to remain neutral, but I think they were still in shock.

Later I asked Lori how long I was out there with the media, thinking it had been about fifteen minutes. She said I spoke to them for almost an hour and half. I do remember the surreal quality of going from one cluster of reporters to the next, the breakneck relentlessness of it.

But it wasn't relentless in an unkind way at all. Alison was one of them. They all knew it, and they treated me like I was their dad, too. Responding to their questions was double-edged; their questions allowed me to focus on my newly acquired mission, but while those questions gave me a sense of purpose, telling them about Alison's life, again and again, caused me nothing but heartache.

The intensity of the press whirlwind helped keep my heartache in check until I met Andrea McCarren from WUSA9. There was a photographer with her, as well as a service dog named Bunce. She later explained that she helps train service dogs. As she prepared for the interview, Drew, who had been hanging back and absorbing the media circus, became a dog whisperer and quickly befriended Bunce.

Andrea's lead question caught me completely off guard.

"How does the coolest dad in the world lose the coolest daughter in the world?" she asked.

It was unexpected and touching. I lost it.

Most of the time I'm not surprised by a reporter's question, but every now and then I'll get a "gotcha" question. I don't think it's their intent to knock me off my pins, and that was certainly the case here. But Andrea's question cut right through me like a hot knife through butter.

I used to remind Alison in a teasing way that her dad was way cooler than any of her friends' dads. She would scoff and say, "Yeah, sure, Dad," but deep down, I hope she thought it was true. I took great pleasure in cutting up in front of her friends and watching her mock horror at my sometimes (well, often) juvenile behavior. I think Alison's friends thought I was funny, but she didn't want to let on that I actually might be.

Andrea clearly did her homework, but it was the first time a journalist called me and Alison cool. I regained my composure somewhat, but I can't recall what I said. I hope it was coherent and worthy of the compliment. Whatever I said, it ultimately didn't matter. Like a game of Jeopardy, the question was more important than the answer.

The mental picture I have of Drew kneeling down and petting Bunce while I listened to the sweetest compliment I'll ever receive will stay with me forever.

In truth, I don't think I'm the coolest dad in the world, but I did do a lot of things that other dads didn't. I had been a professional actor. Alison was only a baby when I was in my last professional show, *Pump Boys and Dinettes,* at the Kennedy Center. But in 2013, she did get to see me play Javert in *Les Misérables* for the community theater that Barbara and I helped start. I'd been loath to do anything short of a professional production, but after TheatreWorks quickly proved successful, I was impressed enough by the local talent to give it a go.

I had also been in politics, winning my first election to the Henry County Board of Supervisors by one vote. A run for the Virginia House of Delegates wasn't as successful, but Alison had a good time going out stumping with me at the Ruritan clubs and local lobster fest.

The acting, the politics, the travel, the spontaneity, and lots of downright goofiness were all part of the sense of adventure I always tried to incorporate into my life. She knew I was different from her friends' dads, and we were kindred spirits.

Alison never said, "Dad, you are so cool." It might surprise you to learn that she also never said, "Dad, I love you." In retrospect, I wish I'd told her "I love you, Scooter" over and over again. But we were the kind of family that didn't feel the need to verbally express those feelings. We were so tight-knit that we all knew the love was there.

So, was I the coolest dad in the world? I did help raise Alison, so maybe I can lay claim to the title after all.

7

HONORING ALISON

The JMU and Virginia Tech games were among the first events to honor Alison, but they wouldn't be the last.

Chris and I arrived home Friday night, September 11, with just enough time to sleep in our own beds, repack, and get ready to head to Richmond the next day. It was the Richmond 500 and the JMU/Alison car was making its debut.

While we were gone, Barbara had been doing all the hard stuff related to Alison's affairs, dealing with the funeral home, the death certificate, and all the other horrible little details that must be addressed when someone passes. Even though the Xanax was helping me sleep, I wasn't in any shape to handle a death certificate and the cremains of my beautiful girl.

As we later discovered, Barbara's Lexapro regimen is what enabled her to function. She had been taking it for several years, primarily because it minimized menopausal hot flashes and the desire to beat the living hell out of me when my occasionally obtuse behavior would have otherwise compelled her to do so.

As I mentioned earlier, some people thought Barbara's initial absence from the media spotlight meant she was intentionally avoiding it, but that was never the case. Fortunately, she made this next trip with us.

The day of the race was gray, the rain threatening to wash out the track or at least delay the start time. We arrived at the speedway entrance that afternoon and followed a golf cart of security guards around the grandstands and through a tunnel. We emerged in the track infield and were instructed to park and give our keys to one of the security guys there. I'd had good parking in my two prior visits to the Martinsville Speedway back home, but having your vehicle literally parked in the middle of the action was pretty impressive. All around us, various crews had tents set up with food and drinks available for corporate sponsors and other VIPs. We were led to a tent and saw Ron Devine, the owner of the Alison car; he introduced us to all kinds of well-wishers. Given my stance on guns, I wasn't sure how we were going to play to a NASCAR crowd; a NASCAR race isn't exactly considered a hotbed for progressivism. However, we were greeted warmly, total strangers coming up to us and offering their support.

In an unusual encounter, Joe Gibbs, former head coach of the Washington Redskins and now a race team owner, came over and introduced himself. We were in the middle of the usual small talk when without warning, he grabbed my arm and Barbara's, closed his eyes, and broke into an impromptu prayer. I knew he was religious, but I didn't realize he was *religious*. We were taken aback, but we appreciated his sincerity. Instead of a politician's empty words, Joe meant business with his "thoughts and prayers."

Ron asked if we wanted to see the car before they got it into position to start the race. We were eager to, so we followed him through an impressive array of tractor trailers and race cars, along with the high-tech equipment that kept them running.

And there it was. I had imagined that her face was going to be on the side of the car, but I suppose that would've been a little over-the-top. Instead, her picture was like a vanity plate on the rear end, and it was so lovely. Where the driver's name was usually painted over the doors, Alison's name was printed instead. It was another emotional moment for all of us. Barbara and I had never had a favorite NASCAR team or driver, but you'd better believe we were all in for BK Racing and the Alison/JMU car.

Ron, while not a neophyte, was still new to racing. His team was making progress, getting better with each race, but we all knew it would take a miracle for the car to win. We just didn't want her to finish last.

After a photo op with the car, Ron escorted us to a big tent where all the teams were gathered for the prerace briefing. As we headed inside, Chris recognized Tom Graves, a congressman from Georgia. The congressman introduced himself and his young son who was with him. The boy had a kayaking T-shirt on and Chris asked them if they paddled. Graves said they did a little and Chris mentioned how much we love paddling.

After putting the politician at ease, Chris then expertly pivoted and asked Graves why he voted against recent legislation meant to overturn the Dickey Amendment. Jay Dickey was the congressman who championed a 1996 restriction on federal funding for gun violence research. In recent years, Dickey had publicly admitted that the bill that bore his name was a terrible mistake.

As a journalist, Chris had felt compelled to do a deep dive into the nuts and bolts of the politics of gun safety. He was deep in the weeds of gun legislation while I was still standing at the periphery trying to fire up my string trimmer. As a talented reporter, he devoured knowledge and knew how to use it. I'd seen this on full display the previous week while I watched him eviscerate Bob Goodlatte, peppering him with questions he couldn't answer. Graves said nothing. We politely said our goodbyes and walked away.

We were seated in the front row and watched the drivers and their crew chiefs file in. I recognized Dale Earnhardt Jr. and Jeff Gordon. My NASCAR knowledge was exhausted at that point, but Chis was able to point out Tony Stewart. One young driver paid his respects to us, but that was it. A NASCAR official who was also a college football referee gave me the coin used for the toss at midfield.

The man sitting next to me was Walt Ehmer, the CEO of Waffle House. "Our family loves Waffle House," I remarked. "Wish we had one in Martinsville." Walt had no idea who we were, but he smiled, reached into his pocket and produced two cards good for a free side dish at any Waffle House. I graciously accepted the coupons and chuckled inwardly; I guess he hadn't seen the news.

The NASCAR official overseeing the race called the meeting to order and proceeded to introduce the special guests in attendance. When we were recognized, Ehmer leaned over, his face ashen.

"Oh God, I'm so sorry," he said. "If I'd known, I wouldn't have done that," referring to his gifts.

"Hey, don't worry," I said smiling. "We'll still use them."

After watching a safety film and listening to a rules overview by the NASCAR official, we started filing out of the tent, where we were greeted by a downpour. Weather radar showed it was going to move out, but it was definitely going to delay the race. The delay was going to complicate things for us because I had connected with Levar Stoney earlier in the week to let him know we would be in Richmond and see if his offer to get together with the governor was legit. It was. The plan had been to watch a few laps of the race and then head over to the governor's mansion. Now I was in quandary, unsure of what to do if there was a huge delay. *Should I be ungracious to Ron Devine and leave early, or should I be late for a meeting with the governor?*

We made our way to Ron's luxury box at the track, and Barbara and I planted ourselves on a plush couch and watched football on a big-screen TV. While Barbara and I watched Virginia Tech play Notre Dame and chatted with a few of the other folks in the box, Chris went to locate the pit boss of the Penske team. Harry Hurst worked with them in public relations and wanted us to say hello. By that point, the rain had stopped and the track was being swept with specially designed trucks equipped with massive blow-dryers. From the box, it sounded like jets winding up on the tarmac.

Chris called me from the pit and told me to meet him at the Penske tent. I made my way from the box through the tunnel and back up to the infield. Even though we had badges, I wondered how in the world we would be let through with the race about to begin. My question was answered as Chris and I approached the Penske area. A security guard told us this was as far as we could go. We told him we understood completely, then backtracked a few paces, slipped between two trailers, clambered over the cables snaking back and forth, and hopped the crash barrier. After walking onto the track and passing several teams and their cars, we made it to Penske.

Ryan Denny, Penske's marketing services manager, was waiting for us and took us to meet the Penske driver, Brad Keselowski. We waited patiently while he stood with his longtime girlfriend and their newborn daughter, doing media interviews and getting photographed. The more I waited, the more out of place I felt. When Chris and I were finally introduced, I wished him luck and congratulated him on the new baby. I'm not completely sure he knew who we were or why we were there, but he was certainly nice enough, though he might have been a little preoccupied with mentally preparing to win the race without crashing his car. After we were photographed with Brad, Ryan was more than gracious and thanked us for coming down.

You never know how you'll touch people. Chris later told me that after Ryan met us, he and his wife named their new daughter Parker.

It was now two hours past the scheduled start time, and the dilemma I pondered earlier was now approaching a crisis. I had texted Levar earlier that we were running a little behind because of the rain delay, but now we were well and truly running late. I now texted Levar that we would arrive about 8:00 p.m., and he quickly texted back: no worries. We were back in the box to see the race start at about 7:45. There was only time to watch a few laps before we had to leave.

I'm so glad we watched that handful of laps. It was exhilarating to see the car honoring Alison race around the track. I imagined her sitting in the passenger's seat, loving every minute. This was her car. Her name was on it. She was going to flash and dash. Alas, the car wasn't destined to win or place, but she was going to show.

Before we left, we said goodbye to Ron and thanked him for his kindness. He completely understood our rush; you can't just cancel a meeting with the governor. We retraced our steps and were back in the infield, only this time there were fifty cars screaming around us, the deafening roar vibrating our very bones. From the stands, it must have been an odd sight to see all the action on the track and a lone Honda Ridgeline driving out of the infield and into the tunnel.

We pulled up to the guardhouse, situated right in front of the stately 1813 governor's mansion that sits on the state capitol grounds. After we identified ourselves, we were told by the guard to park right next to the front door. Levar was at the open door waiting for us, and we stepped inside a veritable museum. My eyes were immediately drawn to the familiar large portrait hanging in the center of the opposite chamber, a vast room that appeared to be a great banquet hall. It was George Washington in his first military uniform. To the left and right were sitting rooms filled with portraits of notable figures from our state and nation's history.

"The governor should be here any time now," Levar told us. "He's coming from the game."

So much for my fear of keeping him waiting.

Levar volunteered to show us around while we waited for the governor to arrive. We went from parlor to parlor as Levar gave us the grand tour. He told us that the governor's mansion was the oldest one in the country still used for that purpose, and he pointed out various portraits, including renderings of Pocahontas and Elizabeth I. As we made our way to the dining hall, Levar pointed out matching sets of stairs on opposite sides of the foyer. "Take a look at each staircase and tell me what's different about them," he said.

"One staircase is narrower than the other," I said.

"That's correct. And why is that?"

We were momentarily stumped, but I surmised correctly that the narrow side was for the servants, who, when the house was built, were of course slaves. It was a fascinating piece of historical architecture.

We were about to head into the dining hall when the governor burst through the door with his teenage kids in tow, along with a couple of his old friends. One was a longtime aide, while the other was his oldest friend from law school.

"Hey, guys, how ya doin'?" the governor exclaimed, clearly exuberant at the prospect of hosting some friends. "Has Levar shown you the house?"

I told him we had just started on the nickel tour, and McAuliffe said he'd take it from there. It was like watching Walt Disney show off the wonders of Disneyland for the first time.

McAuliffe led us into the great dining hall and straight to the silver collection on display. "When we moved in, Dorothy and I found all of this in a closet," he said. "It's the silver service from the battleship *Virginia*. It was a shame to keep it all in the closet, so we had shelves made in here to display it. The guild got all torqued about it 'cause they want to keep the house the way it has been historically. But ya know, I thought we did a pretty good job with these shelves. It looks like they've been here all along."

The man was justifiably proud of his home improvements. It was his house, after all.

After the tour drew to a close, we all plopped down on couches and chairs in the parlor adjacent to the dining hall. It looked a bit less formal than the other rooms, although that wasn't saying much. After a few moments, a butler entered, giving McAuliffe the opportunity to introduce us to Tutti. "Tutti's an institution," McAuliffe said proudly. "He's served nine governors. What do you guys want to drink?"

We all ordered cocktails, and before Tutti walked out, McAuliffe's kids appeared. "What do you guys want to eat?" the governor asked them. "Why don't we just get Cook Out?" Turning to us he said, "Is that OK with you guys? You hungry? Dorothy's out of town, so we're kinda baching it."

We were stuffed from the food at the race, so we politely declined. But it was charming to see the governor, his kids, and his old friend from law school collaborating on a to-go order from a burger joint. It didn't take them long, either; they were well-versed with the menu. The kids left, Tutti returned with our first round of drinks, and then he headed off to pick up the burgers.

Our surreal adventure continued. It's common knowledge among Virginians that McAuliffe is friends with Bill and Hillary Clinton, so I asked him how he came to know them.

"Oh, we go back to the eighties," he said. "I was just out of law school and wanted to work on a campaign, so they hired me. I've been with 'em ever since. Played golf with Bill yesterday as a matter of fact. We're not worth a shit, but love to hit the ball around."

I told him I'd qualified for and played in two Virginia State Senior Opens. "I was scheduled to play in a qualifier the week after Alison was killed," I said. "I don't know now when I'll get back to it. It just doesn't matter anymore."

While many of the guys I used to play with at Forest Park Country Club came to the celebration of life, I knew they were not of the same political bent as me, even before Alison's death. It would have been uncomfortable playing with them again, even in better circumstances. I knew there was no way I could ever return to Forest Park.

"We still paddle, though, and always will," I said, pulling out my phone to show him pictures of us paddling on whitewater rapids.

Of course, we talked politics.

"You've seen Hillary's numbers," I said. "Why does she come off so stilted in public?"

"Yeah, I know," McAuliffe said wistfully. "And the damnedest thing is that she could be sitting here with us and be like a different person, much more relaxed. Some people just don't do well in public, and she's kinda there. It's a shame, but she's really a good person."

OK, I thought. *I'll give her the benefit of the doubt.*

More politics came up (a shocker, I know). It was such an incredible diversion, an amazing opportunity to get a peek through a window that few get the chance to see.

McAuliffe asked about my background, and I gave him the not-so-short version. I told him I had been a headhunter for the last fifteen years and had been a professional actor in my past life. This, as always, became an instant curiosity, and I regaled him with my stories of life on the road and in the Broadway company of *The Best Little Whorehouse in Texas*. McAuliffe and his friends seemed genuinely fascinated.

By now, we had been at the mansion for more than two hours. Tutti kept bringing us drinks. I could easily see why nine governors had wanted him on the payroll. It seemed like we were just getting warmed up.

The conversation turned to the political dynamics in Virginia.

At that time, the entire General Assembly was up for election. McAuliffe had controlled the Senate until Senator Phil Puckett resigned a year earlier; it had been a fifty-fifty split between Democrats and Republicans, and McAuliffe's Democrat lieutenant governor, Ralph Northam, was the tiebreaker. I'd met Puckett once before while at a Board of Supervisors conference. He'd resigned from the Senate on June 9, 2014, citing "family reasons." His resignation gave the Republicans a 20 to 19 majority. Puckett's resignation coincided with an alleged offer by the Virginia Republican Party to appoint him as the deputy director of the state tobacco commission, which provides grants intended to boost the economy in areas of the state that are struggling. Following criticism, however, he announced he would not accept the appointment. Puckett's departure, McAuliffe said, had done the Democrats no favors.

"We've got to pick up at least one seat this time," McAuliffe said. "Two would be better. There are two races where we think we can pick them up."

Earlier, we had told the governor that Barbara and I were scheduled to meet Michael Bloomberg the following Friday.

"Listen," McAuliffe said, "when you see Bloomberg, I want you to ask him for a million dollars for my PAC so we can get those seats."

I was taken aback, but in a good way. "Well, I've never gone for quite that much before, but you know I'll ask," I said.

"I know you will. That's why I asked you to do it."

As the conversation became strategic, I mentioned that Chris was considering running, maybe even against Bob Goodlatte.

McAuliffe's head snapped toward Chris.

"That would be terrific," he said. "Let us know when you're ready and we'll help."

McAuliffe's aide, who had been very quiet all night, turned to Chris and said, "As soon as you announce, I'll stroke you a check for $5,000."

Chris was off to a pretty good start, I thought.

We had been at the mansion now for almost three and half hours. There was no body language from the governor indicating that we'd overstayed our welcome. If fact, he looked like he wanted us to stay longer. But it had already been a long day, and we were running out of gas.

We said our goodbyes and the governor waved from the front steps as we got into the Ridgeline and drove off. There was silence for a moment, and then as we cleared the gate, I sighed.

"I don't know about you," I said to Barbara and Chris, "but for me that was pretty surreal."

I had evolved over the course of that evening. I started out as a grieving parent, then became an entertaining drinking buddy, and finally transformed into a political operative. That McAuliffe had asked me to pitch to Bloomberg for money had left my head spinning. I guess my past life in politics had provided the opening. I was amazed and flattered, and maybe he knew I would be. I had clearly gotten to know McAuliffe on a personal level. It was a welcome rush and a much-needed stroking of my ego. I was a player again, even if I hated the way I'd gotten there.

While we were in the governor's mansion, I could feel Alison's presence. "Hey, Dad," I imagined her saying, "this is cool and so out there."

Yeah, Scooter. It was *very* out there. It was a much bigger game than I'd ever imagined, and I was in it for her.

———

Alison's next honor came on September 26, 2015, a month to the day after her death.

Dancing with the Valley Stars, a popular Roanoke fundraiser that benefits the Salvation Army, was scheduled for that night. It was an evening I had looked forward to a month and a day before. Now Barbara, Chris, and I were scheduled to attend the event that Alison had been bound to win.

It was a big deal in Roanoke to be one of the local celebrities selected to compete in Dancing with the Valley Stars. With her typical gusto, Alison had been determined to win it. She was paired with Pedro Szalay, the artistic director of the Southwest Virginia Ballet in Roanoke. Pedro was a former company dancer with the Richmond Ballet and had been an instructor in their Minds in Motion movement program that Piedmont Arts had sponsored for thirteen years in Martinsville. It was an ingenious way to get kids to participate in dance/movement at an age when they were still unencumbered by self-consciousness. Alison was involved for three years, and because she was already in a private dance class, she excelled.

In her last year of eligibility, Minds in Motion did a themed program around a newspaper. Alison was cast as the star of the show and I was pressed into service as the offstage narrator. It was our first and only time together in a show, and I could only watch her from the wings. Consider it foreshadowing that she was the star of a show centered on journalism. In her first time in the spotlight, she demonstrated the fearlessness and perfection she would carry the rest of her life.

Alison and Pedro had decided on a tango combined with ballet. Alison was going to wear pointe shoes. She found the perfect costume on eBay, of all places, and I ordered it for her, a fiery red feathery thing. Shortly before the costume arrived, Alison happened to be in town and she asked me to take a photo of her in her ballet slippers.

"Hurry, Dad, because it's been so long, I'm not sure how long I can hold it en pointe." She pointed and unfurled her graceful arms to create a beautiful, athletic tableau. It was the last time I saw her in a dance position. I saw the costume when it arrived, but I never saw her in it.

As a tribute to Alison, Pedro asked one of his students to dance in Alison's place at Dancing with the Valley Stars. She was of a similar build, and after a slight alteration, she wore Alison's red costume.

The event was held at the Jefferson Center in the same space where the nondenominational memorial service took place less than a month earlier. Barbara and I took seats in the back; I knew what was ahead for me, and I wanted to position myself where I could make a hasty retreat into the foyer should the need arise. The event would have drawn the press anyway, but it drew even more due to the circumstances.

Thankfully, Pedro and his new partner were the first contestants. Before they danced, the emcee made the announcement from the stage about Alison's replacement. A giant screen descended behind him, the lights dimmed further, and there was Alison. The screen showed her recital video, in which she performed to "Walking in Memphis."

I had seen that video so many times when she was alive; watching that grace and beauty always gave me a lump in my throat even before her death. Now, I had to watch the video again.

As of this writing, that was the first and last time I have seen a video of Alison after her death. I just can't do it, regardless of when, where, or why it was recorded. Videos bring her back to life for me, but I know it's not real, like when you have a wonderful dream of a missing loved one and wake up to the cold, stark reality.

Barbara and I sat quietly in the dark, holding onto one another. Then Pedro and the replacement dancer performed a powerfully athletic and graceful dance. In my mind's eye, I could almost see Alison on the stage, dazzling the crowd with her smile and effortless motion. Tears streamed down my face, and when it was over, I bolted for the exit.

I found a staircase around the corner from the main lobby and sat on the plush red carpet. I was briefly alone with my aching grief, when Brie Jackson, a reporter from the local NBC affiliate, found me and put her hand on my shoulder. "It's OK," she said. "It's OK."

I appreciated her kindness, but it wasn't OK and it never will be. My daughter was supposed to wow everyone while her proud dad watched her inexorable march to greatness, happy to sit on the sidelines. Instead, a man with a crushed soul was sitting on the stairs, averting his teary eyes from everyone who passed by.

8

ON CALL

On our way home from one of our many trips to Richmond, we took a side trip to Harrisonburg. In less than a month, Alison's scholarship had grown to more than $150,000, and it was still gathering steam. It had become the fastest growing scholarship in JMU's history. We were there to tape a well-deserved "thank you" video that JMU was going to send to all the donors.

Parkhurst, Alison's favorite professor, met us at the entrance to the JMU School of Media Arts and Design and led us back to the studio. After Barbara and I filmed the piece, we piled back into the truck to head home.

About an hour into the drive, I got a call from Lori Haas.

"There's been a mass shooting in Oregon," she said. "It was at a community college."

Oh shit, I thought. *I just can't believe this.* Soon enough I learned that it wasn't all that hard to believe, that an average of 342 people are shot every day in America, 96 of them killed. But this day was different. This was a mass shooting, and it was the first high-profile incident since

Alison's murder such a short time earlier. It was a punch to the gut. I felt sickened, and then the rage came. *How can this continue? How can this just keep happening?*

I didn't have long to ponder that rhetorical question. Just as it had a few weeks earlier, my phone started blowing up with calls from television news producers. *Why are they calling me?* I wondered.

And then it dawned on me: I was the new face of gun violence prevention. I was now considered an expert on tragic shootings. It was an international story, and I was now the media's go-to guy. If I was going to be that guy, I wanted to make the most of it. It kept Alison's name and memory out there.

Steve Lewis, an MSNBC producer, was the first to reach me. He asked if I could be on Lawrence O'Donnell at 9:00 that night.

"Steve, I'm on the road headed back from Richmond," I said. "I can do it, but you're going have to find a different studio than the one we used last time in Roanoke."

I had done the show the previous month at the NBC affiliate in Roanoke. In what seemed like the ultimate case of strange bedfellows, they shared a studio with the local Fox affiliate. Both were planning to move into their own spaces, but their arrangement at the time looked like the *Wayne's World* set when compared to WDBJ's studio. The earpiece they provided didn't fit in my ear and kept popping out. It was plugged into a technician's iPhone, and even when the earpiece did stay in, I could barely hear O'Donnell's questions. I wasn't going through that again.

"What about the NBC affiliate in Greensboro/Winston-Salem?" I asked.

"Let me work on it and I'll get back to you," he said. He called me thirty minutes later and said, "How about Raleigh?"

By then I'd become amused at how geographically challenged many of these bookers are. They were used to New York, used to quick studio access. I often had to explain that I lived in the boonies a full hour away from Roanoke or Greensboro. Raleigh was more than two hours away.

"Steve, I've been on the road most of the day," I said. "I just can't make that drive. What happened to Greensboro?"

"No uplink capability," he said. "There's a production company in Raleigh we use quite a bit that can do it. If I can get a car for you, would you do it? I can put you up overnight because they want you on *Morning Joe* the next morning."

"OK, that works," I said. "Thanks for being accommodating."

As soon as we ended the call, Jennifer Henderson from CNN called me. By now, the network had given her "ownership" of me for all their programming. She worked for Poppy Harlow's show, but she teed me up for CNN's whole slate.

"I need you to go on *New Day,* then Carol Costello tomorrow morning," Jennifer said.

This was insane.

"Jennifer, I've got a car picking me up shortly to take me to Raleigh to do Lawrence O'Donnell tonight. They're putting me up so I can do *Morning Joe* tomorrow. I could sandwich it all in if the production companies can work it out with you. But there's also the matter of who pays my expenses."

"We shouldn't have any problem," she said. "Give me your contact at MSNBC and I'll work it all out."

It might have been the first time in history that opposing networks split the travel costs of a guest.

For the second time in my life, I was chauffeured. The Lincoln Town Car that picked me up wasn't nearly as flashy as the gaudy stretch limo that had ferried Jonas and me the month before, but it was comfortable and I wasn't driving, so it was perfect. The driver dropped me off at the studio, which was housed in a modern low-rise office complex. We weren't sure we were in the right place at first; there were no lights on, no cars in the parking lot, and the entrance was locked. Fortunately, I had the contact's phone number and he came to the door to let us in.

I had made it to Raleigh with about twenty minutes to spare before I went on air. Jay Chapman, the studio manager, took me to the studio, made sure my tie was straight, and got me miked up and into my chair. It was an impressive setup. I even had a digital backdrop of the nighttime Raleigh skyline behind me.

This time I could hear O'Donnell's questions and the interview went much more smoothly. I reinforced my theme and added some new stuff; I felt it was the best way to keep the message fresh.

After my interview, Jay came up to me.

"You know," he said, "I've never thought about gun control much. I own a gun. But what you said made so much sense. You're not advocating taking everybody's guns away."

"No, I'm not," I said. "Just trying to keep the guns out of the hands of the wrong people. See you tomorrow, Jay."

If Jay's response was any indication, my message seemed to be registering. I went to the hotel, crashed for a few hours, and prepared myself to do it all again the next day.

———

The Umpqua Community College shooting created another duty for my new "job." I was to be the spokesman for gun violence prevention whenever a tragedy struck. It wasn't a requirement so much as an obligation I felt to Alison.

Most people learn of a mass shooting by way of updates on Facebook or Twitter. I find out when my phone starts ringing off the hook, or when I'm traveling out West and wake up to a text message from a producer on the East Coast, which was how I found out about the mass shooting in Las Vegas.

Every time my phone begins buzzing like a nest of hornets, I think to myself: *Here we go again.*

Let me be clear: it's not a complaint. I owe it to Alison, to every victim of gun violence, to provide whatever nugget of insight I have, to try to make sense of the senseless and provide some measure of hope, however small. As long as the media gives me a platform, whether on television or in op-eds, I will use the bully pulpit without complaint.

I've been in front of so many cameras that I get recognized on trains, planes, and even at Beal's Lobster Pier in Southwest Harbor, Maine. When Barbara, Chris, and I were in Los Angeles to tape an episode of *The Doctors*, I could see the Uber driver looking back at me in the rearview mirror.

"I've seen you on the news, but can't remember what it was about," he finally admitted.

Well, it is LA, and people watch TV. But am I that visible? I brought him up to speed. "Man, I'm so sorry," he said. "Keep up what you're doing."

I've had journalists from Japan, Germany, and France travel to my home. The international press has an almost voyeuristic attraction to gun violence in this country. Maybe it's because the concept is so alien to them, so alien to anyone from a country other than the United States. They are morbidly fascinated, like when you come across a grisly car accident and just can't force yourself to look away. Their questions are all pretty much the same:

"Andy, after this latest shooting do you see a tipping point?"

"If nothing happened after Sandy Hook, do you really think anything will ever change?"

"Is there any hope for progress?"

And then there's the one that always gets me choked up:

"What do you think Alison would say?"

I didn't have a satisfactory answer to the tipping point question until the fall of 2017. When I was asked that question during an interview on HLN, a part of CNN, following the shooting inside a church in Sutherland Springs, Texas—where a gunman killed twenty-five people, including a pregnant woman—I provided an answer to anchor Erica Hill that probably came as a surprise. I told her that I believed we had reached the tipping point, but it wasn't the latest shooting, it was the Virginia state elections the previous month, when polls showed that the gun issue was number two in importance to voters.

After the Parkland shooting on Valentine's Day 2018, I was asked it again. This time I modified my answer. "The tipping point was Virginia in 2017," I said. "The Parkland kids have now put this movement on steroids."

Most of the time, the television host sticks to the issue, but they occasionally ask about Alison—what she meant to me, to others, her legacy. It happens most often with print journalists. I try to answer with a concise testimonial, but I always have difficulty adequately expressing my feelings.

Every time I do an interview, and they typically come in bunches, I come away exhausted and emotionally drained. I can't tell you how much concentration it takes, how much effort, to sound professional and knowledgeable while discussing a topic that rips open a wound that can never fully heal. It's part of the reason I've never watched any media I've done. I don't need to revisit it. If I did watch, I would probably find myself analyzing my performance, beating myself up for omitting some important point. Early on, Barbara watched all of them. Her only critique was, "You've got to stop saying 'you know' so much." I worked on it, figuring I'd have plenty of opportunities to shake the bad habit. Tragically, I did.

With few exceptions, the media has been kind and gracious. They know now that I've never seen the video of Alison's murder. They know it's out there in perpetuity, and when they include it in part of their story, they do their best to shield Barbara and me from seeing it.

A good example of this happened prior to the airing of the *CBS Sunday Morning* segment we did. CBS had trailed Barbara and me to record B-roll at various rallies, so they had supplementary footage of us. I didn't meet Erin Moriarty until she came to our house the morning of our interview. Erin is a reporter for *48 Hours Mystery*, but Alison's story had such an impact on her that she made a special request to be involved in the *CBS Sunday Morning* segment. In the run-up, I had developed a nice rapport with Jay Kernis, the show's producer. In another of those unusual six degrees of separation occurrences, it turns out that Jay had worked at NPR with Frank Tavares, my eternal friend, college roommate, and the best man at my wedding.

When the segment's airdate was set and production was finished, Jay called me.

"Andy, it's a great piece," he said. "Very powerful. But if you watch it, don't watch the first couple minutes. You know why."

"I understand, Jay. It's part of the story. I wish you didn't have to air it, but I get it. And I appreciate the heads-up."

Because of the prestige and production values of *CBS Sunday Morning,* and because of Jay and Erin's terrific work, I had planned to break my rule and watch my own interview. When Jay gave me that news, I stuck by my rule. I didn't watch it.

Barbara and I have done a few student forums for aspiring journalists at JMU, and I always impress this story on them. Once they get that gig out in the real world, I tell them, don't forget to be human. Have respect for the people you interview and always protect your sources.

Alison always did. So did Jay Kernis.

I also tell the story of what happens when you don't have that respect.

One early summer day in 2016, I was scrolling through my Facebook news feed. At the time, I had autoplay enabled, meaning that as I scrolled over a posted video it started playing automatically. As I went down the page, I scrolled across the trailer for the Katie Couric-produced documentary *Under the Gun* that one of my gun violence prevention friends had posted.

Chris and I been filmed for it in DC in September when we were there for the Whatever It Takes rally, but that was the last time I'd had any contact with them. I'd forgotten about the whole thing until I saw the post for the movie trailer.

As my mouse hovered over the post, the trailer began. To my horror, I saw Alison, seconds before the moment she was killed. I averted my eyes before I saw too much, but I had already seen more than I ever wanted.

The video was like a spark, inciting a rage inside me. *How could they just put it out there without telling me?* I knew the video of Alison and Adam's shooting was on the internet in perpetuity, but I also knew how to avoid it. To have it appear in a trailer for a documentary I had appeared in was like getting ambushed by someone I was supposed to trust.

I immediately called Chris Kocher at Everytown. "What the fuck is this?" I yelled.

He explained that he was unaware of the trailer and had not seen the clip in the documentary previews the film crew had screened for Everytown.

"Well, it's in the trailer, and I'm livid."

Chris said he would track it down. An hour later, he texted me that they had taken down that trailer and replaced it with a trailer without the clip of Alison. Incredibly, he asked me if I would participate in the film's promotion by being on a panel.

"Are you kidding me?" I barked. "Absolutely not. You think I'd want to be a part of anything with that in it? They may have removed it from the trailer, but it's in the goddamn film." Chris said he understood, but I was dumbfounded that he'd even asked.

The next day, I saw another post of the trailer from a different friend. This time, I had disabled autoplay and started slowly scanning through the trailer frame by frame. I'll be damned if I didn't come across the same frame, Alison frozen in time seconds before her death.

I went ballistic and called Kocher again. He had no idea how it had happened, but I later learned that people were still able to post the older version of the trailer, and that was what I had stumbled across a second time.

Through the film's marketing director, I was able to contact the film's director, Stephanie Soechtig. She took full responsibility, but since Katie Couric was the executive producer, I placed the ultimate blame on her shoulders. She never returned the message I left.

Whoever was responsible for putting that trailer up without informing me of the contents was Alison's antithesis. They were also the antithesis of Jay Kernis and Erin Moriarty, consummate, caring professionals.

Every one of these shootings is a punch to the gut, but I think the worst one for me was the slaughter of the journalists at the *Capital Gazette* in Annapolis, Maryland, in June 2018. I didn't know any of them, yet it felt like I had lost people close to me. They were part of the journalism family. I spent two days in constant interviews, all the time wading through deep, personal sorrow.

I suppose my longevity as the go-to guy is in part due to my ability to put together a couple of reasonably intelligent sentences in a five-minute hit. But I also think that because Alison was a journalist, she was a member of that aforementioned family, and her fellow journalists haven't forgotten her. On many occasions, I've had young television or radio journalists start an interview with me only to melt down in tears.

I've become not just the guy who's on call; I've developed lasting friendships with many journalists, wonderful, hardworking, kind-hearted people who Donald Trump vilifies as purveyors of fake news and enemies of the state. Like Alison, they report with ethics and integrity in a country where they find themselves under attack, both literally and figuratively. They have allowed me to be a conduit for Alison's voice, and for that I'm eternally grateful. And in a cruel, ironic twist, I've become a journalist following in my daughter's footsteps.

In 2015, Barbara and I attended another ceremony at the DC Newseum, an event honoring all the journalists who fell that year. Many of their families were there, including Adam's parents, Buddy and Mary Ward. I spoke on behalf of Alison. I spoke about how proud I was, how I wished I wasn't standing at the podium that day.

Alison's name was etched into a translucent glass wall, and the effect was ethereal. I think she would have approved of the placement: front and center, eye level, and striking.

9

SCOOTER WINKS

On September 19, Barbara and I were headed to Roanoke for the annual Greek Festival. WDBJ had been an official sponsor of the festival for many years, and the station has a booth near the entrance to the festival site, held on the grounds of the Holy Trinity Greek Orthodox Church. The booth is continuously manned with local news personalities, bringing good PR for the station and an opportunity for viewers to see their favorite TV friends in person.

I knew the event was going to be excruciating for me.

The year before, Alison had become a fan favorite at the Greek Festival. It reminded me of a conversation we had before her first appearance for WCTI in Jacksonville, North Carolina, in 2013. It was shortly after she started with the station, and she preparing to attend an event at the Chamber of Commerce. WCTI had provided her with a stack of her glossy headshots to sign and hand out.

"Dad, this is stupid," Alison said. "Nobody's going to want me to give them my picture, signed or otherwise."

"You'd be surprised," I'd told her. "Remember, you're on TV.

People think you're a celebrity, even if you don't think of yourself that way."

Alison was astonished that people wanted her autographed photos and wanted to be photographed with her. The one that really shocked her was when a little Asian woman approached her table, speaking haltingly in broken English, and asked if she could take a picture of Alison.

"Sure," Alison said. As the woman snapped a few photos of her sitting behind the table, Alison said, "Why don't we take a picture together?" The woman beamed as one of her daughters took a snapshot of the two of them.

"Dad, she didn't think she would be allowed in the picture with me," Alison told me later. "It was so touching."

Alison's career in the spotlight had begun. On a visit to Jacksonville later that year, I ended up playing golf with the mayor. When he found out who I was, he told me in no uncertain terms that Channel 12 needed to stop messing around and make Alison the official face of the station. He wasn't being patronizing; I could tell he meant it.

At the Greek Festival in Roanoke, Barbara, Chris, and I were back where Alison had held court just one year before. Her fans loved her, but the Greek organizers were especially taken with her. Certainly, they loved the publicity that her live morning reports provided in the lead-up to the festival, but it went much deeper than that. As she did with so many, she had made a connection, a bond. No one loved her more than Charlie Tarasidis, one of the festival organizers. Charlie is big athletic guy with a bald head and a distinctive goatee, jet-black above his mouth and gray below it. He could pass for a Spartan.

We passed the carnival photo cutouts where the year before I'd stuck my head in place of the discus thrower, and we briefly stopped at the WDBJ tent to say hello. Then we made our way through the crowd to find Charlie, stopping along the way to speak with well-wishers who recognized us. Chris received particular attention since so many people saw him on WDBJ each day; people stopped him to offer a few kind words and even a few hugs. As usual, it was both heartwarming and gut-wrenching. We had become walking emotional triggers for anyone who knew us even faintly.

We spied Charlie on the patio at the corner of the grounds. He was hovering over a massive grill covered with lamb and chicken kabobs, the smell delicious and intoxicating. As he had the year before when Alison introduced us, he gave me a bear hug and then put my face between his two big hands, giving me the traditional Greek kiss on both cheeks.

"I was hoping I'd see you here," he said, his eyes watering. "It just crushed all of us. She was part of our family."

"Thanks, Charlie," I said. "We had to be here. She would have wanted us to be here, and I know she loved you guys. Of all the events she covered, this festival was her favorite."

Charlie smiled. "Go get some food and I'll meet you at the table," he said.

On the way to the food line, I bought a Greek beer and a bottle of Greek white wine to share. We filled our trays with the wondrous offerings and sat down at one of the many long tables set up under a massive tent. We were interrupted several times by well-wishers; while they were strangers to us, to them, we were part of their extended family. They had lost Alison too, in their own way.

Charlie joined us midway through the meal. Barbara poured each of us a glass of wine then put the cork back in the bottle. As I talked to Chris and Barbara talked to Charlie, I missed the first of what I've come to think of as "Scooter's winks," little bits of unexplained phenomena. As we spoke with one another, the wine bottle's cork popped out, landing in Barbara's lap.

Barbara and Charlie just looked at each other, frozen in a *what the hell just happened?* moment.

"Did you see that?" Barbara asked. Chris and I hadn't, but the look on Charlie's face told us she wasn't making it up. There was no explanation for it, just Alison letting us know she was there in spirit with her family and friends.

When we were too full to eat another bite, we thanked Charlie for his hospitality and then said our goodbyes. It was the first time since Alison died that I felt her soul was still with us, and it granted me a small sliver of peace.

Scooter continued to wink at us in the weeks and months that followed, a series of little noncoincidental coincidences. Before Alison's death, I'd always been skeptical of "signs" from the afterlife, wherever that is. I'm a believer now. Those "winks" happen. Some people will think this is nonsense; had I not experienced them, I might say the same. But Barbara, Chris, and I have experienced the unexplainable.

For example, Alison once told Barbara that she thought it would be cool to have a pet snake. We ended up getting Clarisse, a friendly corn snake. After our meeting with Michael Bloomberg, we came home and discovered that Clarisse had shed her skin and then vanished from a completely escape-proof aquarium. Maybe an octopus could have found a way out, but the aquarium's lid was sealed tight.

A month later, just as we were about to hit the road to scatter Alison's ashes, guess who showed up? Clarisse was in our bedroom, headed underneath the dresser when Barbara retrieved her. How Clarisse escaped her tank remains a mystery, but the timing of her return felt like a sign.

There is an iconic picture of Alison, a screenshot that Barbara captured of her sitting at the anchor desk, a wistful expression playing across her delicate features. I printed and framed two copies of the screenshot, one that sits on my desk, the other on Barbara's.

For weeks, the picture on Barbara's desk would turn slightly, maybe an inch at a time. It happened during the day and it happened overnight, and sometimes it happened multiple times per day. I put a business card holder parallel to the base of the frame to gauge the movement. Sure enough, within a day, they would be out of parallel.

I jumped up and down next to the desk, trying to see if the movement caused by walking could cause the picture to move. It didn't, and besides, we weren't walking around in the middle of the night, and the picture still moved. I don't know how else to explain it.

One of my favorite winks occurred in April 2016, when paddlers in the area were able to take advantage of the rain and hit one of our favorite spots, Kibler Valley. It was a reunion of sorts, since I hadn't seen any of them since Alison's death. One guy I'd known for some time—we'll call him "Nick"—gave me a hug and issued the standard, "Sorry for your loss."

"But I don't agree with what you're doing," he added in the next breath. I was so taken aback that I don't even recall what my response was. It was probably the standard, "Look, nobody's coming to take away your guns" line.

We all put in and made it through the first big rapid. There's a drop-off between the first rapid and the second. It's not particularly difficult to navigate, even for an inexperienced paddler, but lo and behold, Nick—an experienced paddler—flipped his kayak. He burst from the water, huffing and puffing, as he dragged his waterlogged kayak back to the riverbank. I asked him if he was OK, but it was clear that his pride was the only thing injured in the spill.

I paddled over to another friend, Delane Heath, who had heard my exchange with Nick earlier.

"Nobody swims there," I said to Delane. "I think Alison flipped him."

Delane laughed.

"Yep, she sure did."

In addition to paddling, I go on a hike or do strength training almost every day. This deeply ingrained workout ethic continued after Alison was killed, and it is critical to my physical and emotional well-being.

After a workout, I like to I reward myself with a cold beer and an evening dip in the hot tub. Prior to Alison's death, the hot tub was simply a place to relax, think, and occasionally have an epiphany of some sort, usually work-related. The hot tub took on a new function after Alison was killed; it became a conduit of sorts, a place where I could have conversations with Scooter.

I climb in with my beer, stare up at the sky, and say, "Hey, Scooter." She always replies, "Hey, Dad."

I don't know if our conversations are real. Maybe I'm simply inventing them. But they happen. I only hear her voice in my head, but wherever she is, I know she hears me. When I'm in the hot tub, I can feel her presence nearby. I may sound like a goofy medium, but our family always has done things a little differently.

Hot tub o'clock is when I commune with Alison. I gaze up at the stars and ask her how she's doing, and from somewhere within my head, I hear her reply. Depending on the day, I melt down. I've probably filled that hot tub with tears over the years since her death.

As I sat in the hot tub one clear night, I was in a dark place, darker than normal. The usual unrelenting heartbreak had been replaced by acute agony, the pain of her loss so incredible that I felt like I was being crushed. I sobbed uncontrollably, barely able to catch my breath.

Not knowing what else to do, I pleaded to the stars above.

"Scooter, let me know you're there," I rasped. "Please, let me know you hear me."

The words had just left my mouth when, suddenly, a brilliant meteor streaked overhead and split into three magnesium-bright branches, scratching fire into the sky. It was more spectacular than any meteor I've seen before or since.

It was no coincidence. Alison heard me.

Another day I was sitting in the hot tub in the afternoon. The clouds coalesced into the unmistakable form of a winged statue holding a globe. We'd found out a month earlier that Alison had been nominated for an Emmy for Best Live Reporting. It was not a token gesture; it was for her work. The award ceremony was the following month.

I hadn't asked Alison for anything that day, and I wasn't even thinking about the Emmy Awards, at least not until I saw that formation. It was Alison telling me that she was going to win.

And she did.

Later that summer, our dog, Jack, became really sick. He was losing weight, not eating, and having trouble relieving himself: the telltale signs of cancer. When I left him at the vet to be tested, the results were already clear to me; I was a blubbering mess. I couldn't bear another loss.

I climbed into the hot tub that afternoon and wept.

"Please Scooter, don't take him yet," I said. "I know you want to meet him at the Rainbow Bridge, but I just can't take it right now."

I looked skyward, hoping she'd hear my plaintive pleading. Through bleary eyes, I watched as the clouds formed the unmistakable image of Jack's head.

The results came back. Jack didn't have cancer, just an easily treatable bout with colitis. Whatever she did, Scooter bought Jack another two years. When he fell ill a second time, there were no signs in the clouds. This time we knew. They're at that Rainbow Bridge now.

When Jack's time did come, I changed my desktop background image. It had previously been a picture of Alison and me standing atop the Mayan pyramid at Coba, but I changed it to an image of Alison and Jack on the bank of the Smith River. They both had big smiles, and the photo, though wonderful, made me long for the days when they were both on this earth, paddling together.

I figured I'd leave that background on my desktop for the foreseeable future. Two months later, Barbara and I decided to get another dog, a golden retriever puppy we named Bailey, Alison's middle name. After selecting him, we had to wait a month until he was old enough to take home. Around the same time, my desktop background reverted back to the picture of Alison and me at Coba. It just did it by itself. It was as if she was telling me, "Dad, I like that picture of us better."

But the occurrence that took my breath away happened shortly after. I bought an Apple Watch and paired it with my phone, setting it to cycle through more than thousand images in my phone's photo library. The first one that popped up on the watch's screen, however, was Barbara's screenshot of Alison at the anchor desk, a wistful, thoughtful expression playing across her face. It's the same photo that inexplicably moves across Barbara's desk. That wink left me speechless.

I know, I know. All this sounds made-up, like a load of BS. But I promise you, it's not.

10

NEW FRIENDS

Governor McAuliffe's press secretary called on Monday, September 28, and informed Barbara and me that the governor was holding a press conference on Wednesday to announce some executive orders, and he wanted us to be there.

Who were we to say no to our hospitable new friend? I called Lori Haas and booked a stay at the Haas *haus*. By now we were staying with Lori and her husband, Channing, nearly every time we went to Richmond. Their house was fast becoming a second home to us.

"Do you have any idea what he's going to do?" I asked Lori.

"No, but it must be something pretty big," she said. "He's asked a lot of us in the gun violence prevention movement to come."

We arrived at the Capitol and entered one of the large staterooms. A battery of television cameras lined the back of the room. Rows of chairs were beginning to fill with people, many of the faces already familiar to me. Even people I didn't know knew me. State police, police chiefs, and sheriffs lined the walls to the right of the podium. Brian Moran, Virginia's secretary of public safety and homeland security, followed us in and greeted us warmly.

We were about to sit down when McAuliffe's press secretary found us.

"Oh, no, we don't want you in the audience," she said. "We want you standing next to the governor when he makes his remarks." We had been upgraded from attendees to conspicuous window dressing. As we took a place next to the podium, Senator Tim Kaine entered the room with Virginia Attorney General Mark Herring. It was good to see Kaine again, and it was our first time meeting Herring, a tall, silver-haired man with a kind face and rugged good looks. We exchanged greetings as the governor entered.

By now the room was ringed with law enforcement officers from all over the commonwealth, so Barbara and I took our places flanking the podium. Brian Moran warmed up the audience and was followed by Tim Kaine who, as always, spoke without notes. In his eloquent remarks he touched on the story of the professor at Virginia Tech who survived the Holocaust only to be gunned down protecting his students during the 2007 massacre. Kaine was governor when the Tech shooting took place, the worst mass shooting the country had ever seen, up until the Orlando nightclub massacre, followed by the Las Vegas Strip massacre (may that hideous record never be broken). The Tech shooting and the story of the professor had profoundly moved Kaine and catalyzed him to action. He then alluded to Alison's murder, calling on the need to do something to stop the madness.

Then it was McAuliffe's turn. He spoke clearly and confidently, rarely referring to his notes. He proudly boasted about the "F" grade he received from the NRA when he ran for governor before announcing a series of executive orders. Among other actions, the orders prohibited weapons in government buildings, but truthfully, they didn't put much of a dent in the gun violence problem. It wasn't McAuliffe's fault, of course; he had done all he could within his power. Well-meaning as it was, the event was more of a publicity stunt, although the orders were a step in the right direction that I could certainly get behind.

After the governor's enthusiastic speech, we were directed to a desk with the orders laid out for his signature. As Barbara and I stood behind him, McAuliffe signed the orders and then turned around and presented the pen to Barbara. It was a very cool moment.

People call McAuliffe a showman—and make no mistake, he is—but you can tell when someone genuinely cares. I could tell he genuinely cared about Barbara and me, and about the gun violence prevention effort.

I love this guy, I thought. I knew Alison would have been impressed too.

Press conference over, McAuliffe went into the corridor to field questions from the press. When they were done with the governor, it was our turn. It was something I had expected, and by now, I had the drill down and the sound bites memorized. It was the first time Barbara fielded questions too, and she did a wonderful job (probably better than me).

We chatted briefly with the governor, bade him farewell, and then followed Lori to Mark Herring's office for a sit-down. We were in a large corner office with a great view of the Capitol grounds, Herring seated at his desk across from us.

"How do I address you?" I asked. "As General?" It was sort of a joke, but on the other hand, I'd never spoken to an attorney general before.

"Call me Mark," he said, smiling. "The formal way is just too cumbersome."

We talked about our involvement in the upcoming election, how we were willing to participate any way we could. He was not up for reelection that cycle, but he mentioned how he squeaked in the first time. The architect of his narrow victory was sitting with us as well: Kevin O'Halloran, a tall, young, professorial type.

"It was just a few hundred votes after the recount," Mark said. "The funny thing was, we got more votes from the recount."

"I didn't have a recount, but I sure had you beat on the close-race comparison," I said, telling him about my Henry County Board of Supervisors victory. "I won by one vote. My friends dubbed me 'Landslide.'"

At the end of our conversation, Mark walked us through a maze of corridors and back outside. Shortly after, we found ourselves back at Lori's house for cocktails.

It's not part of the mission, and it's probably not a psychologist-recommended coping mechanism for grief, but drinks do make things easier. Not getting sloppy drunk, just having a few to take the edge off. Always the accommodating host, Lori had her bar stocked with the latest flavors of Deep Eddy Vodka, brought back from her trips to Austin, Texas, to see her son Townley, now an Olympic gold medal–winning swimmer.

Crashing at Lori and Channing's home was like wearing a comfortable old pair of jeans. The Haases are as warm and caring as anyone I've ever met, and Barbara and I remain grateful for their hospitality and friendship.

———

In early October, I went back to Washington, DC, this time with Barbara, to meet Mark Kelly and Gabby Giffords. The drive already felt routine.

We met Mark and Gabby at a trendy restaurant near Dupont Circle, arriving early on a warm, sunny day. As we waited on the patio next to some big ferns and funky furniture, we saw a big black SUV pull up, a Chevy Tahoe of the type favored by government officials, dignitaries, and television dramas like 24. Several aides jumped out and then Mark Kelly emerged. Flanked by an aide, he helped Gabby get out and escorted her to the entrance.

I was well aware of the congresswoman's injuries, but this was the first time I'd seen the effects of her wounds. She leaned on a cane and was able to walk under her own power, but it was clear she had to have help negotiating steps and sitting down. It was painful to see, and infuriating that someone so vital had been cruelly robbed of the ability to function normally.

I shook hands with Mark and turned to Gabby, who had not yet been seated. I gave her a hug, and then, unexpectedly, she gave me a kiss—not on the cheek, but on the lips. No words were spoken. Although she can speak, it's still difficult for her. That kiss was both genuine and obviously platonic, a way to express the powerful emotions she felt but had difficulty communicating verbally.

We took our seats, Mark facing me, Barbara on my left, and Gabby on my right. Gabby's right hand is virtually useless, but she reached over with her left hand and grabbed my hand with a firm grip. We talked with Mark about what their PAC, Americans for Responsible Solutions (ARS), did, and we discussed how Barbara and I could help. Other than wanting Barbara to participate in an upcoming conference, they didn't need anything from us.

It was apparent that ARS was a very different deal than Everytown. I had intended to angle for some kind of paid association with ARS. I wasn't trying to get rich; I just had to make a living somehow in the new normal, and it would be an understatement to say that my heart was no longer in corporate headhunting.

It was clear though that a gig with ARS wasn't going to happen, and I certainly wasn't disappointed. Mark and Gabby were the stars of the show for good reason. They didn't need anyone else to go on the stump. Gabby was the living embodiment of the movement.

We finished lunch, Gabby holding my hand the whole time. We

walked them to the waiting Tahoe and once again Gabby gave me a smack on the lips. I saw her again twice more in the coming months, and she greeted me with the same heartfelt kiss each time. It was inspiring to be around Gabby and Mark. I loved our new friends. I had met two heroes.

We had only two days back home before our next trip, this one to New York City to meet with Michael Bloomberg. We arrived in New York on Thursday morning, September 17, and cabbed it to the Everytown offices. They are housed in of one the buildings owned by Bloomberg, but there is no marquee, only an address. An armada of security guards behind a counter took our pictures for temporary ID badges.

A young woman descended on the escalator to collect us. We followed her through the security gates and back up the escalator to a bank of elevators. We got on, she swiped her badge, and we ascended to an unmarked floor. Only Everytown employees are supposed to know where each other's desks are, but I wonder if even they get lost. They take no risks at the Everytown office, and when you consider their opponents, they're right to do so.

We emerged from the elevators into a large, open office with a lot of young people working next to each other in long rows of workstations. Some were sitting and some were standing, using the latest in stand-up desk technology. I'd never seen an arrangement like this, and I was told it was the open office environment that Mayor Bloomberg preferred. The place was bright and airy, abuzz with activity from the millennials hard at work.

We were greeted by Chris Kocher and taken to one of the glassed-in conference rooms on the perimeter of the open office. A parade of young people came through, briefing us on various projects and policies. It was an overwhelming amount of information. I felt like I was drinking from a fire hose.

After our dizzying orientation, it was time to meet the big man. Back down the elevator, down the escalator, and out the door we went, pausing only to give our badges back to the omnipresent security guards. Chris Kocher escorted us around the block to another building. It was the official Bloomberg headquarters, with the same security set-up and elevators. The next open office we arrived at was twice the size of the one at Everytown. Monitors were everywhere, some displaying the Bloomberg financial network, while others displayed CNN and a slew of other news channels. We were standing in the intelligence headquarters of one of the richest men in the country. I remembered McAuliffe's request, asking me to pitch to Bloomberg for a million dollar donation. Hell, the man probably made a million a day just in interest.

John Feinblatt, a longtime Bloomberg aide and now president of Everytown, led us back to a lounge area at the corner of the office space. I vaguely remembered meeting him at the rally in DC the previous week. We had barely sat down when Bloomberg rounded the corner and greeted us.

"Mr. Mayor, it's an honor," I said.

"Call me Mike," he replied. I was astonished at his grace and informality.

He talked about how touched he was by Alison's death and how strongly it affected him; he has daughters, and it hit close to home. After a little more small talk, I changed the subject.

"Mike," I said, "we spent some time last weekend with an acquaintance of yours—Governor Terry McAuliffe. I told him we were going to be seeing you and he asked if I'd do something for him. He wanted me to ask you for a million dollars for his PAC for some key state senate races he thinks he can win. But since I found out Ed Gillespie was kicking $500,000 into those races, I'm afraid I'm gonna have to ask you for two million."

Bloomberg just smiled. "We'll be there," he said.

There was no commitment, but I felt good about his response. A brief feeling of triumph washed over me. I'd just pitched to Michael Bloomberg for more money than the governor had asked for. I knew Alison would be impressed.

The conversation shifted to the presidential race. Bloomberg wasn't enamored of any of the candidates, and Trump's name didn't even come up. Back in those simpler days not so long ago, he was still considered a joke candidate. Bloomberg said Jeb Bush was his preference as far as the Republican slate went, but he didn't care for Jeb's stance on guns.

After twenty minutes, it was time to go. We thanked Bloomberg for his time and started to head out. As we walked out of the lounge area, I turned to see him take off his coat, put it on the back of a desk chair at the end of the long row of workstations, and sit down at his spot, just another member of the crew in that vast open office. I was astounded and impressed. I conveyed my amazement to Feinblatt.

"He's got an office upstairs that takes up a whole floor of this building," Feinblatt said. "He never uses it. We have this big food court downstairs and he stands in line to get his lunch just like everybody else."

He's just a genuine human being, I thought. I sure can't imagine Trump working and eating alongside the commoners.

After our meeting with Michael Bloomberg, we returned to the Everytown office for a sit-down with Chris Kocher. I put my cards on the table. I told him I couldn't go back to what I was doing before Alison was killed, that I couldn't go back to being a corporate headhunter. It didn't seem important anymore. I needed to be a full-time advocate. Chris said he would run it up the flagpole, and he asked me how much money I needed. I told him I only needed enough to survive. I had no intention of becoming rich off of advocacy. It was a calling, not a job.

With that, we left the offices and headed back to our hotel. During our previous family trips to New York, we stayed in New Jersey and took a bus into the city each day, even when I was doing pretty well financially. Now here we were, staying in a nice hotel on Manhattan's East Side. It was a convenient treat, but I'd be lying if I said there wasn't a layer of guilt.

We had dinner at Joe Allen, our restaurant of choice since the seventies, and Barbara wanted to see a show. I'd tried every avenue I knew of to get *Hamilton* tickets, but it wasn't happening. Aside from that, there wasn't much I cared to see. Barbara wanted to see *Hand to God*, a comedy about a puppet ministry in Texas where the puppet is possessed by the devil and turns against his high school puppeteer. It was a wickedly funny show, but while Barbara enjoyed it, I simply couldn't. I wasn't yet ready to laugh, to be entertained. As I stood to stretch my legs during intermission, a couple of women seated behind us caught my attention.

"We just want you to know how sorry we are for what happened to you," one said. "We want you to know how much we admire what you're doing."

Jesus, I can't believe I'm being recognized in New York, I thought. *Maybe people do watch the news. Maybe I am having an effect.*

11

ASHES

October 10, 2015, was the second worst day of my life.

On a gloomy, overcast day that matched our moods, Barbara, Chris, Drew, and I headed back to the Nantahala River. We were going to scatter Alison's ashes.

Every time we headed to the river, we passed by a series of large contemporary homes that appeared to be part of an exclusive development. A little arched bridge connects the property to an island that splits the river, a beautiful gazebo perched on its banks. Its serenity and location make it the perfect setting for a riverside party.

Or a wedding.

Only six weeks earlier, Alison was playing tour guide for Chris as we all passed the spot in our kayaks and rafts. After seeing it, she and Chris talked about getting married there one day. The scene had captured their hearts and imaginations. This river was already special for her, but now the gazebo became the focal point for a major milestone.

Now, however, we were not going to the gazebo to see Alison and Chris exchange vows as family and friends looked on. We were there to release her ashes into the frigid water.

We picked the day so that her close friends Katy, Heather, Georgina, and Sasha could all be there. It was a good time to take a break from the breakneck pace of media appearances.

Earlier, I had called the Nantahala Outdoor Center to find out who owned the gazebo, and they immediately put me in touch with Tom Hurd, the property manager for Mystic Lands property, the developer. When I asked if the eight of us might be able to access the gazebo for our little ceremony, Tom said "absolutely." I thanked him and asked if he had any lodging recommendations.

"Give me a bit and I'll call you back," Tom said. Within a couple of hours, he called and offered to put us up at one of the Mystic properties free of charge.

"That's very gracious of you, Tom," I said.

"We and the property owners are all glad to do it," he replied.

There was little debate about when we would have our ceremony. It needed to happen the day we arrived. None of us could bear drawing it out for the two days we planned to be there, especially me. We got to the Nantahala Outdoor Center around 3:30 p.m. and I alerted Tom. We then caravanned to the entrance and, to our surprise, entered a large contemporary clubhouse instead of a residence. Tom greeted us and we made small talk, thanking him again for his kindness. Through the sliding glass doors, the river, the island, and the gazebo were in view, and the already somber mood darkened further. I felt like a condemned man staring out at the noose swinging from the gallows.

Leaving Tom, we crossed a footbridge that arched over the small fork in the river and set foot on the little island, the gazebo canopied by trees.

I couldn't help but imagine the wedding that should have been taking place. I imagined Chris, his parents, and Barbara standing in front of the gazebo's big fireplace, the rest of the small gathering standing on either side of the pathway leading up to the structure. A string quartet would be playing, of course, and I would cross that footbridge with my Scooter on my arm, my gossamer angel. The reverie was so painful that I pushed it from my mind.

It was only a few yards from the bridge to the gazebo at the water's edge. The closer we got to the riverbank, the more I started to spiral into an abyss of anguish. I didn't have a plan for our ceremony. Thankfully, Barbara did. We gathered and held each other in a tight circle, all of us in tears. Chris managed to choke out a few words, and then Barbara passed small pewter tokens to everyone.

She had run across the tokens years earlier and given a bag of them to Drew and Alison when they graduated high school. Each bag contained five small tokens marked with symbols: a heart for love, a peace sign for hope, an acorn for a long and healthy life, an angel to watch over you, and the world, because the future is in your hands. She also gave everyone pieces of Alison's favorite turquoise necklace. Each person lining the riverbank would say something about Alison and then toss the token or turquoise into the clear, shallow water.

I think all I could muster was "I love you, Scooter."

Barbara opened the box that held Alison's ashes and passed it around, each person taking a handful. The sight and touch of my handful, all that remained of her, was more than I could take. I immediately tossed her ashes into the river. I couldn't say a word. I was too wracked with grief, the same black wave of emotional devastation I felt the day she died crashing over me once again.

The ashes left a residue on my hands, and I was struck with an odd compulsion to smell them. Maybe I thought I'd be able to pick up a trace of her essence. I figured the scent would be startling in some way, either good or bad. It was neither. There was no scent, but there did seem to be an odd freshness, a purity I couldn't define. Maybe *that* was her essence.

The members of our grief-stricken party released her to the river, and we all wandered away from one another in an unspoken understanding, taking up solitary positions on the island to become lost in our thoughts. I found a large tree trunk that had been fashioned into a stool and I sat there, staring upstream, imagining I could see my Scooter paddling her kayak around the bend. I was transported back to the day she died, looking at the same tableau on the Smith River. I felt as though every drop of my soul had been wrung out, left to drift down the Nantahala toward parts unknown.

I finally staggered back to the clubhouse and joined the others. We milled about the patio, barely speaking, before we departed for the River's End restaurant. I don't remember much levity or any Alison stories being told. It was as if we'd all run a competitive marathon and had nothing left in the tank.

Before we got back into our vehicles to return to our cabins, Chris stopped me.

"She was with us before we went to the gazebo," he said. "As I was parking the car, Sirius started playing her favorite song. She winked at me."

At their wedding, Alison had wanted her first dance with Chris to be to that song, Ed Sheeran's "Thinking Out Loud."

It was an exhausting day, but it was over. I wasn't in the hot tub, but I could easily imagine Alison's voice.

"Dad, I love you and I know your heart breaks for me. But I want you to try to have a little fun tomorrow."

The gloom of the dark, cloudy day mercifully faded into night, and the following morning was bright and sunny, the balm we all needed as we prepared to run the Nantahala with Alison as our spiritual guide. As we gathered at the put-in, we took a group photo, the rest of the crew holding me up horizontally like some enormous fish. We were going to have fun. It's what Alison wanted and we were going to oblige.

With Drew in a ducky (a one- or two-person raft, a bit like an inflatable canoe), me in my kayak, and Barbara at the helm of the six-person raft, we embarked. It was Heather and Sasha's first time on whitewater, and Barbara was able to navigate them through the first big rapid, Patton's Run, without incident. A few wave trains later, we approached the gazebo, the site of such sorrow the previous day.

Yet the vibe was totally different. We didn't pull over. We didn't need to. On this brilliantly sunny day, as we passed the gazebo, we all said hello to Scooter. We knew she was with us when we saw a solitary yellow butterfly hovering over the raft. I often see yellow butterflies dancing nearby when I'm on the river or in the hot tub, in the places where I feel closest to Alison. It flapped lazily overhead as we continued our journey down the river, before it fluttered away in the direction of the gazebo.

Those yellow butterflies seem to be Alison's preferred way to touch us. Almost three years later, Barbara hit a spot on the river that flipped her. As she was trying to find a place to get out of the frigid water, a yellow butterfly fluttered in front of her, leading her to a safe spot on the shoreline.

The big finish at Nantahala is the falls. It's big class III+ (which means it can get pretty difficult) that provides a thrill for those in rafts and duckies. It's a natural Disney adventure. But even if there is a mishap and the boat flips, the take-out is not even thirty yards away. It's one reason the river is so popular with paddlers; there are big wave trains, but no consequences other than the occasional bruise (or bruised ego), and a great climax at the falls.

Until my last trip to Nantahala, to celebrate Alison's birthday, I had never flipped at the falls in all the years I'd run it, but on the last day I ran it before we headed home, it got me. Adding insult to injury, I couldn't hit my roll and had to bail out. I gathered my kayak and dragged it to shore, banging my shin on a boulder in the process. It was a bizarre feeling, and looking back, it might have been an omen. Something just didn't feel right that day, although sometimes the river will smack down even the best paddlers when they least expect it. Just like Burt Reynolds said in *Deliverance*, "You don't beat the river." I found out a few days later that life, too, smacks you down when you least expect it.

This time I eddied out just above the falls and watched the raft blast through them, accompanied by the whoops and hollers of its crew. It was time for me to run it and I was as apprehensive as I'd ever been. I needed to get back on the horse that threw me, but I was nervous about it. Before peeling out into the current, I reached out.

"Help me, Scooter," I said. "Get Dad through it."

She did, and I was exultant. It was the perfect run for all of us.

That evening, we gathered once more at the River's End to have our last dinner together before heading back the next morning. As dinner progressed, the topic of conversation turned to Katy's employer, a Republican congressman. She was one of his staffers, and she said he was a great guy to work for.

I admonished her. "Katy," I said, "one of your best friends is dead and your boss won't do a damn thing about addressing any gun legislation. You need to tell this guy what happened. Seriously. Maybe it will have an impact."

Regrettably, my rant continued.

"Frankly, I don't see how you can honestly work for a guy like that," I said. "I couldn't do it in good conscience after what happened. I don't know how you can justify it, either."

She sat there with tears in her eyes and didn't say a word. My pent-up anger had erupted, and I had taken it out on a sweet young woman who was just trying to establish her career in Washington.

I realized my effrontery pretty quickly, and later in the evening, before we went our separate ways, I apologized to her for my outburst.

She was gracious, but I think I inflicted lasting damage on the relationship. We haven't seen her again.

"You can't do stuff like that," Barbara later told me. "You want people to be sympathetic. You don't want them to think you're an asshole."

She was right, of course, but my state of mind was such that I often didn't care what I did or said. Bitterness and anger can turn you into a raging asshole if you let it. And I let it.

There were consequences far beyond Katy. I abandoned friendships because of my friends' stances on guns and their antagonism toward President Obama.

I had particular issues with the guys I golfed with. A few of them were my friends, but for the most part, we only spent time together while on the course. My family doctor was an exception, since he shared my politics and my outlook on life. All I ever heard from most of the other golfers I played with was that Obama was a terrible Muslim. I thought they were idiots, but I didn't want to get into it. I just wanted to play golf. I never socialized with them. Play golf, pay off your bets, then go your separate ways.

Several months after Alison's death, I tried to play again. I loved to play, and I was good at it. But my first day back on the course, I was paired with two assholes, one of whom was a gun shop owner who went out of his way to disparage my advocacy. I don't think they even took the time to offer up an insincere "Sorry for your loss." After informing me that my new career as a gun violence prevention advocate was a foolish endeavor, the gun shop owner mentioned that Barack *Hussein* Obama was trying to take our guns away.

"If he was going to do that, he'd have already done it," I said. "He's your best salesman, for Christ's sake."

"He's a Muslim," the gun shop owner replied.

Oh, for fuck's sake.

If I hadn't been at the farthest point from the clubhouse, I'd have walked back right then and there. I played the last few holes, wishing I could be anywhere else. When I finally returned to the clubhouse, I paid my ten dollars for the team bet and told the pro that I'd never be back.

A few months later, I received an invitation to an outing I'd participated in the year before. I thought I'd try to get back into the game. There was no harassment, but my heart was no longer in it. The very next day, I put all my golf equipment on eBay. Maybe one day I'll go back. I dream about playing from time to time, but I've never once missed it.

One of the most perplexing losses was a friend named Brian, an avid outdoorsman and conservationist. We had worked together to get weekend water generation at Philpott Dam and he was with me on August 25, 2015, the day of the big announcement, that triumphant day before The Day that now seems like it occurred one hundred years ago.

I knew Brian owned guns. It never bothered me before, and it doesn't bother me now. I've never had an issue with responsible gun owners. But like so many people in rural Virginia, Brian had a yellow "Don't Tread on Me" Gadsden flag license plate, a specialty plate available in Virginia that has been co-opted by the Tea Party.

Through a Facebook exchange with Barbara, we discovered that in spite of everything we loved about him, Brian was of the conspiracy mind-set. He seemed to think that the government was coming to take all the AR15s away and that we needed to prepare for the uprising. He had been a close friend, and having to walk away from that friendship was painful.

I left my recruiting business behind because, like golf, my heart was no longer in it. Friends like Brian were discarded; not many, but enough. They were pieces of a former life, and now I was living in a tribal place.

12

THE HIGH BEFORE
THE STORM

The day after our return from Nantahala, Barbara and I were back on the road to Washington, DC. Barbara was to be a featured speaker at a women's conference hosted by Gabby Giffords and her PAC, Americans for Responsible Solutions. It was Barbara's first real opportunity to emerge from my shadow and take center stage; I was there primarily for moral support and window dressing.

As usual, Gabby greeted me warmly, and I took my place in the audience. There were many powerful women from the gun violence prevention movement in attendance, like Donna Dees, who started the Million Mom March in 1999. Many of them would later become good friends of ours, but at that point I was still trying to remember who was who. One of the worst gaffes I've ever made was asking Lucy McBath, who also spoke, how her son was doing.

"My son is dead," she replied icily. In that awful moment, I realized I hadn't done enough homework. I had confused her with DeAndre Yates, whose son had been shot in the head from a stray bullet; he survived, but was left in an almost vegetative state.

"Oh damn, I'm so sorry." I said. "I apologize." I hoped my newbie status would serve as an excuse, or at least an explanation. At the time, Alison's death was fresh on everyone's minds, and they all knew the circumstances. Even so, a faux pas like that must have been wounding for someone like Lucy, whose story was the subject of the documentary *3½ Minutes, Ten Bullets*. When I was finally able to bring myself to watch it, I understood that she had been involved in this for a long time, and had perhaps suffered more than we had. Now that we were the focus of national attention, I had let myself get lazy with the homework I should have been doing to familiarize myself with the other members of the club. I had empathy, but my own selfishness made me believe our loss was more important than anyone else's. In my world, Alison's life was more valuable, and the way she died put her in a different league.

Barbara's speech was terrific, as I knew it would be. She knows how to write and deliver an impactful speech, and she was certainly at the top of her game that day. We mingled with the attendees for a bit, then spent the rest of the time walking around DC, enjoying a beautiful fall day.

As we ate dinner that evening at a sidewalk café, I was struck once again by how surreal our lives had become.

"Scooter would think this attention and travel is all so cool," I told Barbara. "I just hope she's out there somewhere enjoying it with us."

The sunset over the DC skyline cast a brilliant pink and orange hue over the city. I looked up and thought, *Yes, she is here with us.*

After another brief pit stop at home, we were back on the road, this time to Richmond, where we again set up camp at Lori's house. The time had come for us to engage in the two key Senate races identified by Governor McAuliffe and the Everytown political team. My request to Mayor Bloomberg a few weeks earlier had resulted in a $2.2 million contribution to McAuliffe's PAC. If Dan Gecker and

Jeremy McPike could win in their runs for the Senate, it would give the governor a Senate majority. The House was hopelessly gerrymandered, as so many states are, creating a huge artificial Republican majority. But if the Dems controlled the Senate, there would at least be a possibility of going on the offensive instead of being stuck using the governor's veto power against the ludicrous progun bills being passed and sent for his signature.

We spoke at Gecker's rally in late morning after being introduced to the candidate. Dan Gecker was an attorney and had been on the school board in the Richmond suburbs. He was a soft-spoken, articulate man with a professor's intellectual demeanor. He told me he had been drafted to run; he hadn't really sought out the opportunity. A nice, smart guy, I just hoped he had the fire in his belly.

Earlier, Everytown's political team had asked me how far I'd go in the campaign.

"Use me like a cheap suit," I said. "I'll do ads, appearances, you name it."

Jon Blair, Everytown's director of elections, prepared a series of television ad copy for me the following week. It was right in my wheelhouse and I couldn't wait to film the spots.

After the rally, we drove to a house in an upper middle-class development to shoot the first of the spots. It was the home of a Democratic supporter who had offered up its interior to serve as our set. Cables were strewn everywhere, and the place was lit up like a modeling shoot. I had brought a few different options from my wardrobe, and once they picked what they liked, I suited up and headed to see the makeup artist.

We were ready to roll. I had been given a basic script in advance, but there wasn't much to it. The director told me we were going to shoot multiple versions of the spot with different phrasing for each, some sets for Gecker, the others for McPike. Most of the versions were with me, some with me and Barbara. I had originally thought we'd be in and out in an hour, especially since I had a teleprompter. That turned out to be wishful thinking.

The director knew exactly what he wanted, and it wasn't what I initially had in mind. I spoke my first lines:

"I'm Andy Parker, and my daughter was gunned down on live television."

The words seethed with barely contained rage. I was speaking from the heart. I was ready to pound the living hell out of the opponents. But it was too over-the-top, the director said, and asked me to dial it back.

Three hours and a hundred takes later, we had struck the right chords and given the production company enough material to edit and compile for multiple spots. It was mentally and emotionally exhausting. Imagine having to say, over and over again, "My daughter was gunned down." Barbara and I were glad the director liked our delivery, but the day took its toll.

The following day was blustery and cold as we spoke at a rally for Jeremy McPike in Manassas. Jeremy has a warm smile and an earnest, enthusiastic disposition. He was every bit as approachable as Gecker was aloof. I got the sense that his heart was in it, that he was willing and eager to do the hard work necessary to win. We gave his canvassers a pep talk after doing interviews with the local TV stations.

The following evening was the Coalition to Stop Gun Violence dinner, the big annual fundraiser for Lori's organization. I was the featured speaker, and this time, I had time to memorize my remarks. It might have been my best speech yet.

Our stay at Lori's continued through the next day with a debate between Gecker and his competition, Glen Sturtevant, as the final event. Our visibility at the small college auditorium provided moral support for Dan Gecker and let the opposition know we were not going away. As we filed into the tiered lecture hall with the audience, mostly college students, I heard a voice behind me say, "Mr. Parker, sorry for your loss." I glanced back and saw that it was Sturtevant, a tall man with elfin features. We kept walking and he turned to go to the stage to be seated.

He can't even come up to me, introduce himself, and offer his condolences to my face, I thought. *Instead, he just throws it out like an aside.*

The debate was a debacle, but not because of Gecker's unemotional responses or Sturtevant's priggish, preppy demeanor, and the fact that neither of them came off as particularly likeable. What created the sideshow was the Libertarian candidate, Carl Loser. Even though he pronounced it with a long "o," his buttons and literature all read "Loser for Senate." The man was a stand-up comic's dream. Gecker and Sturtevant at least had coherent, though divergent views on the issues, but Loser's responses were so off-the-wall that he frequently evoked laughter at his own expense. The highlight came when he veered off on a tangent about the danger of adoption, claiming that adults were stealing children. It was so bizarre that it was almost funny. However, Loser's involvement diminished the whole debate. It was a gigantic waste of time for the real candidates, even if it was weirdly entertaining for the crowd.

I would later run into Loser roaming the halls of the General Assembly during the 2016 session, passing out literature that suggested anarchy was the best solution to our nation's problems. Shortly thereafter, he sent me a private message on Facebook telling me I was a piece of shit. I politely told Carl that I knew going through life named "Loser" was a bit like the Boy named Sue, but in his case, it doubled as an accurate descriptor.

After the disastrous debate, we were back home for a few days, but it felt like a month. We'd been caught up in the road show for so long that we didn't know how to act when we were alone, how to decompress. Barbara and I were both speaking at a Brady summit in DC that weekend, and Sunday was the Emmy Awards ceremony for the capital region, which included all the press from DC, Baltimore, and Virginia. We knew Alison and her cameraman Adam Ward were to receive the Ted Yates Award, named for an outstanding journalist who had been killed covering the Israeli Six-Day War in 1967. The honor typically went to a journalist for lifetime achievement; recognizing journalists as young as Alison and Adam was highly unusual.

A few days before our trip up to DC, Everytown informed me that they had booked us on Meredith Vieira's daytime talk show in New York the morning after the Emmys. As I mentioned earlier, I had been approached only a few days after Alison's murder by a producer at *The View* who wanted me to appear on the show. At the time, I wanted to do network news interviews, and I was also concerned about overexposure. I feared that an appearance on *The View* would seem opportunistic. I politely thanked the producer, but declined. It was her job as a booker to ask, and she completely understood my reasoning. Going on a daytime talk show, no matter how legit, still had me raising an eyebrow. But Meredith had been a journalist, and Everytown assured me it would be tastefully done. Barbara, Chris, and I accepted the invitation, knowing that it would be a race from the Emmy Awards to catch the last flight to New York that night.

The Brady summit was the first time Barbara and I addressed an audience together, albeit with separate remarks. Barbara talked about Alison's life and how she died, and spoke of Alison's legacy. I called out the usual cast of political villains who do nothing to prevent acts of gun violence. As would often happen, Barbara provided the nails while I brought down the hammer.

After the Brady summit, we headed back to the hotel to grab a drink at the bar and prepare for the Emmys. We were staying at the Kimpton Topaz, a trendy boutique hotel that oozed class and atmosphere. I wasn't worried about drinking too much because Barbara was accepting the award at the Emmy ceremony. Then again, I seldom worried about drinking too much anymore; it seemed I could drink like the proverbial fish and never appear inebriated. The only thing the alcohol did was dull the pain for a while before fueling my rage when I sat in front of my laptop screen.

Consider that foreshadowing.

When it came time for the Emmys, we changed into our black-tie attire and entered the large banquet hall in the West End's elegant Fairmont Hotel, just outside of Georgetown. It soon become clear that many of the winners' acceptance speeches were going to be a recounting of their entire professional lives. As the evening wore on, I worried that we might miss the last flight out of DC to New York, but told myself, *If we miss it, we miss it, and that's okay.* What I refused to miss was seeing my daughter honored by her colleagues. Leading up to the Ted Yates Award, each of the winners received what looked like a silver engraved plate; I had expected the usual winged statue.

At long last, it was our turn. Gordon Peterson—a longtime anchor and a fixture in the DC market who had recently retired—gave some introductory remarks, as photos of Alison and Adam were projected behind him. I was still uncomfortable by the idea of any video of her being shown, and they understood completely. It was hard to even see the photos from where we were sitting, but still I began to melt down as soon as I saw the first one. I also spotted Adam's mother, Mary, and his brother, Jay, in the crowd, there to accept Adam's award.

I don't remember much of what Gordon said, but it was eloquent. There were very few dry eyes in the house. When Gordon's speech drew to a close, he introduced Barbara. She delivered a beautiful tribute, and I could barely see through my tears. As I sat slumped and sobbing in my chair, a veteran reporter from Baltimore came over to the table, put her arms around me, and held on tight.

To my surprise, they did not hand Barbara one of the silver plates we had seen earlier; they gave her a winged Emmy statuette. Jay Ward then offered an equally eloquent speech, and then the moment was over. Barbara returned to the table and handed me the Emmy, the first I'd ever seen, much less held. It was a heavy, substantial piece of hardware.

We were now dangerously close to our flight time at Reagan National Airport. After whispering a few polite goodbyes to the people at our table, we raced out of the room. Mary and Jay Ward saw that we were leaving and followed us to the lobby, where we shared a few hugs and tears, and then we stopped at the Emmy backdrop and got someone to take pictures. Barbara's Lexapro allowed her to smile; as proud as I was of Alison's achievement, I should have been beaming, but I didn't have it in me, and neither did Chris. We made it to the gate just in time and took our seats on the plane, our fellow passengers probably wondering why we had dressed in black tie for a late-night flight out of Reagan.

After a short night's sleep, we were on the *Meredith Vieira Show* set in front of a live studio audience. It seemed like it went well, but it's hard to say; I can never gauge these things in the moment. As I looked out over the audience, I saw plenty of teary eyes, people clearly affected by our story; after the segment, many of them reached out to grasp our hands as we left the studio. Meredith was quite gracious as well, and I could tell by looking into her eyes that she was truly touched by our story. I didn't know if anybody would watch the show, but quite a few of our old friends across the country caught it and reached out to us over the following days.

As soon as we finished the show, we were taken to Grand Central to board a train back to DC, retrieve the Kia Sportage, and make the familiar drive home. Colin Goddard, who had accompanied us on the trip, sat with Chris on the train, and Barbara and I found a couple seats in front of them. I sat down and had just started to check email on my phone when a man knelt right beside me in the aisle.

"I want you to know what you're doing is courageous," he said, "and there are so many of us with you."

13

TWELVE-DOLLAR BILL

It had now been over a week since we shot our TV ads for Gecker and McPike, and the election was less than two weeks away. We had barely walked in the door from New York and our appearance on *Meredith Vieira* when I got a call from Governor McAuliffe.

"Hey, buddy, have you heard anything about the ads?" he asked. I found that amusing, as if anyone would tell me when they were going to air before telling the governor of Virginia.

"No, Governor, I haven't heard a thing."

"Damn, we've got to get these things out there," he said. I told him I'd see what I could find out, and then hung up and called Jon Blair from Everytown.

"Jon, the governor is getting nervous about these ads," I said, "and he's calling me to find out what the plan is."

"They're going to hit tomorrow," Jon said. "After we edited them all, we wanted to show them to focus groups to make sure we were going with the right tone. We're running with your solo spots and also one with you and Barbara. The strategy is to wait until the last possible moment so we can hit them hard in the final week. We got a deal on the McPike ads, but we ended up buying $2 million in airtime."

"I'll let him know," I said.

Jon told me that he'd send me a link to the ads as long as I'd promise not to post them to Facebook before they aired. He emailed a link to the ads that night, and when I watched them I was blown away; they were outstanding.

They cut to the bone. The director had picked the takes with just the right amount of anger and outrage without being over-the-top. I knew they would be effective, and I knew there would be plenty of blowback from the online crazies. I didn't care. I wanted to punish the do-nothing, bought and paid for politicians. I wanted to rub their noses in it. Within days, my face would be on televisions across half of Virginia.

And the next day when the ads aired, I did rub their noses in it. Fueled by righteous fury and alcohol, I began trolling Facebook. First I posted on Hal Parrish's page; I'd never met him, but I knew he was running against Jeremy McPike. I recall posting a link to the ad and snarkily suggesting that he "get some of this," and I did the same thing on Sturtevant's page.

As the evening wore on, I turned my attention back to my favorite loathsome target, Virginia Senator Bill Stanley.

I've heard that in some circles, Bill Stanley is known by the moniker "Twelve-Dollar Bill." The name was coined by a local wit who once calculated that it cost each Virginia taxpayer about $12 per year to pay for Stanley and his staff. Considering the quality of Stanley's representation, the person said, Virginia residents represented by Stanley would be far better off if they had no representation at all and just received a check for twelve bucks from the state each year.

My utter disdain for Twelve-Dollar Bill began a year before Alison's death. The first time I met him was while tagging along with Barbara as she visited legislators during Arts Advocacy Day in Richmond. As the name suggests, this is the day many nonprofit arts organizations send their representatives to fight a losing battle for state money. The first time I went, the recently elected Stanley was "too busy" to meet Barbara.

That was strike one.

The next year, he did meet us. I was initially struck by how much he looked like the villainous Biff from the Back to the Future series (who, coincidentally, was modeled after Donald Trump, at least in the second movie). I soon discovered that in action and character, he was Biff with all the oily charm of *Leave it to Beaver*'s Eddie Haskell.

That same year, I personally experienced "Biff/Eddie" Stanley in action. I had taken on a new cause, the Freedom to Float legislation that was making its way through the General Assembly. For any other state in the country, this bill would not be necessary, but in Virginia we have a peculiar holdover from colonial times. It seems that not long after Virginia became a colony, the British Crown gave property owners in a few isolated areas in the state exclusive rights to bodies of water under King's Grant status. This made access to some rivers and creeks prohibitive to those without the grants. The King's Grants were never changed or challenged, and it gave rise to some non-King's Grant property owners who didn't fully understand the law deciding they owned a river, even if a paddler accessed it on public property.

Senator Dave Marsden was the chief sponsor of a bill dubbed the "Freedom to Float Bill" that would decriminalize recreational floating on certain waters. He also happened to be a paddler who had gone through the Upper Gauley in an open boat, which was pretty impressive. A tall, affable man who is a dead ringer for a fiftyish Franklin Roosevelt, Marsden was running into absurd hypothetical property rights arguments almost exclusively from, wonder of wonders, Republicans. Dave once told me, "There are two kinds of Republicans in Virginia: the crazy ones, and the ones who pretend to be crazy."

Bill Stanley was the latter, and he also had a mean streak. He was the kid that you catch breaking windows who turns around and blames you for the vandalism.

I saw both types of Republicans on display in January 2014 when I testified for Marsden's bill in front of the Senate committee. I listened to the ridiculous "what ifs" before the committee barely voted for it to go before the full Senate. A week later, I was in Stanley's office with Barbara when she was pitching him her funding request for Piedmont Arts, but all Bill wanted to talk about was how he was planning to go to bat for me when the Senate voted for Marsden's bill. He was so smooth, I actually believed him.

Later that week, the Freedom to Float Bill was soundly defeated. Not only did Stanley vote against it, he spoke out against it. He might as well have aimed a triumphant middle finger at me as he spoke. The experience reaffirmed what I later found out from others: Twelve-Dollar Bill was a lying cretin.

A reporter friend of ours once told us that he has seen Bill give speeches promising to take one action, and then days later address a different group with divergent interests and promise to do the opposite. He could usually get away with it because the opposing sides rarely crossed paths.

A couple of days after the McPike and Gecker commercials were rolled out, I felt on top of the world, and I started trolling Stanley's page. He had posted photos of events attended by a handful of people, coupled with captions like "Big turnout today." I commented on the small size of the crowd, linking it to his small stature. I think Stanley had the textbook symptoms of a Napoleon complex.

After posting my snarky comments about the size of his audiences, it occurred to me to scroll back on his timeline to see what he posted on the day of Alison's murder.

"So tragic," he'd written. "Our thoughts and prayers go out to the family."

I felt myself pushed over the edge. That was all these NRA-backed politicians could say: thoughts and prayers. It was self-serving bullshit, a way to say, "See, we're paying attention and we care." Yet every day, I'd see a Stanley ad sponsored by the NRA pop up on my USA Today app. I realize it was geographically targeted, but it felt like he was taunting me, rubbing my face in his NRA ties when I just wanted to read the news.

I detested Bill Stanley. He wasn't the only local politician with a pocketful of NRA blood money, but he was the worst of them, the apotheosis of the smarmy, slimy, double-talking politician.

When I came across his post after Alison was killed, I was in a hubris- and alcohol-fueled rage. Before I could calm down and think, I lashed out.

"You sorry little coward," I posted. "You didn't even have the decency to reach out to offer a lame condolence after my daughter Alison Bailey was murdered in your district. When you see me again, you best walk the other way lest I beat your little ass with my bare hands."

About a minute later, Barbara came storming in from the bedroom. She wasn't asleep yet, and my post had popped up in her feed. I hadn't yet figured out that when you post on Facebook, regardless of the page you post on, everyone who follows you can see it.

"You've got to take that off right now!" Barbara said. She was right, and I knew it was over-the-top, so I dutifully deleted the comment and went to bed.

I thought that was the end of it. No one visiting his page would see it. The post was gone, deleted, and it had only been up for a minute or two.

The truth is, as much joy as I would no doubt get from beating the living hell out of him with my bare hands, I would never do it. I'm not a violent person; I just don't have it in me.

Although I had deleted my comment, unbeknownst to me, the page moderator could still retrieve it.

The next day, Sheriff Lane Perry pulled up in our driveway. He asked if I was receiving any threats.

"No, Lane," I said. "It's been pretty quiet."

He seemed a little confused. "Well," he said, "we heard there was something about a threat and just wanted to make sure everything was OK here." He drove off, leaving me confused, too.

Moments later, my phone started ringing. As usual, if I didn't recognize the number, I let it go to voice mail. The call was from a reporter from the *Richmond Times-Dispatch*, a right-leaning paper. The reporter said that Stanley had published my post and now he was fearing for his safety and that of his family. He asked if I could please comment.

Fuck me.

I was stunned that Bill would take my rant seriously, or at least pretend to. As I realized what I'd done, the dominoes began to fall in my mind, one by one. I had besmirched my own reputation as the good guy, the grieving father with a powerful message. I had possibly sabotaged the chances of the two candidates I was trying to get elected. My act of stupidity was going to reflect poorly on Barbara, on Chris, on Governor McAuliffe . . . hell, it was going to reflect poorly on just about everyone who had ever stood next to me. Everytown would probably kick us to the curb.

And worst of all, there was the possibility that I had damaged Alison's legacy.

I was devastated, completely embarrassed, and also stunned at the cruelty that Stanley's faux distress had inflicted. He was Biff breaking windows and blaming me; he made Eddie Haskell look like the Beaver.

It was fight or flight now. I had to call Chris Kocher at Everytown and let him know. He quickly got Stacey Radnor on the call, and she told me not to speak to the press about it, that her team would handle it.

I've always felt I needed to fight my own fights, to explain myself, but this time I deferred to her judgment. I shut up; not only to the press, but to everyone. I was so ashamed of myself that I went into a self-imposed exile from the world, including my family and friends, for the next two days. I wouldn't talk to anyone except Barbara, and that was only because we lived under the same roof. Chris Hurst and Chris Kocher worried about me. I couldn't bear to talk to them; I was afraid I had completely ruined my life and possibly their lives as well. Next to the day Alison died it was the lowest point in my life, and it came about because of a toxic combination of my own hubris and Bill Stanley's cravenness.

My worst fears were confirmed when the story took off all over the state. Stanley had managed to turn me into the bad guy. I had played right into his hands. He told the press that he felt the need to get a concealed carry permit.

Of course, Stanley seemed to forget that just a few years earlier, he had made a threat of his own. In an October 17, 2011 *Roanoke Times* article by Mason Adams and Michael Sluss, it was reported that Stanley was asked if he had seen any members of incumbent Democratic Senator Roscoe Reynolds's campaign staff investigating to see if Stanley was living in his new house, since there was some question as to whether he had bought a house he had no plans to use in order to have a residence in a district he thought he could win.

"Not that I know of," Stanley replied, "unless they want to get a face full of my Glock."

Stanley later claimed that comment was a joke. Threatening to brandish a firearm at your opponent's campaign staffers sure is a knee-slapper.

Nonetheless, Bill was making political hay while I was lying low.

My only response was one crafted by Stacey, apologizing for my inappropriate remarks.

The story lasted another day, but this time the governor had my back. I picked up the *Martinsville Bulletin,* and the headline, in big block letters above the fold, said it all: "Governor to Bill Stanley: 'Man up.'" It was just the balm I needed. McAuliffe's words were strong, nearly belittling Stanley and all but calling him a wuss. I was finally able to emerge from my hole.

"Look, it was bad, but these things last three days in a news cycle, then they're over," Chris Hurst told me. "Nobody will remember."

I hoped he was right, but I knew I would remember. And I do think there was lingering damage done. My reputation wasn't completely sullied, but I wasn't going to be seen as the same saint who appeared on *Meredith Vieira.* Social media was quick to fill up with posts saying I was unhinged, and maybe they were partly right. Driven by my grief, my quick temper had finally gotten the better of me. From here on out, it was going to be a constant struggle to prevent myself from lashing out at perceived injustices, and I was still going to lose that struggle on occasion. All that was left was to wait and see how much damage I had done.

After this episode passed, I thought I was done with Bill Stanley, but about five months later, I discovered that he wasn't done with me. On March 26, 2016, I got a call from reporter Mark Bowes at the *Richmond Times-Dispatch.* He asked me if I was aware that I was under investigation by a special prosecutor.

At first I thought it was a joke, but it quickly became clear that he was serious. I was dumbfounded.

"For what?" I asked.

Bowes told me that Bill Stanley had initiated the investigation in response to my "threat" the previous year.

My jaw dropped. Once the initial shock wore off, I was livid.

"So you didn't know anything about this, and you haven't heard anything from the commonwealth's attorney?" Bowes continued.

"Not a word," I said. "And I can't believe Stanley would do this after I apologized for my remarks."

Bowes quoted me in what he wrote:

"If there was anything to this, you would have thought I would have heard something by now—or somebody from state police would knock on my door. But nobody has. And I have to think that Stanley's behind it. . . . He's doing everything he can to ruin me. He's searching everywhere he can for a friendly [commonwealth's attorney] that will take the case and appoint someone to look into it. That's the only thing I can think of, because there is absolutely no merit to it."

After hanging up with the reporter, I immediately called Ward Armstrong, a friend and local attorney who had served in the Virginia House of Delegates for twenty years, including nearly five years as House Minority Leader.

"Ward, looks like I'm gonna have to lawyer up," I told him, and I explained the situation.

Ward told me to keep my mouth shut and let him work on it. He said he doubted it would go anywhere, and even if it did, a judge would probably throw out the case. No jury in the world would find for a conviction.

Thankfully, Ward said he'd do it pro bono. Had it gone further, I'm sure he would have relished going after Stanley in court.

My immediate desire was to find Bill and kick his ass, but as much as it would have been deserved (and probably applauded in many quarters), that kind of thought was what got me into trouble in the first place. I was never going to play into Stanley's hands again. I did, however, allow myself to enjoy the mental image.

Meanwhile, I was pleasantly surprised to find that Twelve- Dollar Bill was taking a beating in the court of public opinion. Dan Casey, a columnist for the *Roanoke Times*, wrote a satirical piece mocking Stanley's proclaimed fear that I might come after him and his family. I got in touch with Dan and thanked him for going to bat for me in such a clever way. He told me he was glad to do it; Stanley had been a featured buffoon in some of his past pieces.

Two days later, Guns.com referred to Casey's satirical piece, but incredibly, they took Dan's over-the-top *Onion*-esque satire as fact. More fuel had been added to the dumpster fire Stanley had started, and it served only to tarnish his character. At best, Bill's investigation made him look like a coward; at worst, it made him look like a man pretending to be a coward because it was politically expedient. Neither was a good look.

In response, Dan penned another dagger. It savaged the Guns.com crowd and made Stanley's supporters look guilty by association.

I later found out from some friends in the media that the reason I'd heard nothing from law enforcement was that at the end of the previous year, Stanley had shopped his case against me around the state and couldn't find a commonwealth's attorney willing to touch it. I think Bill decided to just let it go after he couldn't find an ally in his fight against Andy Parker, Violent Human Monster, but then a funny thing happened. The *Richmond Times-Dispatch* reporter was rummaging through old court records and stumbled upon Bill's request for a special prosecutor. Bill's little vendetta became public, and it backfired on him almost immediately.

I kept my mouth shut and sat on the sidelines, watching the outrage get heaped upon Stanley. Of course, his die-hard followers thought he was perfectly justified in his attempts to pursue a grieving, unarmed father. There are plenty of normal, run-of-the-mill, responsible gun owners, but the gun extremists are a different breed entirely, and they operate almost like a cult, totally blind to reality. It's no wonder that Guns.com fell for Dan Casey's satirical column, even though it prominently featured a talking pigeon.

Three long weeks later, a reporter from the *Roanoke Times* called me.

"What do you think about the special prosecutor not wanting to seek charges against you?" she asked.

"It's news to me, but welcome news," I said. "At least they're consistent. I never heard from law enforcement or a special prosecutor during this entire ordeal."

Twelve-Dollar Bill's cruelty and callousness lived down to my expectations. If nothing else, the episode caused a lot of people to finally see the small, vindictive man hiding beneath the charming facade, like one of those little bugs that lives inside a clump of spittle.

After this episode, I felt a bit vindicated after hearing Joe Biden say that if they were both still in high school, he'd take Donald Trump behind the gym and beat the hell out of him. At least I was in good company.

14

MELANCHOLY

Just a few days after the second part of the Bill Stanley story made state news, Chris Hurst was proven correct. My coterie of trolls still remembered the incident, but the media had forgotten about it. No one outside Virginia even knew it had happened. In spite of that, I still felt like I had damaged my image, and I planned to limp along quietly in the background until after Election Day the following week.

To my surprise, that was not to be.

I was scheduled to spend election night with Jeremy McPike and his campaign. McPike was polling favorably, but the Dan Gecker campaign appeared to be in trouble. The Everytown political team wanted me to be seen with a winner, so I was to hang out with McPike.

McPike's victory party was held at a raucous restaurant and bar in Manassas. I arrived just as the revelers were rolling in, expecting a win and ready to celebrate. I, on the other hand, felt strangely subdued. I suppose I was still smarting from the ordeal the week before; all I wanted to do was hang out and drink beer.

Jeremy was sequestered in one of the banquet rooms with his

parents and campaign staff. Everyone else was milling around the bar, anxiously watching the suspended televisions for updates on the poll returns. One political operative was monitoring the results on vpap. org, a Virginia political website, and the campaign staff would periodically update the crowd on Jeremy's progress. It was looking like a done deal. We also started getting updates on Gecker's race. We were stunned to learn that with all but one county left, Gecker was leading by almost two thousand votes.

Can this be? I thought, immediately perking up from my somber mood. *Wow, how cool would it be to go two for two? The ads really worked!* I began to picture myself doing attack ads across the country in 2016, a professional fly in the Republican ointment.

My new career as a pot stirrer vanished into thin air, when the results came in from Chesterfield County, and Gecker's two thousand vote lead turned into a thousand vote deficit. Worse still, Gecker didn't even carry his own county. We were all in shock; he was winning until he wasn't. It reminded me of the defensive back who intercepts a pass and is headed for an easy touchdown, only to get run down from behind by the other guy who hustles down the field and knocks the ball loose before he can score.

The Gecker loss took some of the wind out of my sails, but then one of McPike's campaign staffers burst into the bar to announce that Jeremy had just received a concession call from Hal Parrish. Moments later, Jeremy strode triumphantly into the banquet hall where we were gathered. After a few victory remarks, he graciously introduced me. I gave him an attaboy then quietly slipped out and found my hotel.

The day after the election, Barbara and I were scheduled to fly to New York to speak at a Michael Bloomberg cocktail party. I had expected that the Stanley incident was going to leave me banished from polite society, but not only was I still allowed to come, I was to be a featured speaker. From there, Barbara and I were flying to Texas to attend my niece Regina's wedding. It was something I was dreading on several levels.

My dread had nothing to do with Regina; she's a very sweet young lady who loves us, and we love her. While she didn't spend a lot of time around Alison, she was proud of all her cousin had accomplished.

No, I dreaded the crowning moment of every wedding. I dreaded watching her father escort her down the aisle, both of them beaming, knowing I had been robbed of the same opportunity.

I had known Regina's dad almost as long as I'd known Barbara. He and I always got along fine. He was dating Barbara's middle sister when Barbara and I began our relationship and they had been married almost ten years before Barbara and I tied the knot; Regina came along shortly after Barbara and I married. We would occasionally make the trip to Dallas to see them, spending time in Denison to see Barbara's mother, then move on to Austin to see my sister, Jane Ann, and my mother. This was our routine for many years, since we were the only ones living away from home.

After twenty years of marriage, Barbara's sister and her husband divorced. Her sister's brief second marriage ended when her husband died of cancer, and then she suffered a massive heart attack and died at the age of fifty.

Meanwhile, my ex-brother-in-law met a woman in a bar one night and ended up marrying her. While that sounds more like the setup for a late 1970s country song than a rock-solid basis for a relationship, he just happened to win the lottery. His new bride was an investment banker for Bank of America, and she was pretty high up the food chain. Needless to say, she wasn't after his money; she was making plenty of her own.

Soon they moved to a trendy Dallas neighborhood and Barbara's former brother-in-law, while still dabbling in his graphic design business, was able to live the dream and become a kept man. To the credit of his new wife, she took his daughters under her wing and provided them with an element of stability.

I hadn't spent much time around them until a few years before, when we went to visit the site of their soon-to-be retirement home. They both had quite an affinity for George W. Bush, and they found some land in central Texas where they might be able to rub elbows with the Republican elite.

I guess it goes without saying that they are both massive gun enthusiasts.

Their place was larger than a "spread." It was a compound they named "Kumbaya," which I suppose was perfect for them. My brother-in-law had a shooting range at the compound and proudly showed me his arsenal, a veritable Whitman's Sampler of firearms, including a number of semiautomatic assault rifles. The guns were housed in a three thousand square foot steel and sheet metal outbuilding, which also contained his model trains and a "comms room" filled with antique radio equipment, some of it dating back to World War II. He had a full supply of vacuum tubes to replace any broken components; not easy to find these days, but I think he was preparing for an EMP blast.

I couldn't help but be reminded of the movie *Tremors*, with my-brother-in-law and sister-in-law as Burt and Heather Gummer, the survivalist couple played by Michael Gross and Reba McEntire. For the remainder of this chapter, we'll just call them Burt and Heather.

They weren't preparing for the invasion of giant worms, however. Like so many Tea Party fanatics, they were preparing for a government takeover. I couldn't begin to understand how two seemingly smart, successful people could have such a bizarre mind-set.

That first time we visited the compound, Barbara and I didn't give much thought to Burt and Heather's lifestyle. We thought it was strange, of course, but they were doing well for themselves and took good care of our nieces.

Our opinion changed the day Alison was killed. Heather called Barbara and expressed her condolences before hauling out the NRA's old, weather-beaten cliché:

"You know, Barbara, guns don't kill people, people kill people."

Barbara was so taken aback by the shocking insensitivity of this that she was left speechless.

Neither of us had wanted to attend the wedding, but Regina begged us until we finally relented.

"You're family," she said. "Please come. It will mean everything to me."

Heather's comment compounded the dread we felt as we arrived at Kumbaya for the wedding. I didn't know most of the people there. One flamboyant blonde woman was so pregnant that she looked like she could domino at any minute. She obviously was not from rural Texas, and I later learned she was from Los Angeles; she had interned with Regina at the E! network and later become a producer for the syndicated daytime show *The Doctors*. That was neat, I suppose, but in the moment I didn't care. I wanted to be anywhere but Kumbaya.

The wedding grounds looked like a small festival on the prairie, beer and food trailers interspersed between the big party tent and surrounding oaks, and accented with giant clusters of prickly pear cactus. We took our places on folding chairs facing the biggest oak on the property. It had been a warm sunny day when we arrived, but as the sun began to approach the horizon, a chill set in.

The moment I most dreaded arrived. A small group of musicians began to play as Burt, a large Stetson hat perched on his head, escorted his daughter through the field to take her place at the base of the big oak.

As I watched him experience that magical moment, all I could think of was Alison. I imagined that little gazebo on the Nantahala, Alison on my arm as we crossed the footbridge and approached the big fireplace where Chris would be patiently waiting.

I dropped my head and wept, as silently and discreetly as I could manage. I think only Chris and Barbara noticed. Everyone else was watching the bride and her father.

After a relatively short exchange of vows, it came time for photographs. I reluctantly stood with the family as the photographer snapped away. It was now sunset, and as often happens during the fall in Texas, a norther began to blow in, transforming what had been a warm day into a blustery evening. We headed toward the tent and food trucks and joined the other guests as they ate, drank, and made merry.

Burt mingled with the attendees, strutting around in his cowboy hat like a showy bantam rooster. He came up to me and made some kind of small talk, though I don't remember what was said. I know he didn't ask how I was doing; I think the word had filtered back to him that Barbara and I wouldn't be crushed if we didn't get the chance to speak to him at the wedding. I had tried to avoid him, but with only fifty or so people in attendance, it was difficult to hide.

The sun had now set and the wind had turned bone-chilling. After grabbing a beer and a hamburger, I huddled with Barbara's mother beneath a standing patio heater.

As I ate my burger, I watched Burt, now wearing not only the Stetson but also a ridiculous camouflage outfit, as he gave people tours of the property in his pricey Gator XUV.

Would Burt have turned into this rhinestone cowboy/survivalist caricature if Heather hadn't bought him so many toys, or would it have happened anyway? I didn't know and I didn't care. All I knew was that I was cold and miserable and I didn't feel like socializing.

Somehow Barbara and Chris managed to enjoy themselves a little, even dancing with Paddy Murphy, Barbara's half-sister's husband. I never saw it; they told me later. I was too busy sitting in the car, warming up and feeling sorry for myself. After thirty minutes of that, I went back and told them I was heading to the hotel. Drew came with me; he wasn't having much fun, either.

We drove back down the dark two-lane road. It was Texas-straight as opposed to Virginia-winding, but it provided the same heartbreak I had felt coming back from the marina only a few months before.

Sometime later, Regina confessed to Barbara that she hadn't realized how hard the experience would be for us until we arrived.

———

I could tell that my grief was beginning to have a deleterious effect on my life. I felt like I was treading water, and at any moment, I might run out of steam and slip below the waves. The Bill Stanley incident had done me no favors, and there was mounting tension between Barbara and me.

I decided to seek help.

I found grief counselor Wren Starkey (now Wren West), a robust woman with a kind face and a peaceful demeanor. Her office was relatively small, a cozy parlor with an overstuffed chair for her and an equally overstuffed couch for her patients. She greeted me with a bottle of water, her afghan draped over her shoulders. A white noise machine was whirring somewhere in the room; I felt right at home, since I use one every night. Thankfully, that was the extent of the noise. I was afraid she'd have some new age Gregorian chants or whale songs playing, like you might hear during a therapeutic massage or acupuncture session.

As is my habit, I did most of the talking. I suppose that's what a therapist wants you to do. I told her that I drank, but not to excess (I thought), and was taking Xanax at night to help me get to sleep. We talked about my relationship with Barbara and what I thought led to conflict. I told her that the stress we'd been under was enough to put even the best marriages to the test. Little things turned into big things for no good reason. In spite of that, we always tried to make up before we fell asleep, and we were generally successful. It was never easy, and I knew I was to blame for most of the hurt.

I'd never been to a counselor or a therapist before, so I felt compelled to share one of my favorite jokes with her, if nothing else just to break the melancholy.

"Two psychiatrists were having lunch. One recounted a recent episode that affected him. "'I was standing in line at the airport waiting to purchase a ticket,' he told his friend. 'I became fixated on the rather buxom blonde agent behind the counter. When I got to the counter, I meant to say, 'Miss, I'd like two tickets to Pittsburgh.' Instead, I said, 'Miss, I'd like two pickets to Titsburg.' I was so embarrassed.'

"'Listen, that kind of thing happens all the time,' his colleague said. 'No need to beat yourself up. As a matter of fact, the same thing happened to me just the other day. I was having breakfast with my wife and I meant to say, 'Honey, will you please pass the butter?' Instead I said, 'You fucking bitch, you've ruined my life.'"

Wren hadn't heard that one before and she let out a big guffaw. I could tell I had found the right counselor for me.

I told Wren that being on the road advocating for sensible gun legislation was the only tonic to keep our minds off the despair that was always lingering like a chronic disease. We went on to talk about steps I could take to keep small problems from escalating. She encouraged me to ask Barbara questions instead of trying to dictate. She also suggested meeting with Barbara, which I thought was a very good idea. When she mentioned it, I thought, *Well, she'll see I'm not the problem here,* which was total bullshit, of course, but it was the first thing that came to mind.

I had my marching orders and an appointment to come back in a month. It was more than I expected, which wasn't a lot, and confirmed that I was dealing with my loss about as well I could.

On February 22, 2016, I paid my last visit to Wren. We both agreed

I was handling myself and my relationship with Barbara the best I could under the circumstances. She validated what I had thought from the start, that there will never be healing, just managing daily despair.

There is a contemporary bronze sculpture by Albert György in Lake Geneva, Switzerland. It depicts a man sitting on a bench. His arms are crossed and resting on his thighs. The arms and shoulders outline a vast empty space, his head drooping into the void where his entire torso should be. The statue is named *Melancholy*.

I can't speak for everyone who has lost a loved one to gun violence, but I know how I feel. From the outside looking in, it may seem like I carry on with my life just as I did before The Day. I may even have moments of joy and happiness, a shared laugh with good friends. I may seem "normal." But like that statue, I have a hole inside me, one that will never be filled, and there isn't a moment that goes by that I'm not conscious of it.

15

SWAMP THING

It was the middle of July 2016, and across the country there had been a rash of ambushes on police officers. In the wake of the carnage, the mayor of Roanoke, the chief of police, and a prominent pastor decided to hold a town hall meeting to discuss how to defuse dangerous situations.

While Roanoke didn't have a spotless record regarding overuse of force by the police, it was a fairly solid department in comparison to many others in America. The gathering also provided an opportunity to interact with the community and burnish the police department's image in the process.

The event was not publicized to a great degree, but one person who noticed it—and particularly noticed the roster of guest speakers—was Catherine Stromberg, my Moms Demand Action partner in advocacy. She gave me the heads-up that none other than Bob Goodlatte was going to speak. Senator John Edwards was also going to be there to address the predominantly black audience and answer questions. I wasn't surprised that Edwards would be there to pander to his base, but Goodlatte? The man was so unwilling to do town halls that he had become a joke in Roanoke. His face even adorned a series of "Have You Seen Me?" posters that some prankster once taped up all over downtown.

This was too good to be true. Two of my favorite politicians were going to be in one place, just waiting for me to call them out. I knew my presence would come as a complete surprise.

Barbara and I arrived at the church where the meeting was held, right before the program started. There were about three hundred people seated in the pews. I found Catherine and a couple of the other moms; they were sporting their Moms Demand Action T-shirts, and their presence in the crowd was hard to miss.

We listened to the mayor, the police chief, and the pastor deliver their remarks. They touched on violence, but they seemed reluctant to discuss the preferred method: guns. John Edwards was seated in what appeared to be a deacon's chair behind the podium. He was certainly doing his best deacon impression, nodding solemnly at the proper moments as if he'd just heard a righteous line from the scripture and had to offer up an "amen."

Goodlatte was the last to speak, and the Q and A was to follow his remarks. He took the opportunity to ramble on about nothing of substance, commenting that we all need to learn to live together and treat people well. It was banal and off-topic, and it sounded like he had written the speech while gazing down a hallway full of junior high motivational posters. It didn't play well with the audience, either. After his speech, he received a smattering of polite applause and sat down.

As he ended his drivel, I was already standing in the aisle like a racehorse in the paddock, primed and ready to run. When the moderator gave the word, I walked swiftly down the red-carpeted aisle to be the first to speak. I wanted to address the audience without the aid of the microphone, but the pastor insisted that he hold a mike up to my face. I could tell he was afraid of what was coming.

I went to the front of the stage and stared down at Goodlatte, who was sitting in the front row to my left.

"Congressman, I at least have to applaud you for showing up at this venue," I said. And then I launched in. To the audience, I ran down the list of Goodlatte's nonactions, including his refusal to hold hearings on any of the one hundred plus gun violence prevention bills collecting dust on his desk.

But it was a Q and A, after all, so I felt compelled to ask the man a question.

"Bob," I said, "how do you sleep at night?"

Goodlatte looked like he'd swallowed a lemon. He didn't respond. He merely sat there scowling. I know a coward when I see one, and I knew a response wouldn't be coming. People applauded as I walked back up the aisle and returned to my seat.

Next, John Edwards rose and talked about his great record on gun legislation. It was nothing but hot air, half-truths, and bullshit. I unleashed on him from the back of the room.

"That's just a lie," I said as he attempted to explain himself, and then Catherine tagged me out and took her own turn lighting him up.

Were we disrespectful? Probably. Was it warranted? Absolutely. I felt jacked up. It was good to finally get the chance to vent at politicians I despised.

Goodlatte was never going to change. After Trump claimed he was going to "drain the swamp" (which I suppose he did, in the sense that it's now so full of swamp creatures that they have displaced every last ounce of water), I dubbed Goodlatte the "Swamp Thing." He exemplifies everything that's wrong with Washington, a political craven more interested in lining his pockets than representing the interests of his constituents. My public confrontation with Goodlatte preceded the similarly angry town hall meetings that would follow in the wake of

Trump's election. Having seen a glimpse of the writing on the wall, I expect it reinforced his decision to refrain from holding town hall meetings. Goodlatte's Facebook page is inundated with comments from outraged constituents.

In hindsight, the town hall may have been the turning point for John Edwards. In the 2017 General Assembly in Richmond, Senator Edwards redeemed himself. He sponsored a bill that would make it a misdemeanor for an unlicensed firearm dealer to sell a gun without first completing a background check on the customer. It closed a loophole that had been a source of contention since the Virginia Tech massacre a decade earlier.

Barbara and I frequently met with our legislators on Lobby Day to tell them about issues that were important to us, and while we were making our rounds in 2017, I suggested to Barbara that we pay Edwards a visit. He had finally done the right thing, and I felt we needed to make peace with him and offer him a pat on the back.

When we got to Edwards's office, it was the end of the day. He didn't have any visitors, so we went right in.

"Senator, you know I've been particularly hard on you," I said.

Edwards flashed a big smile. "Hey, it's politics. I'm used to it."

"I want to let you know you did the right thing," I said. "I'm on your side."

He was very gracious, and we went on to talk about our families—and of course, about Alison. I couldn't have known six months earlier that one politician's heart and mind might be changed at that town hall meeting.

Many Republican politicians continue to shy away from town halls, some (like Morgan Griffith) claim they're afraid of paid rabble-rousers and deranged protestors. Maybe they're really afraid that they'll discover the other side has a valid point.

16

THE ANTI-NRA

Before my episode with Bill Stanley, Everytown decided to hire Barbara and me as consultants. I thought the Stanley incident would torpedo the deal, but to their credit, they kept me on for a ninety-day trial. Our compensation was to start in the middle of November, but while I was grateful to have a source of income again, I was uneasy about my role. I'd previously had the freedom to say whatever I felt needed to be said—occasionally to my chagrin—and I had a suspicion that that was about to change.

My advocacy created a much-needed sense of purpose and routine that had been missing in action since Alison's death. I still had those unavoidable breakdowns whenever something reminded me of her, but the activity provided a distraction. As part of my duties for Everytown, I led conference calls to rally the troops (or moms as the case may be) in advance of the Senate election. Colin Goddard wrote the scripts and I helped edit. This became a routine for every appearance or call on behalf of Everytown. As time went on, I found myself doing more editing and adding more content. I didn't want the message to become stale. I understood the need for repetition, but as I told Everytown on several occasions, "You can't just keep repeating the same story over and over. People know my story by now. You have to inject some fresh material to keep people interested and motivated."

It was around this time that I was cautioned to be more politically correct with my messaging. To many, the term "gun control" implied that we wanted to take their guns away. Everytown uses the language, "gun violence prevention," and wanted me to do the same. I understood their reasoning and intention, and never uttered the words "gun control" while working on their behalf, but I often found myself thinking, *Trying to keep guns out of the wrong hands* is *gun control.* I felt like we were tiptoeing around the issue. No matter what language you use, the only thing the other side will hear is that our intention is to take their guns away.

I also began to chafe at the notion that gun violence prevention was not a partisan issue. It shouldn't be, but you will be hard-pressed to find a Republican who cares about gun violence prevention more than shilling for the NRA, and the financial backing that goes with that. My handlers at Everytown winced whenever I attacked the Republican Party. I'll be the first one to give a politician a big attaboy as soon as they see the light—just ask John Edwards—but until then, I'm going to keep criticizing them for valuing money over human lives.

Within a month, I began to feel like Everytown was a chafing muzzle strapped to my head. I felt like I couldn't go to the bathroom without checking with them first. *You brought me on as a consultant,* I thought to myself. *Trust my instincts and let me be a consultant.*

In 2017, I started a blog on HuffPost. This led to my writing a series of op-eds that were used by various news outlets. One was published by the *New York Daily News* in December of that year. Early on, I had been reluctant to collaborate with the *New York Daily News.* I never saw their immediate front-page coverage of Alison's murder, but Chris, ever the protector, told me I didn't need to see it. It turned out they were on my side in a big way; they reached out to me, they were abundantly cooperative, and they were willing to run my op-eds. In the first op-ed I wrote for them, I called the Republican leadership treasonous.

Everytown went ballistic.

"You should have run that one by us," their communications director Stacey Radnor said.

"Stacey, it's a little late for that," I said. "I said the same thing last night on CNN. Besides, it's true. They are a bunch of traitors, and Everytown needs to come to grips with it. You're never going to convince these assholes unless you call them out for what they are."

Later in the day, I got a call from Steve Lewis, the producer at MSNBC, asking if I could appear on the *Last Word with Lawrence O'Donnell*, to discuss the recent shooting in San Bernardino, which was the same reason I'd been on CNN the night before. I'd been on O'Donnell's show a couple times before, and I told Steve it would be my pleasure. An hour later, he called me back to tell me that Everytown had nixed my appearance. They wanted someone different on the show. Neither of us understood why; we were both perplexed, and I was pissed off.

Several weeks before, I had shared all my media contacts with Stacey Radnor. Everytown has plenty of media contacts, but after the whirlwind I'd gone through in late 2015, they didn't have a Rolodex like mine. I was perfectly happy to provide her with the info, and she asked that I defer any future media contacts to her. The explanation was that Everytown would make sure I wouldn't get double-booked with media appearances. I had managed to do quite well on my own, and I valued the relationships and friendships I'd formed with journalists and producers, but I agreed to her request.

I certainly wouldn't have been double-booked if I'd accepted

Steve's invitation to go on Lawrence O'Donnell. I had been blocked from doing a program with a producer who wanted my voice on the show, not someone of Everytown's choosing.

When I spoke with Chris Kocher, he also chastised me for writing the *NYDN* op-ed without first running it by them.

"You can't call them traitors," Chris Kocher told me.

"Of course I can, and I did," I responded. "You guys have got to quit being so timid. I know you keep preaching that this is not a partisan issue, but goddammit, it is. That's the reality. And how is it that Everytown now decides when or if I do interviews with these people who want me on their shows? That's crazy, Chris, and you know it."

He didn't have much of an answer for that one. It hadn't been his call to pull me from Lawrence O'Donnell.

I realized my relationship with Everytown was not going to last. I figured they'd fire me in January. I wasn't too far off; they ended the relationship that March.

Let me be clear: I don't want you to think I hate Everytown—I don't want anyone to think this. We're on the same side. We want the same things. They have done a lot of great work, and they were doing it before I came along. But I felt they weren't pushing hard enough. I think over time they started to realize that, too. Maybe that realization came after endorsing Republican senators Pat Toomey, Susan Collins, and Jeff Flake for cosponsoring a bipartisan bill that would have prevented potential terrorists on the "no fly" list from buying guns. It was a commonsense bill that Americans wanted, but other Senate Republicans killed it. That left Everytown in the awkward position of having endorsed candidates who were weak on universal background checks and other sensible bills, in the vain hope that they could pull their colleagues along. Everytown had tried to meet the Republicans halfway, supporting members of its party to make a dent in fixing gun laws, and that still failed. The party at large refused to budge.

Even the most well-intentioned organizations can make painful missteps, of course. In July 2018, I was contacted by a woman working on an ad campaign for the Giffords' organization, Giffords: Courage to Fight Gun Violence, which had formerly been known as Americans for Responsible Solutions. Just a few weeks before, Barbara and I had joined Lonnie, Sandy, Laurie, and several other "club members" for a DC roundtable discussion with the organization's new outreach director. They were attempting to get into the advocacy game rather than remain solely a PAC.

The ad producer told me about a new campaign they were working on—a short film that was going to be shared through social media—and provided me with the following description:

"Our goal is to connect with Americans who believe guns are a viable asset for protection. They believe that guns make them safer, even though we know the opposite is true. In order to help shift perceptions among this group of people, we have built a powerful campaign centered around the CDC and FBI statistics that show how few gun deaths, comparatively, are intentional or justified, compared to the many more that are homicides, suicides, or accidental. Specifically, only one in every 137 gun deaths is actually justified. Of the rest—83 are suicides, 51 are homicides, and 2 are accidental deaths.

"The film will illustrate the real-world consequences of gun violence, by featuring 136 photos of real people who have lost their lives in unjustified cases of gun violence; these photos will represent the 83 people lost to suicides, the 51 people lost to homicides, and the 2 people lost to accidental death. We will fire 136 bullets, 1 at each photo. Filmed in slow motion, this video will be a dramatic and powerful representation of the message."

They wanted me to provide a picture of Alison. The producer admitted she hated to even ask. My response was an emphatic "no." After all we had been through, they wanted Barbara and me to provide a picture of Alison, my Scooter, so that she could be shot all over again. I was furious that they would even ask.

I called Mark Kelly and shared the story with him. He said he was aware of the campaign, but he didn't realize how they were going about it.

Sure, maybe the campaign would have been effective, would have raised awareness. But it was ghoulish and gruesome, a terrible burden to place on the families of those 136 victims. The idea was quietly shelved, and justifiably so.

Events like this illustrate the point my friend Lenny Pozner (whose six-and-a-half-year-old son, Noah, was killed at Sandy Hook Elementary School), makes: "Unless you've paid the price of admission like we did, you just don't understand." Even the most well-meaning people sometimes don't consider the consequences for those of us left behind.

After my Everytown departure, I exchanged messages with former Everytown executive director Mark Glaze. He was there when things were less constrained, but he got burned-out.

"Mark," I said, "they wanted me to be a consultant. Isn't the role of a consultant to provide his input and voice? I felt like they wanted to control every sentence."

I thought I was the only member of Everytown who felt stifled, but after Barbara and I parted ways with the organization, we learned of others who had similar experiences. Perhaps the most visible branch of Everytown is Moms Demand Action. Its precursor was the Million Mom March conceived by Donna Dees after she saw young children being led out of the Los Angeles Jewish Community Center following a shooting there in 1999. Through her tireless effort, Million Mom initially joined forces with the Brady Campaign to Prevent Gun Violence. Together, in the days before social media was the powerful, galvanizing force it's become, they somehow managed to create a national network of Million Mom chapters.

Social media had truly arrived when Shannon Watts, founder of Moms Demand Action for Gun Sense in America, started posting on Facebook after the Sandy Hook shooting in 2012. One of the things Moms Demand Action took on was to organize "craft campaigns." The first one encouraged people to write "Moms Demand Action" in chalk, photograph it, and email or Tweet the photo to Moms Demand Action and the creator's representatives in Congress. The photos went viral. Later, Donna graciously gave the infrastructure she had built for Million Mom to Shannon, and Moms Demand Action took on a life of its own.

Donna moved on and created the Concert Across America to End Gun Violence, and Shannon developed Moms into a hardworking machine that increases awareness and provides a conduit for volunteers.

Moms Demand Action has since become the face of Everytown, but when people tell me they're frustrated and want to do something, anything, to help end gun violence, it's the group I point them to. They have the structure and provide a great introduction to the resistance. They are Resistance 101. However, some friends like Kate Ranta, a gunshot survivor, and Catherine Stromberg, a former Moms leader in Roanoke, whom I worked with at Everytown, are more like me. They said they were booted from Moms Demand Action for being too rabidly outspoken.

Don't get me wrong, I believe there is value in having a scripted, even-keeled response to these issues, and I applaud anyone willing to take the time and effort to fight gun violence. But I believe we also need people who are willing to rattle a few cages and criticize those who deserve it.

Doing this, though, can open you up to a world of different outcomes. Lonnie and Sandy Phillips had a particularly bad one. After their daughter Jessi was killed in the Aurora shooting, they worked with the Brady Campaign to sue the dealer, an online company, that sold more than four thousand rounds of ammunition to the killer without running a background check.

A judge dismissed the case, citing the Protection of Lawful Commerce in Arms Act (PLCAA), which protects gun dealers from liability, and ordered the Phillips to pay more than two hundred thousand dollars to the defendant to cover the company's legal fees.

They had to pay the people who sold the ammo that killed their daughter.

The Brady Campaign was born out of the earliest gun violence prevention organizations. Sarah and Jim Brady became involved in preventing gun violence after Jim was grievously injured in the attempted assassination of Ronald Reagan on March 30, 1981. Sarah began working with Handgun Control, Inc. (HCI) and later became chair of it and its sister organization, Prevent Handgun Violence. After a seven-year battle in Congress, President Bill Clinton signed their proposed legislation, the Brady Bill, into law in 1993. It required background checks for all handgun purchases at federally licensed firearm dealers. In 2000, HCI renamed its organizations the Brady Campaign to Prevent Gun Violence and the Brady Center to Prevent Gun Violence.

The Brady organizations seemed to be making some initial headway in the nineties when the Brady Bill was passed, but this momentum was cut short when they ran into Wayne LaPierre's NRA grinder; LaPierre is executive vice president and CEO of the NRA.

In 2014, it seemed the Brady Campaign wanted to make a splash by filing suit on behalf of the Phillips. The Brady Campaign covered the Phillips's legal expenses and told the couple that they had a great case.

Sadly, as a result of the PLCAA, the case was doomed before it started. Sandy and Lonnie not only lost, they also found themselves on the hook for unexpected legal fees. In the face of colossal expenses, they had to file for bankruptcy to protect what few assets they had.

Despite the failure of the suit and the terrible consequences, Brady is still a player in the movement. Their biggest contribution is one that goes unnoticed by those who are not down in the weeds; it's that Brady's legal team is probably the best out there. They failed in the Phillips case, but they have won settlements against the NRA and consistently beaten back questionable legislation promoted by the NRA. The Brady Bill was eventually diminished by the NRA's politicians, but it was a first. More recently, in the wake of Parkland, Brady has been beating the drum to bring back the assault weapons ban, which was enacted in 1994 and expired in 2004.

Among other influential gun violence prevention organizations is Mark Kelly and the amazing Gabby Giffords's Giffords: Courage to Fight Gun Violence, which I've discussed, and also the Coalition to Stop Gun Violence.

In my opinion, the Coalition to Stop Gun Violence is the little engine that could. I've told its executive director, Josh Horwitz, a dozen times: "If you had Bloomberg money, we'd be way ahead of the game." I've told Lori Haas the same thing. Lori is the coalition's boots on the ground in Virginia, while Christian Heyne, who lost his mother to gun violence, oversees the coalition's efforts in the rest of the country. Even though Lori's focus is on Virginia politics, she has networked across the country. I've never seen anyone work harder on our fight.

True to the organization's name, they build coalitions, working with the Giffords' organization and States United to Prevent Gun Violence, a grassroots effort with thirty-two state affiliates around the country. As Christian explained, "We go in where there is a local group in place and ask them 'How can we help you? What do you need us to do?'" It's a stark contrast from other organizations that go in and tell the local groups exactly what they're going to do.

Josh might be the biggest policy wonk I've ever encountered, but he knows his stuff and he knows which issues to push. Back in 2013, Josh was working on Extreme Risk Protection Orders (ERPOs), a type of "red flag law" that pushes to make it easier to take guns away from people whom police or family members believe is a danger to others or themselves. They are starting to become law in several states and have gained traction across the country. ERPOs exist under different names in different states, but all have the same goal. Had one been in place in Virginia in 2015, maybe Alison would still be doing the news. Or maybe Parkland would be just another Florida city you'd never heard of. But thanks to Josh, Lori, Christian, and others, the momentum for such commonsense legislation is finally here. Thanks to their hard work, we will never know about the tragedies that have been averted.

Two organizations that formed in the wake of Sandy Hook are Newtown Action Alliance and Sandy Hook Promise. Newtown Action Alliance is an all-volunteer grassroots organization comprised of advocates, families of victims, and survivors of gun violence, and is focused on gun violence prevention through a broad range of efforts. They host a national vigil in DC every year to commemorate all victims of gun violence. Sandy Hook Promise was started by Mark Barden and Nicole Hockley, parents who each lost a child in the shooting, and Tim Makris, whose son narrowly escaped. They decided their focus should be developing mental health and wellness programs that identify and help at-risk individuals, and they also promote gun safety practices that ensure that firearms are kept safe and secure. It's a noble approach that has had a measure of success.

To me, the fight to reduce gun violence parallels the civil rights movement in many ways. Just as the organizations I've written about cooperate to battle the NRA, they had their counterparts in the twentieth century. Some, like the National Association for the Advancement of Colored People (NAACP) and those led by Martin Luther King Jr., urged caution and patience. Others, like Malcolm X in his earlier years and the Black Panthers, were more radical. Eventually and cooperatively, they got the job done, although in the age of Trump, it's easy to see pockets of unbridled racism that still burble beneath the surface of society and all too frequently ooze out into the light of day. Tragically, there will always be racism, just as there will always be deaths caused by guns. The goal is to lessen the degree.

A few days after Alison's death, I asked Harry Hurst to paint me the landscape of gun violence prevention organizations, to explain how they interact. He explained that there are three major players: Everytown, Brady, and Giffords. Then there were the next-tier groups, like the Coalition to Stop Gun Violence and the Newtown Action Alliance, followed by a host of smaller organizations.

I asked myself and others, why can't we form one super organization to combat the NRA monolith? I still ask that question, but the answer is that it's just not that easy.

The main problem is that everyone loves their own brand. This, of course, is not a problem unique to gun violence prevention organizations; it's just human nature, and anyone who has worked in the nonprofit world is intimately familiar with the issue. It happens in big cities, small towns, and everywhere in between: One person will create the Widget Protection Coalition, and someone else will create the Save the Widget Society. Both groups have the exact same goal and do extremely similar work—and they may even collaborate on occasion— but if you tell them that they would be stronger together and try to get them to join forces under a single umbrella, they'll bicker over which group has to change its name and buy new business cards. It just isn't going to happen.

I've already said that even though I have a different way of communicating than Everytown does, and even though we butted heads, I still respect their work. If at any point it sounded like I'm bitter, that I still suffer heartburn over my experience with Everytown, I'd like it to be clear that I don't. I will always appreciate the way they stood by me during the Bill Stanley fiasco and I'll always appreciate the opportunities they created for me, Barbara, and Chris. They created an additional platform for us and sent us across the country to get our message out. They provided us an income when I feared we'd go deep in the hole.

Maybe the most important thing they ever did was connect us with other "club members," people like Lonnie and Sandy, Wayne and Judi Richardson who lost their daughter Darien, and Patricia Maisch, who isn't technically a club member but more than earned an honorary membership when she helped tackle and disarm the lunatic creep who shot Gabby Giffords.

All of these gun violence prevention groups are forced to focus on fundraising, push the brand, get there first, and get some quantifiable results to share with their donors so they'll keep on giving. Under Wayne LaPierre, the NRA presents a unified front and a thirty-year head start. While these other organizations have to produce results and explain nuanced legal concepts, the NRA only has to do one thing to survive: convince its faithful followers that somebody's coming to confiscate their guns.

It's a facile message, but as the NRA and the Republican Party well know, abstract fear is a hell of a marketing tool.

The prevention movement, however, has a powerful new arrow in its quiver.

The Parkland Never Again kids have been a game changer for the movement. Their message and their bravery are awe-inspiring. It's one thing to hear parents say they fear for their children's lives. It's another thing entirely to hear young people say they fear for their own lives.

During a CNN interview I did with Alisyn Camerota at the March for Our Lives event, the student-led demonstration following Parkland that an estimated 1.2 to 2 million people attended (not including the eight hundred sibling events), she asked me about the Parkland kids:

"Andy, I know we've asked this question so many times, but is Parkland the tipping point?"

"Alisyn," I said, "I still believe the state election in Virginia last fall was the tipping point, because gun violence was the number two issue. People have finally had enough. And what these kids have done is take that outcome and put this issue on steroids."

When the Parkland students came out swinging against gun violence, I penned an open letter to them that ran in the *New York Daily News*. Here's an excerpt:

> To the students and families of Marjory Stoneman Douglas High—thank you. Thank you for standing up in the wake of a tragedy that has become too commonplace in our country. "Some of you believe that it may take until your generation is in charge to fix this scourge. I can't bear to wait that long. I don't think you want to, either, but your voices are helping us move closer to the day we can live in a safer country.
>
> Your immediate and persistent outrage was and is spot on. This should not be a partisan issue—both Republicans and Democrats are demanding change. But sadly, the Republicans that want reasonable change don't hold political office. And that is why nothing gets done.
>
> After my daughter, Alison, was killed on live television on Aug. 26, 2015, I was outraged like you. I tried to reason with her congressman, Bob Goodlatte, chairman of the House Judiciary Committee. Without remorse, he told me he was not going to hold any hearings on the 100-plus gun bills he had the power to consider. Not one.
>
> In the November blue wave here in Virginia the GOP lost fifteen House seats, holding on to their majority by a single seat. They promised a new

spirit of bipartisanship. That promise lasted only until the opening gavel of the General Assembly session. . . .

Take it from someone who's been in the trenches for a while. Never apologize for speaking the truth. Calling out those who are willing to accept young people as collateral damage to the Second Amendment is not something that needs an apology. I was proud of the way you as well as your parents demanded during CNN's town hall meeting that [Marco] Rubio answer for his failure to act on bills that could save lives.

If I can offer some advice, here it is:

Keep calling out Republican lawmakers, but concentrate on participating in the fall election to get Democrats elected. They are no longer afraid of running on the gun violence issue, which was the number two concern for voters in Virginia. Many of you can't vote yet, but you can influence and encourage people who can.

Don't hold back. Two years ago in the national media, I called the NRA a terrorist organization and politicians who take money from them traitors. I still stand by those statements and I'm right there with you on your "No BS" mantra—just like Broward County Sheriff Scott Israel.

Demand change. Call "BS" on anyone who suggests that what happened to us is the "price of freedom and democracy." Your life, liberty, and the pursuit of happiness take precedence over the right to own assault weapons.

Thank you all so much for your bravery. Stay strong, and be relentless. Even most gun owners want what we want: To end this madness.

I met many of the Parkland students in Blacksburg, Virginia, in August 2018, when they were traveling around the country leading town hall meetings. There they drew a huge crowd, as they had on previous stops. I found them to be mature beyond their years and as committed as they had been the day after their classmates were killed. I'm encouraged by their relentlessness and bravery. They have exponentially amplified the message.

———

While there are many organizations and individuals who desire to take a measured, levelheaded, even-keeled approach to combating gun violence, I can't help but relish my role as a pot stirrer, a persistent yellow jacket spoiling the NRA's picnic.

In the spring of 2018, I found out that Ted Nugent would be performing in Roanoke on July 17. Although Nugent was once famous for his music, since about 1977, he has largely been famous for being a gun nut and NRA spokesman who makes the news every once in a while for saying something exceptionally cruel about a gun violence survivor. The son of a bitch actually said that the Parkland kids were soulless.

Nugent was to appear at the Berglund Center, a Roanoke entertainment venue that offers a variety of performing arts and sporting events. Alison spent many hours covering their events for WDBJ, and I was disgusted at the thought of this violent reprobate coming to Alison's home.

Thanks to a successful crowdsourcing campaign, I was able to launch a rolling billboard through the streets of Roanoke on July 2 and 3, which asked the citizens of Roanoke if they were comfortable having a has-been gun-toting draft-dodging pedophile invited to their hometown. If not, the billboard suggested, perhaps they should boycott the Berglund Center.

In the days before the concert, I even staged a "die-in" at Berglund's box office. The campaign made the national news.

Ted certainly got the message. During his appearance, he singled me out as a "dumb fucker," among other epithets. But at least he dedicated a song to me, which I thought was mighty considerate.

In a separate act of buffoonery, Nugent had encouraged his fans to bring their firearms to the concert to exercise their Second Amendment rights. Berglund Center is a public building so under commonwealth laws its staff could not refuse entrance to people carrying firearms, yet when the doors to the venue opened, the Berglund management scurried out to the line of people waiting to get in and announced that there were no guns allowed inside. The local NBC affiliate, WSLS, reported that Nugent's management had made the decision not to allow guns inside and Berglund was honoring their request. As he's prone to do, Nugent flipped out. He posted the following on his Facebook page:

> Dear God in heaven & damn the fakenews [sic] lying bastards! I gave the direct order tonight that guns were absolutely welcome to my concert. The media cannot be trusted. They are consumed with hate and dishonesty. We had a phenomenal concert tonight as I offered prayers for the soulless crazed hateful protesters. America be aware that the media is infested with America haters and liars. Meanwhile thank you Roanoke for a wonderful #6703 ultimate rockout! God bless you all. To hell with the lying punks.

Of course Nugent blamed the media. He learned from his orange führer. But there was proof that it was Nugent's own management that directed Berglund not to allow guns at the show. Berglund's manager was interviewed on local television and confirmed that the decision was not theirs, but Nugent's team's, saying, "We have to take direction from . . . the people who are leasing the facility [Nugent's management] . . . Ted probably felt more comfortable if his audience did not have firearms in there."

The interview is pretty remarkable. The whole thing is now available online. WSLS reporter Shayne Dwyer says, "So I just want to make sure I'm understanding—so it came from the promotion folks . . . or Ted's folks?"

The Berglund Center manager responds, "Ted's folks."

It seems the chicken hawk loves guns until they show up at his concerts, and when he's called on it, he claims the media is spreading fake news. Unsurprisingly, many of the witless morons following him chimed in on social media to attack the media with him. There is a certain segment of this country, the Trump-loving, gun-worshipping, anti-science crowd, that will never see the light of day. They will merely howl with approval whenever Trump repeats his dangerous message that the media is the enemy of the people.

The rolling billboard campaign made national news. It was grassroots, inexpensive, and considering how much it seemed to get under the Nuge's skin, pretty damn effective. Until we have a massive, unified anti-NRA force to be reckoned with, the pot stirrers will just have to keep on stirring. And I'm not done writing billboards.

17

THE ANNIVERSARY

It was early August 2016, and the anniversary I didn't want to think about was fast approaching. Mike Bell, who was still with WDBJ in spite of the station's sale to Gray Television, engineered a truly lovely memorial that was built to honor Alison and Adam in an open space on the station grounds. Mike did a magnificent job working with the designer, and Barbara and I will forever be grateful for all he has done for us.

The memorial was a curved limestone bench with pillars on both ends. The left pillar had a metal video camera icon and a plaque beneath with Adam's name. An inscription read, "He filled the world with his smile, laughter and kindness." The right pillar had a microphone with the WDBJ logo. Alison's inscription read, "A light that burned so bright in the world that even now the light remains." In the days after the shooting, many people wore maroon and turquoise ribbons in remembrance of Alison and Adam, and a metal sculpture of the ribbon rose from a bed of river stones. Two metal benches, one facing each pillar, completed the arc.

The dedication was attended by our family, nearly all of Alison and Adam's coworkers, and Buddy and Mary Ward, accompanied by their pastor. It was a somber event and Buddy was a complete mess, and after I read the inscription that Barbara wrote for Alison's pillar, I quickly joined him. Those words wholly described Alison's life and her legacy.

Later that evening, we returned to see the memorial at night. Accent lighting highlighted the pillars and the ribbon sculpture. It had an ethereal quality, and I think she would've thought it was splendid. We haven't had too many reasons to visit the memorial, but when we have, there are always tokens or coins in the river stones and a flower atop the pillars. Her death affected many people whom we have never met.

Two days later, Barbara and I were back in DC; this time as guests of Bill McCarren, the executive director of the National Press Club, for the National Press Club Awards dinner. We were there because Bill wanted to recognize us. That alone was a kind gesture, but we were surprised and honored to learn that we had been made lifetime members of the National Press Club. By that point, I'd been writing quite a few op-ed pieces for the *New York Daily News* and contributing regularly to HuffPost, so it was a true honor to be inducted into the journalism family that Alison had loved so dearly.

The following day we stopped by Senator Tim Kaine's office, less than two weeks before he was formally tapped to run as Hillary Clinton's VP. We knew his name was on the short list, but when I asked him if he was ready to run, he only offered a coy smile.

"Hey, I've got a great office here," he said, grinning. "I'd hate to leave it."

Unfortunately, Senator Kaine got to keep his office.

On August 9, 2016, we were back at the WDBJ studio for another interview. This was going to be a particularly tough one. The interviewer was Brendan King, a reporter whom Alison befriended when they were both in New Bern/Jacksonville, North Carolina. He helped us move her out of her apartment when she got the job at WDBJ. I somehow made it through the interview, but it was only the first in a string of "anniversary" interviews I'd be doing. It was tough to keep going, to relive the horror, but I knew it would keep the light shining.

The following week we went back to Nantahala for what has become Alison's annual birthday party on the river. Her close friends Katy and Georgina didn't join us this time—it's just too tough for them emotionally—but Chris, Sasha, Heather, and some WDBJ pals made the trip with us. We placed a stone memorial at the base of a tree adjacent to the gazebo, right at the water's edge. The stone was etched with the words "Alison Forever," and the roots formed a perfect cradle, almost as if the tree had been waiting for it. I thought I was going to melt down again, but this time was different. I felt a comfort I hadn't felt when we scattered her ashes. Barbara said it was as if we'd had unfinished business, and after placing that stone, it was completed. I think she was right.

We drove back from Nantahala on August 26, 2016, the anniversary of The Day. I think I fielded a couple calls from journalists, but I mainly focused on the drive.

One call I did take was from Mark Barden. His son Daniel was one of the children killed at Sandy Hook. Mark and I had played phone tag for a week, and I was glad to finally touch base. Like so many of our fellow club members, we only see each other in passing at the events we attend and we don't get enough time to talk.

I asked him if he was going to be in New York for the Concert Across America to End Gun Violence. He gave me a curious answer: "They asked me to play in it, but I'm not sure if I'm going to make it or not."

Play in it?

"Mark, what do you do for a living?" I asked.

"I'm a professional musician," he said. "I play guitar gigs in and around New York, from sessions to Broadway shows."

I'd had no idea. I told him we had a shared background and shared a bit about my theater career.

"I know the Truthers latched onto that when they immediately called me a crisis actor," I said.

"I was probably the cause of the hoax thing to begin with," Mark said. "They found out I was a musician, and therefore an entertainer, so [they thought] the whole thing had to be made up. That's why you got the same treatment."

If it hadn't been Mark, it would have been someone else. I've long since stopped reading the posts and comments from the truther crowd, but I still can't help but marvel at their absolute depravity and breathtaking cruelty.

During the call Mark told me about Sandy Hook Promise and said he'd welcome my participation. I told him I'd consider it, and I did, but in the end, I felt my calling was on the side of the issue that lessens gun violence by instituting commonsense gun legislation, instead of on the mental health side, though that is also incredibly important.

A few days later we went back to see our amazing, cherished friends at the Roanoke Greek Festival, which we return to each and every year. From there we went to New York to attend the first Concert Across America to End Gun Violence.

Donna Dees, the creator of the concert, has a journalism background, both on-air and in production at the network level. She knew everyone and was respected by everyone. When she graciously offered to put us up for the weekend, we gratefully accepted. We were on our own now, and travel was becoming expensive. Having a free place to stay meant we could fly to New York instead of drive and stay out in New Jersey.

When our cab pulled up to Donna's Union Square apartment,

there were photographers on the sidewalk in front and television live trucks lined up across the street.

"I could be wrong, but I don't think they're here for us," I joked to Barbara. "Unless Bill Stanley decided to have me prosecuted after all."

The red brick apartment building looked like a luxury hotel with an attached parking garage and a covered drive-through. As soon as we exited the cab, I walked over to one of the photographers and asked what they were there for.

"We're on the Weiner watch," he chuckled, referring to disgraced Congressman Anthony Weiner, who had been busted yet again for sexting. "He lives here. We've seen his wife come and go, but not him."

I asked the photographer whom he worked for and was told the *New York Daily News*. When I told him my connection with *NYDN*, he gave a sad look.

"Oh, wow," he said. "Yeah, we all remember that day."

I told him I planned to see the paper's editor-in-chief, Jim Rich, while we were there and would say hello. "Good luck with finding the Weiner," I added. Weiner never appeared at the front door during our stay, and although the live trucks dwindled, the photographers were always out front. Our Weiner banter was renewed every time we left the building.

Donna told us she had plenty of room, and she wasn't kidding. The three-bedroom apartment was big by the standards of any city, much less New York. It even had a huge patio with potted plants and trees. We didn't get to spend much time with her, though; she was sequestered in her room, working furiously on the concert logistics. Marc Cohn, Eddie Vedder, Jackson Browne, and Rosanne Cash were performing.

Over our only dinner together, Donna provided some interesting insights into the various gun control advocacy groups. Her take confirmed what I had concluded; while they mostly cooperated, there was a lot of turf fighting going on. Donna got tired of the infighting and just did her own thing. Even working on her own, her efforts resonated not just in New York, but across the country. She lined up a *People* magazine webcast interview for us, as well as one with WABC that happened during the concert.

The evening concert at the Beacon Theatre was the headliner, but there were smaller ones taking place all day across the country. That afternoon, there was a concert not far from Donna's apartment at the Church of St. Francis Xavier, and she asked if Barbara and I would go to take some pictures.

I figured there wouldn't be much to it, that we'd snap a few photos and be out of there. We were in for something much more emotional than I expected.

The interior of St. Francis Xavier was massive and ornate without being over-the-top. It even made a non-churchgoer like me feel awed. We got there a little early and told an usher who we were and that we wanted to get some pictures. He took us down to the front, and he must have spread the word to the organizer, because we were recognized by the emcee as the concert started. Barbara always carries an 8 by 10 inch framed photo of Alison when we attend any of these events, and we sat with the photo facing the choir and orchestra.

Hearing the music was like an emotional gut punch for me, a group of musicians comprising strings and brass playing "Ashokan Farewell." When the music rose triumphantly, I went downhill. As I sat weeping, a woman in the pew behind me put her hand on my shoulder and squeezed it.

Later that day we headed to the Beacon. It was my first visit, and the theater reminded me of a smaller version of the Pantages Theatre in Los Angeles. Like many old New York City buildings, the exterior of the Beacon wasn't impressive, but once inside, I immediately understood why it is called the "older sister" of Radio City Music Hall. It was splendid.

The venue was sold out, and as people started filing in, Marc Cohn's manager came out to greet us. "He's not going to play "Walking in Memphis," the manager said. "Just wanted to let you know in case you were expecting it."

"That's OK," I replied. Honestly, it would have been difficult to hear.

"We'll see you after the show," he said.

We took our seats and the show started. None of the performers played their hits, concentrating instead on songs about social issues. I particularly enjoyed watching Eddie Vedder, not for his music but for his rant. He blasted the living hell out of the NRA. I'm probably the only Eddie Vedder fan who can't name any of his songs.

As Eddie's set was winding down, I got a text from Donna. WABC wanted to interview us right after they interviewed Eddie. We were told that they wanted to do it in front of the theater, so out we went onto the sidewalk as traffic whizzed by on Broadway. As the interview drew to a close, the young journalist asked me two questions: "Why do this?" and "Why do people need to be involved?"

I gave him the answers I've given so many times before: I do it to honor my daughter through action, and the reason people need to be involved and fight with us is because you could be the next victim, or a member of your family, or one of your close friends. Gun violence affects people exponentially.

We finished, thanked the crew for keeping our story front and center, and started back into the theater. I had taken about three steps that way when a total stranger stopped me. He reached out and put his hands on my shoulders as if to make sure I had his full attention. I did.

"You have no idea how many lives you've touched with your efforts," he said. "No idea." I was stunned. I've received compliments on my advocacy before, but never like that. I was at a loss for words before I finally managed to fumble out, "Well, it's Alison really. It's all about her."

"I understand," he said. "But she lives through you." And just like that, he was gone.

I went back into theater, and as his words sank in, I sat and wept for a second time that day.

When I feel like the effort is useless, when I feel like we're not making any headway, Alison seems to guide people to me to lift me up. It's her way of saying, "Keep going, Dad. I'm right here with you."

18

THE OPPOSITION

You're coming to take my guns away. You want to keep law-abiding citizens from purchasing a firearm. You only want criminals to have guns. You're unhinged because you are grief stricken. You're a dumb fucker. You hate guns, but it was a madman who killed your daughter, not the gun. Move to another state. You make no friends with your constant name-calling. You're a fucking libtard. You're a paid crisis actor.

If you check the comments section in any story or video related to me, this is a small sampling of what you'll see. There are plenty more I'm forgetting, but you get the drift. Those comments aren't even the worst. I've received plenty of death threats.

The first time I saw those comments, I was stunned. Most news websites allow people to comment under their Facebook profiles. You can click the little picture next to the hate-filled message and learn all about the person who typed it. Some of their profile pictures are adorned with guns and Confederate flags, so it's easy to understand where their warped mind-set comes from. But others look like ordinary people, like a soccer mom or a grandpa whom you would walk past in the grocery store without a second thought. The anonymity of the internet emboldens them, and you can see a disturbing glimpse of the howling, hateful id beneath the seemingly normal facade.

I'm often asked how it is that people who can otherwise seem perfectly normal and rational can come completely unglued when guns are brought up. My only answer is that for nearly thirty years, Wayne LaPierre and the NRA, armed with millions of dollars of funding from a variety of domestic and foreign sources, have done an incredible job of building a paranoid citizen army equipped with highly lethal weapons.

One of my favorite pieces of nonsense was expressed by Ted Nugent when he opined that owning an AR15 was "a God-given individual right guaranteed under our sacred Second Amendment." Unless historical records have somehow omitted the awe-inspiring moment in which God Himself appeared before Thomas Jefferson as he was penning the Declaration of Independence and handed him an AR15, I'm pretty sure the only God-given rights mentioned are life, liberty, and the pursuit of happiness. Christian nationalists who proclaim such a strong pro-life agenda appear to look the other way when it comes to guns, or even concur with LaPierre's absurd notion that "the right to bear arms is not bestowed by man, but granted by God to all Americans as our American birthright." Instead of claiming to be pro-life, they might as well admit that they just want to get 'em born, then get 'em armed. I haven't heard them speaking out against the gun deaths of so many innocents. Pro-life, hell.

This attitude might as well condone gun violence, or even encourage it. When the response to gun violence is not a strong, clear message that it is not okay, that it should not become the new normal, and that concrete gun safety legislation needs to be urgently enacted, the path toward continued acts of mass shootings is reinforced. And the people keeping us on this path look at me like I'm the crazy one.

What gets to me as much as the reaction to shootings being to send thoughts and prayers, are the claims that it's okay when people are killed, because their deaths were part of God's plan—as if God plans mass shootings and the murders of innocent people.

In the wake of the mass shooting at the church in Texas, the response from many of the surviving members of the congregation seemed to be that the deaths of their family members and friends was part of "God's plan." Even worse, other churches in the area suggested a solution consistent with their worship of guns first and God second: arm the congregations. If the deaths were part of God's plan, why arm at all? Unlike the Parkland kids who were outraged and rabid in their grief, just as I was in mine, the reaction here was resignation, not outrage.

On Fox News, Ken Paxton, the gun-worshipping attorney general of Texas, made the insane comment that Texans should respond to the shooting by taking advantage of concealed carry laws and suggested that arming parishioners and congregants is a good path forward. Piers Morgan, former CNN anchor and current *Good Morning Britain* anchor, suggested that only a brainless moron makes such a comment. As anyone in the military or law enforcement will tell you, he who shoots first wins. The "good guy with the gun" swooping in and saving the day is a false narrative the NRA continues to employ. Of course, gun nuts lionized the man who chased down and shot the killer in Sutherland Springs, even after it was proven that the killer ultimately took his own life. Perhaps because of this defeatist reaction, the Sutherland Springs shooting was a virtual blip on the media radar.

In his speech to the state GOP convention, Texas Governor Greg Abbott promised he would protect gun rights.

"The people of Sutherland Springs, they looked me in the eye and they insisted, they said, 'Governor, do not let them use this to take away our guns,'" Abbott said.

In an Associated Press article following the Sutherland Springs shooting, Cal Jillson, a political science professor at Southern Methodist University, said the response was to be expected. "It is remarkable how consistent the playbook is in red states," Jillson said. "Let time pass, let attention pass, then declare that current law has this under control. That's the normal playbook and that's what we saw here."

In 2008, then-candidate Barack Obama took serious flak about remarks he made during a campaign stop. He described the bitterness of some small-town folks who "cling to guns or religion or antipathy toward people who aren't like them."

But guns and religion are intertwined. Just look at the incredible hypocrisy of the Republican support for Alabama Senate candidate Roy Moore in 2017. It was the model of a philosophy that has gone sideways. These are people who evoke the name of Jesus and "love thy neighbor" while advocating for looser gun regulations, dismissing those in need unless they look like themselves, despising anyone who doesn't speak English, and voting for a man who preyed upon teenage girls.

Once people have made up their minds, the facts are meaningless. If reality doesn't line up with their fantasy, they reject reality and double down on fantasy, especially if others reinforce and encourage those beliefs.

I saw this firsthand during President Obama's town hall meeting, Guns in America, with Anderson Cooper in January 2016. The president had just issued some executive orders regarding gun violence prevention—small efforts, but all he could do within his limited executive powers. Barbara, Chris, and I were seated in the small audience. The president took questions from the audience and answered them all in a deliberate, thorough manner.

Time expired before I could ask my question—"What is your take on the 'good guy with a gun' narrative?"—but similar ones were posed by Taya Kyle, the widow of famous *American Sniper* Chris

Kyle who was murdered at a shooting range, and Kimberly Corban, a rape survivor and rape victim advocate. Corban asked the president, "As a survivor of rape, and now a mother to two small children—you know, it seems like being able to purchase a firearm of my choosing and being able to carry that wherever my—me and my family are—it seems like my basic responsibility as a parent at this point. I have been unspeakably victimized once already, and I refuse to let that happen again to myself or my kids. So why can't your administration see that these restrictions that you're putting to make it harder for me to own a gun, or harder for me to take that where I need to be, is actually just making my kids and I less safe?"

The president calmly told her that there's nothing he proposed that would make it harder for her to purchase a gun. He just wants everyone to have to pass a background check. He told her that if her assailant gets released from prison, he wants to make it harder for that guy to get another gun.

For the umpteenth time, the president had to debunk the usual NRA propaganda that any gun control legislation will "only make it harder for law abiding citizens." He was more diplomatic than I would've been. In his calm, professorial voice, he replied, "Well, Kimberly, first of all, obviously—you know, your story is horrific. The strength you've shown in telling your story and, you know, being here tonight is remarkable, and so—really proud of you for that. I just want to repeat that there's nothing that we've proposed that would make it harder for you to purchase a firearm. And—now, you may be referring to issues like concealed carry, but those tend to be state-by-state decisions, and we're not making any proposals with respect to what states are doing. They can make their own decisions there. So there really is no—nothing we're proposing that prevents you or makes it harder for you to purchase a firearm if you need one."

The NRA must have followers to be successful, and the more

uninformed those followers are, the more the organization flourishes. They also rely on the true believers, the millions of members of the Cult of the Holy Semiautomatic who make Scientologists look like Presbyterians. Of course, the most potent of these and the most intractable are Republican lawmakers across the country. As of now, they are the party of the NRA.

Early on, I was of the mind-set that Republicans who voted for crazy gun laws and against any commonsense bills were doing it because they were hooked on NRA cash. I didn't see how anyone capable of critical thinking could actually believe that they were doing the right thing. Surely, I thought, they were simply hypocrites and cowards who cared about adding to their coffers more than saving lives.

For some, I think that is the case. There are those politicians out there, such as Bill Stanley, who do know better, but are completely amoral.

Others are simply true believers.

As part of our routine when Barbara and I are in DC, we like to go on what I call the "Go Fuck with 'Em Tour." We walk into the office of Bob Goodlatte, or Morgan Griffith, or even Paul Ryan, tell the staff who we are, watch the look of shock on their faces, and then leave a card that says "#WhateverItTakes: Barbara and Andy Parker, Advocates for Commonsense Gun Legislation." On the back of the card we've written, "We're Not Going Away." I'm not sure they do anything with that card but toss it, but that's OK. At least they know we're out there.

We visited Louisiana Congressman Steve Scalise's office on one of our tours. Scalise was among those shot at a practice game for the 2017 Congressional Baseball Game for Charity. I thought that after surviving a shooting, following a brush with death, Scalise would have had an epiphany. Nope. He doubled down, insisting we need more guns to keep us safe. Instead of the usual young female staffer at the receptionist's desk, we were flanked by two men in their thirties on each side of the office foyer. Judging by their haircuts, they looked to be ex-military, and they certainly didn't seem at all happy to see us.

I said to one of them, "Ask Steve if he's going to wear a pistol on his baseball uniform the next time he plays."

In a tone dripping with contempt, the aide replied, "Do you *really* want me to ask the congressman that?"

"Yes, as a matter of fact I do," I said. And before things got too heated, we left.

Perhaps my favorite example of this lunacy came from Virginia Delegate Todd Gilbert, majority leader of the Virginia House of Delegates. He's a bald, burly man with a close-cropped goatee and a malicious countenance that would fit right in at an alt-right rally.

Here's the backstory: Virginia has more specialty license plates than any other state. If a group has enough signatures and applications paid in advance, the themed plate goes to the General Assembly for consideration. These plates range from "Colonial Williamsburg" to "Fight Terrorism" to "Choose Life" and, of course, "National Rifle Association." Plates like these are routinely approved by the General Assembly; it's essentially a rubber-stamp process.

But when a new plate saying "Stop Gun Violence" was introduced, based on the reactions from many Republicans, you would have thought it said "Kill Whitey." Gilbert was the most outraged. Even though the plate was overwhelmingly approved, Gilbert and seven of his fellow wing nuts voted against it. Even modest bills, such as a proposal requiring day care centers to have any guns on the property locked away, are seen as efforts to chip away at a fundamental constitutional right. Gilbert said, "The agenda toward taking firearms away from law-abiding people is ultimately insatiable."

The most hilarious example of the lunatic fringe was aired by Showtime in July 2018. On his brilliant show *Who Is America?*, Sacha Baron Cohen punked Philip Van Cleave, president of the Virginia

Civil Defense League, and Larry Pratt of Gun Owners of America. Both organizations make the NRA look like Everytown by comparison. Several current and former Republican congressmen also fell for the ruse and were interviewed in the piece.

Cohen posed as an Israeli anti-terrorism expert who offered plans to arm children and toddlers to prevent kindergarten and preschool shootings. They filmed an infomercial for the program called "Kinderguardians" and Van Cleave was the spokesperson.

I had seen this cretin in action many times. He bragged about killing a bill in the Virginia legislature designed to keep guns out of the hands of children, so it wasn't shocking to watch him go along with Cohen's prank.

"What a buffoon," said State Senator Bryce Reeves (R-Spotsylvania), who received $5,000 from Van Cleave's group for his 2015 Senate bid. "Apparently, common sense wasn't issued with his concealed carry permit. Come on, dude, really?" Yes, Bryce, really. And you and your fellow NRA sycophant Bill Stanley were two of the senators who helped Van Cleave kill that bill.

I've testified several times before the Virginia State Senate committee that considers gun legislation, and I've witnessed Republican lawmakers refusing to budge on guns. During the 2018 session, Barbara and I testified for an Extreme Risk Protection Order bill. After we admonished the committee that "thoughts and prayers" were not enough, that it was time for action, the chairman, Republican Senator Mark Obenshain, said, "We're so sorry for your loss. Thank you for speaking."

Then they killed the bill along straight party lines. They did the same for every piece of sensible legislation, including a bump stock ban, despite tearful testimony from a young woman who survived the horrific mass shooting at the Jason Aldean concert in Las Vegas.

One bill that would have allowed municipalities the ability

to ban weapons from public places—a reaction to the events in Charlottesville in 2017—was voted down despite heartfelt testimony from Charlottesville and Albemarle County law enforcement and Richmond's police chief.

Afterward, I went up to the officers and said, "I'm sorry these assholes make your jobs that much harder and less safe." As I said the word "assholes," I motioned toward Bill Stanley, who conveniently happened to be standing nearby.

The Charlottesville captain shook his head. "I'm just stunned," he said.

"Hey, man," I said, "I've been watching these guys do this stuff for over two years. I'm afraid I'm not stunned or surprised."

As they departed, I threw my hands up in mock surrender and said to Stanley, "Don't shoot, Bill, I'm not armed. Call the special prosecutor!" He laughed nervously and walked off. I would have liked to have seen even one bill pass, but unfortunately, that moment was the highlight of my day.

Since Alison's murder, I've frequently witnessed the exact same behavior from Republican lawmakers. Despite tearful, heartfelt demands for action, they refuse to act.

After Parkland, the situation was slightly different. Instead of the usual "thoughts and prayers," Republicans began promising to listen. Marco Rubio called for a task force.

I suspected that meant Republicans would nod and listen, pretend to review a few studies, wait for Paul Ryan, Mitch McConnell, and Donald Trump to stall for time, and then after the story died down in the news cycle, they would resume their usual business with the NRA. Call me Nostradamus, because my prediction was completely accurate.

Each time a gun bill comes to a vote in Richmond, Van Cleave comes out and speaks against it, and his NRA-funded Republicans dutifully follow his instructions. After the Sacha Baron Cohen "Kinderguardians" piece aired and the world got to witness Van Cleave instructing kindergartners on how to shoot a bad man in the belly, Van Cleave wrote a pitiful missive to his base, saying he thought something was up and was going along with it to see where it went. Cohen humiliated a nice handful of right-wing nutjobs, but Van Cleave was one of the few to try to make excuses.

Cohen's show was truly out there, the setups patently ridiculous. How could these men have been duped so badly? It's because they really and truly believe it would be a good thing to arm toddlers, a view shared by many Republican lawmakers across the country.

When I tell you that the NRA is the biggest force of evil in this country, I do not say those words lightly. Hilariously, the NRA describes itself as "America's longest standing civil rights organization." It was founded in 1871 to promote good marksmanship, and has since provided safety and proficiency training to millions of Americans. Many hunters likely became aware of the group as kids while attending one of its firearms training sessions.

Barbara was one of those kids. She had medals and patches from the NRA proving she was a good shot with a rifle.

Beginning in 1934, the organization began to alert its members about proposed firearms legislation. In 1975, the NRA formed a lobbying arm, the Institute for Legislative Action. In 1980, it endorsed its first political candidate—Ronald Reagan—and began pouring large sums of money into politics.

The situation quickly went from bad to worse. In 2000, a year after the Columbine massacre, actor, and then president of the NRA, Charlton Heston, offered his infamous "cold, dead hands" speech

A friend of mine worked for Heston at the time. It was his suspicion that Heston was already in the early stages of Alzheimer's disease. He announced his diagnosis two years later. "I think the NRA knew this and wanted to take advantage of him," he said to me. "I told him, 'Mr. Heston, if you do this, it will be a lasting stain on your great career.'

He did it anyway, and I told him I had to quit."

With Heston's speech, the NRA's transformation into a political entity was complete. It is unrecognizable from the organization that championed safety, training, and background checks, and has become a leading voice in sowing division and polarizing Americans.

So where does the NRA's money come from? Without getting too deep in the weeds, Wes Siler from Outside Online provides a fascinating detail of the subterfuge and dark money.

"The FBI is investigating what role large donations to the NRA from Russian oligarch Alexander Torshin could have played in the organization's political spending during the 2016 election," Siler writes. "[Maria] Butina [who was accused of being a Russian spy] was allegedly working with Torshin to achieve access to American politicians through the NRA. And, after initially denying it had Russian donors, the NRA sent a letter to Congress in April [2018] disclosing *23 Russian donors. Is it simply a coincidence that the division the NRA is sowing aligns with the goals of Russia's information war?*"

If you believe it's a coincidence, then I have a bridge to sell you. And the NRA is aided and abetted by Republican sycophants in Congress. The NRA long ago ceased being a "civil rights organization" and morphed into, thanks to Trump, a coalition of Republicans, Christian nationalists, and probably the Russians. It has become a state-sponsored terrorist group that can strong-arm Congress without breaking a sweat.

Because of politicians who have lined their pockets with NRA money, Congress has defeated any attempt to:

- Pass legislation to keep potential terrorists on the no-fly list from purchasing firearms.

- Ban bump stocks.

- Fund CDC studies on gun violence. If more than ninety deaths a day were caused by an unknown bacteria, you can be damn sure they'd be throwing money at it.

- Strengthen the National Criminal Instant Background Check System that the NRA helped create in the first place. In fact, they have made every attempt to undermine it.

Here's an example of how the NRA uses coercion and intimidation against those who stray from the script. On our way out of the CNN town hall with President Obama, we stopped to talk with one of the major CNN managers about the evening. This guy was way up the food chain.

He related a story about an acquaintance who owned a gun store. This owner told him that he was completely in favor of the president's push for background checks. The CNN manager asked his friend why he didn't come out and vocally support background checks, especially since it made good business sense; after all, if someone is buying a gun through a private sale or at a gun show, they're not buying it from a licensed gun shop. The gun shop owner replied, "The NRA would kill me if I did. They'd put me out of business through intimidation. You don't screw with them."

I was on Carol Costello's show on CNN the following day, and I recounted the story of the gun store owner. When I got to the part about the NRA "killing the guy," she was momentarily taken aback. I had to clarify that I was speaking figuratively.

When you consider what the NRA has become, you can't blame Carol for taking it literally.

However, the NRA's greatest allies, ideologically if not financially, are the "truthers," those warped individuals who believe that every mass shooting is a "false flag operation" designed to gin up support for taking everyone's guns away—in spite of the fact that, if these were false flag operations, they would be the single most ineffective campaign in history. Just ask the gun store owners who put up signs advertising "AR15s In Stock" in the days after someone uses one to slaughter innocents.

The truthers believe that grieving family members are simply "crisis actors" weeping crocodile tears, and the victims have been paid handsomely to relocate to a different country under assumed names.

Due to my background, the truthers have had a field day with me.

Typecasting is a real phenomenon in show business. Decades ago, when I was an actor in New York and in the Broadway company of *The Best Little Whorehouse in Texas*, I worked with a few theatrical and commercial talent agencies. Getting cast in a commercial was a real crapshoot and a numbers game; the more you auditioned, the better your chances. I was from Texas in a show portraying, at various times, a cowboy and a football player, so agents saw me either as a cowboy or a football player. I wasn't getting roles playing young fathers that were being cranked out daily. Given these arbitrary limitations, I didn't audition that much in New York, but at least I had a steady theater gig.

Football players seemed to be more in demand than cowboys, and I would find myself at an audition in a waiting area filled with guys who looked like the Incredible Hulk. I was six feet, two inches and 190 pounds, but I looked like Bruce Banner in comparison. I would just chuckle and do my scene despite the futility.

On the heels of *Urban Cowboy* and *The Best Little Whorehouse in Texas*, I was able to occasionally find work as a cowboy. Western gear was back in vogue. I auditioned for a Honey Nut Crunch Raisin Bran commercial, and I showed up wearing cowboy boots, a Stetson, and a leather vest. I certainly looked the part. The casting director gave me my line, and it was a short one. I let out the biggest, dumbest "Ooh Whee!" I could muster.

Later that day, the agent called and told me I got the part. It was produced just like a national commercial, but unfortunately, it was run only in test markets to see if anybody was willing to take the plunge on Honey Nut Crunch Raisin Bran. They ended up making the product, and I got paid well for the shoot, but it wasn't the home run I'd hoped for. There were actors I knew who made six figures off residuals for a single national spot. Those days are long gone, and I never made that gravy train. The spot was pretty funny, though.

And then one truther decided that my single "Ooh Whee" was all he needed to construct a conspiracy theory. I was officially Andy Parker, Crisis Actor.

Before Alison was killed, I had no idea there was such a thing as an internet troll. I didn't know about truthers and crisis actors. Conspiracy theorists have been around since the beginning of time, but the only ones I had noticed before were people like the guy with the weird hair on *Ancient Aliens*. He may be little off, but he's not malicious.

Just days after Alison was killed, I received a terrible crash course on these monsters.

Before Alison was killed, I had used YouTube to create an online archive of various Parker family videos resurrected from old tapes and disks. After Alison was killed, for some reason, I decided to check my YouTube page. Maybe it was because I was starting to see a few references online to me being "exposed."

When I went back to my YouTube page, which was public, I was stunned. Every video had been peppered with vile comments. Nothing was spared. It was especially painful to see vulgar, offensive comments on videos of Alison's dance recitals, the glee that people expressed over watching her die.

What human being acts like that? How could someone be so astonishingly cruel? I felt shaken to my core. I was receiving plenty of kind words from people all over the world, but to know that there were also people out there who delighted in Alison's death fundamentally changed the way I view humanity.

The truthers particularly latched onto the old commercials I had done. One clever troll made a montage of my old commercials, presenting it as rock-solid proof that I was a crisis actor. For whatever reason, the Raisin Bran commercial was the biggest hit. The creep that put the video together concluded that my goofy "Ooh Whee!" was proof positive that I was faking my grief.

It was a sickening process, but I removed all the comments and locked the page down so they could no longer post. Unfortunately, the damage had been done; the montages and screen captures had already escaped to the internet, and will likely remain there in perpetuity.

Why do they do it? I think most have nothing else going in their lives, so they are attracted to anything that gives their lives some sort of meaning. They feel like they're among the rare individuals who are in on "The Truth," and that gives them a sense of purpose. These are the same weak minds that fall prey to cults like Scientology—or the NRA, for that matter.

A lot of the motivation is fueled by Alex Jones and Infowars and NRA paranoia. The government is coming to confiscate your guns, so Sandy Hook, Alison's murder, Vegas, Parkland—you name it—are all staged by the government or gun control groups.

Here's the thing: if I were that good, I'd still be making a living as an actor. I never expected to go that route, and I don't regret not doing so. After having the time of my life while working in college as an entertainer at the Country Dinner Playhouse in Austin, Texas, I picked up my Actors' Equity Card doing some professional theater in Dallas. I then made the decision to go pro and move to New York City. Barbara was working as a flight attendant at the time, so we had some income rolling in while I gave it a shot.

I was able to land a show at Radio City Music Hall, and from there I did the national tour and Broadway company of *The Best Little Whorehouse in Texas*. I was also able to do a commercial now and then, which seemed like "found money," and I occasionally got a day-player role on a soap opera. But I swore that the day I needed to start waiting tables was the day I would get out of the business. That day came in 1984, after a year of not working and living on Barbara's salary.

After leaving New York and show biz, I did a few commercials and some theater here and there, but I kept my day job. When YouTube came along, I thought it would be a good way to archive the videotaped commercials, rather than let them deteriorate in a box in the closet.

It never crossed my mind that it would be something for the truthers to latch onto. To them, I had been in show business, and therefore it had to follow that I was a fake, an accomplice in fabricating Alison's murder.

Barbara once came across a truther asking how Alison was liking living in Israel.

"Guess you didn't get the message," Barbara said, in one of her rare replies. "Her ashes are in the river. How do you like living in your grandmother's basement?" And then blocked him.

It's something we do from time to time when we run across a particularly obnoxious comment: the mock and block.

Being called a crisis actor no longer riles me. I was shocked at first, but now it almost feels like a badge of honor. What hurts are the horrific comments about Alison, the soulless bastards who express vicious glee at her murder. That's when I'd like to find one of these guys and open a shoe store in his ass.

One YouTube video popped up in a search related to our foundation, For Alison. A troll made a video suggesting it was a scam I'd created to line my pockets. I asked Virginia Attorney General Mark Herring what could be done.

"Andy, you're a public figure now, so there's really nothing you can do," he said.

Once you appear on television, there are no holds barred.

A new horror awaited me when I did a YouTube search for "Alison Parker," just to see what would come up. I was disgusted to find page after page of thumbnails of Alison holding the microphone seconds before she was murdered. The titles of these posts made me ill. Some would describe how the shooting was faked because the camera angles weren't right. It was absurd. There were countless pages of this despicable garbage, and it appeared to violate Google's own policies against violent content.

I was already fighting the NRA, so why not take on the most powerful company on the planet? It was time to go to war with Google.

The first contact I had was with an email support representative based in the Philippines. He provided me with a "moment of death" online form I could use to flag the videos. The problem was, I had to watch the videos in order to flag them.

I wasn't going to watch hundreds if not thousands of videos of my daughter's death. The thumbnails were enough.

I shared my dilemma with my friend Bill McCarren, executive director of the National Press Club. He gave me the name of Susan Molinari, former congresswoman and now vice president of Public Policy and Government Affairs at Google. She was very responsive at first, and she had someone from YouTube call me.

The first sign that things were amiss was that YouTube call. The rep had no idea what the issue was. I asked her if she had done a search on YouTube for "Alison Parker." She hadn't.

"You do that," I said, "and you'll see everything you need to know." She told me she was going to get with one of her colleagues and get back to me.

I never heard from her again. I shared that info with Molinari, and another three weeks of silence went by.

In the meantime, I reached out to Lenny Pozner. He is one of the parents of children murdered at Sandy Hook who has been victimized by Alex Jones and his followers.

Lenny had started an organization called HONR Network; it's comprised of volunteers who find these offensive videos, flag the content, and request that they be removed. Because he chose to fight back, he has received multiple threats to his life. One woman who threatened him with death was ultimately prosecuted and sentenced to five months in jail. Lenny offered to help me get YouTube content removed, and I signed a waiver, as did Gray Television (owners of WDBJ), designating Lenny as our digital agent. He started flagging the content I simply wasn't capable of watching.

Lenny and I have discussed the media's responsibility in all of this. We both agree that at some point, Google, Facebook, and Twitter will need to regulate their content. They claim to be neutral content providers, but like it or not, they are news providers, too. They should be regulated as such.

Lenny thought it was good that Megyn Kelly interviewed Alex Jones, allowing him to demonstrate to the world that he is, to borrow an old journalism term, a "fucking idiot." While I agree that the interview served that purpose, it also gave him publicity. For deranged individuals like Alex Jones, any publicity is good.

I hate the notion of being a member of a "protected class," but I think Lenny is correct when he suggests that people who have suffered as we have shouldn't be victimized again. I can ignore it, but Lenny has young kids, and they, like the Parkland kids, are on social media. They should be protected from vicious, often threatening internet trolls.

Once I directed Susan Molinari to communicate with Lenny, she completely disappeared. Lenny and volunteers from his organization had been moderately successful removing content, but they have to constantly fight the algorithms used by these websites. They spend much of their time arguing with scripted responses from robots. And much of the content, including the POV GoPro video that Alison's shooter took of her murder, is still online for anyone to see.

Here is an example of one of Lenny's exchanges with these obtuse robots:

> Hello,
>
> Your identification of the specific copyrighted work at issue is still unclear. If portions of your work appear in this video, what are the specific timestamps in which this occurs?
>
> Regards,
> The YouTube Legal Support Team
>
> Hello.
>
> The entire video is at issue, in that it shows 2 of our employees getting murdered on live TV. This video is a recording of a live broadcast wherein our employee was interviewing a subject for our daily morning show. We, WDBJ-TV, were broadcasting the interview live when a lone gunman walked up to the crew and opened fire on the two employees, Alison Parker and Adam Ward. The woman who was the subject of the interview was wounded but survived.
>
> The author's name is WDBJ-TV
>
> We demand that you remove this video immediately with no further delay, as it is insensitive and distressful to the families of the murder victims shown in the video. Murder of human beings should not be publicly displayed for public consumption and goes against your community standards.
>
> HONR Network is the digital agent for WDBJ-TV, and I, Lenny Pozner, am the owner of HONR Network. The authorizing document

is attached. Audiovisual content in this video was copied from our network-owned video.

I am an agent authorized to act on behalf of the owner of an exclusive right that is allegedly infringed. Attached is the authorizing document. My company, HONR Network, is the digital agent for CBS affiliate WDBJ in Roanoke, Virginia, United States, copyright owner of the audiovisual content.

I have a good faith belief that the use of the material in the manner complained of is not authorized by the copyright owner, its agent, or the law; and this notification is accurate. I acknowledge that under Section 512(f) of the DMCA any person who knowingly materially misrepresents that material or activity is infringing may be subject to liability for damages.

I understand that abuse of this tool will result in termination of my YouTube account.

Lenny Pozner
HONR Network
Digital Agent

Lenny clearly knows his stuff. In spite of that, Molinari never responded to either of us, so I took my case to Mike Henry, Senator Tim Kaine's chief of staff, who bears a striking resemblance to actor Jason Bateman. He arranged a conference call including us, YouTube executive Juniper Downs, and Frannie Wellings, the chief lobbyist in DC for Google. I was relieved that I could finally talk to actual live human beings who, thanks to Mike's intervention, might finally take action.

I told Downs and Wellings in no uncertain terms that I was disgusted with their companies' tawdry practices. I told them that as things presently stand, Google is profiting off malicious content, videos of Alison's murder posted by truthers. The footage is owned by Gray Television and published on YouTube without consent. Images that I own are also being published without consent.

I also informed them that Google is not only violating its own stated policy regarding this type of content (not that it particularly matters to them), but they are likely breaking the law.

By the end of the conversation, they promised to work with Lenny to make it easier for him to flag and remove content. In the meantime, I shared the situation with Lois Beckett, a journalist for the *Guardian*, and Liz Wahl, a former anchor for Russia Today who famously quit because of the fake news they wanted her to broadcast. Liz landed at Newsy and wanted to do a documentary on our travails.

For her part, Lois was only able to get a feeble "we're going to do better" statement from a Google spokesman. Liz's documentary, *Truthers*, ran in December 2017 and got no response from Google.

But Lenny and I were able to make our case. In the last scene of the documentary, I'm holding a copy of the letter sent by Senator Kaine to Google's CEO, suggesting the company clean up its act or risk congressional intervention.

We thought we had a pretty good one-two punch with the combined efforts of Kaine and the press. Unfortunately, Google was cooperative until it wasn't. They worked with Lenny to take down hundreds of offending videos, but for no discernible reason left others that were equally offensive. Communication tapered off, and we got the feeling that once Google got its hand slapped, it would make a show of working with us up until the spotlight drifted away. Our suspicions proved fairly accurate.

Most people would never imagine that Google, a company that

once had an unofficial motto of "Don't be evil," could be guilty of such reprehensible conduct. I always assumed this garbage would turn up on the dark web, but on YouTube? It's truly stunning.

Google's behavior continues to be scrutinized by the press if not by Congress. What Google is doing to me and others in similar circumstances is quite simply monetizing death. Every time someone clicks on a video of Alison being murdered, Google and some unwitting advertiser make money. It's beyond the pale, and Google continues to sandbag us.

And, as we've seen in recent years, Google isn't the only platform that deserves scrutiny. Twitter has increasingly become another cesspool, and Facebook is awash in conspiracy theorists.

Referring to the issue of Holocaust deniers, Facebook founder and CEO Mark Zuckerberg said, "I'm Jewish, and there's a set of people who deny that the Holocaust happened. I find that deeply offensive. But at the end of the day, I don't believe that our platform should take that down because I think there are things that different people get wrong. I don't think that they're intentionally getting it wrong, but I think it's hard to impugn intent and to understand the intent."

What the hell is he thinking? What the hell does that even mean?

Like Victor Frankenstein, Zuckerberg has lost control of the monster he created. This is the world we find ourselves in: a social media landscape that we can't escape, controlled by humans that are every bit as soulless as the algorithms and artificial intelligences that exploit their hate and ignorance.

For all the attacks directed toward me, Chris Hurst gets the same, if not worse. Like me, he just considers it to be a lot of noise mixed with the occasional legitimate threat.

I never personally saw any death threats in the days and weeks immediately following Alison's murder, but I once asked Chris about it.

"Yeah, you had some," he said. "I did too, but the Henry County Sheriff's Department and the Roanoke police had our backs."

We're in good company. The Parkland kids, particularly David Hogg and Emma Gonzalez, are among favorite targets of the truthers, and the vitriol that has been directed toward them is unspeakable.

We lived in a world where Alex Jones duped millions of people and advanced insane conspiracy theories while Google, Facebook, and Twitter were complicit. But on August 5, 2018, things abruptly changed. Apple removed all Alex Jones content from its podcasts. Spotify followed. Then, in a startling reversal, Facebook removed his page and permanently banned him. The dominoes were falling, leaving only YouTube and Twitter. The next day, YouTube, Jones's biggest enabler, removed him. Even Twitter suspended him. The fact that big guys took him down was a sea change.

I wrote a thank-you email to the Google contacts I had. It was as nice as I could muster given our history:

Dear Google Team-

As you know, I've been unrestrained and unfiltered in my criticism of you. But I've always been one to give credit where credit is due. Thank you for taking down Alex Jones' channel.

I'm under no illusions that you did this for any altruistic or honorable reason. After Apple, Facebook, and Spotify kicked him to the curb, you would've been the sole outlier and pariah on social media. I'm sure someone up your food chain recognized this and made a business decision, nothing more. That's all that motivates you.

Nevertheless, thank you for removing the platform for a reprobate and danger to our democracy. It's a shame it took you this long to act. I will continue to monitor your cooperation with Lenny.

We have devolved from the days when we just wanted to share pictures of our vacations and kids and pets. Alex Jones may have been banned, but there is no shortage of cruelty available on the internet for anyone who wishes to see it. As of this writing, Google is still an enabler.

19

COMMON GROUND

The fact that Donald Trump could ascend to the presidency confirms that we live in a deeply divided country. His subsequent behavior and the behavior of his supporters underscores the notion that millions of American citizens are fact-averse, willing to believe whatever nonsense is fed to them by sociopaths like Trump and Alex Jones. I'm not sure there is any hope of bridging the gap with die-hard Trump supporters or the hardcore, gun-worshiping members of the NRA. We live in a country warped by fear and paranoia, a country of gun nuts, doomsday preppers, and flat-earthers, people entirely resistant to meaningful dialogue. When their unhinged base attacks the free press, it only underscores the fact that Trump and the NRA have to rely on support from followers oblivious to reality. There is no point in attempting to reason with these people. Ironically, the best answer to their deranged arguments may come from Proverbs 26:4: "Do not answer a fool according to his folly, or you yourself will be just like him."

That said, there are millions of gun owners who *can* be reached. I recently saw this post on my public Facebook Page:

> I left the NRA a long time ago. I believe in owning any type of firearm (other than full auto), but I also believe in waiting periods, background checks (real ones), safety training, and time on [the] range before being allowed to own. That process should take some time, and not overnight the way the NRA would like.

> Andy Parker thank you sir, I nearly had my head taken off by someone who was ill trained, and thought that gun safety training was for 'Wimps!' He was one of those types running around the mountains of Northern Arizona shooting everything in site [sic]. He shot a neighbor's cat with a compound bow as it walked on the fences just to show his son how to do it! He opened my eyes to the terror of plain ignorance, and he reveled in it! So, nearly winding up dead has a tendency to shape one's opinion, and change one's world view!

> So hang in there sir!

As I've preached since I began my advocacy, we can never stop crimes or murders from occurring, but we can make it harder for the bad guys to get guns. Maybe the best analogy is seat belts. They're not a guarantee your life will be saved in a horrific accident, but you stand a much better chance if you're wearing one.

I truly believe there is common ground between the gun violence prevention movement and responsible gun owners. It's simply a matter of applying common sense. Without going too deep into the weeds, here are a few examples of gun violence prevention measures that are embraced by many responsible gun owners:

- Implement mandatory background checks on every gun purchase or transfer. This one is easy. A national Quinnipiac University Poll in 2017 showed that 94 percent of Americans are in favor of this. To be most effective, it needs to be implemented on a federal level.

- Close online and gun-show ordering loopholes and prevent 3-D printed guns. Most states don't require background checks for firearms purchased at gun shows from private individuals; by federal law, only licensed dealers are required to perform background checks. Virtually anyone can go online or buy a gun at a flea market with little due diligence performed by the seller, yet the NRA is opposed to doing anything about it. What's more, Trump's State Department has now made it legal for an anarchist to sell blueprints for 3-D printed guns. When the Obama administration forced Libertarian activist Cody Wilson to stop selling blueprints for his 3-D printed guns on his website, Wilson sued. When the Trump administration came in, the Justice Department agreed to a settlement, which not only allowed him to keep selling his blueprints, but also paid his forty-thousand-dollar legal fees.

- End permitless concealed carry. A 2016 poll from Strategies 360 showed that 90 percent of Americans are opposed to permitless concealed carry. Even most gun owners aren't in favor of the idea.

- Hold concealed carry reciprocity to the highest standard. While this push lost momentum after Congressman Steve Scalise was shot, congressional Republicans had introduced concealed carry reciprocity bills, meaning that a concealed carry permit issued in one state would be valid in any state. But instead of using a state like New York or California that has a high bar for attaining a concealed carry permit, they want to use the lowest common denominator. In some states, you only have to fog a mirror to get a concealed carry permit. How would that play out in Times Square?

- Require firearms training for first-time buyers. That seems pretty simple, just like driver's ed.

- Prosecute gun owners whose firearm is accessed by a child who accidentally wounds or kills another person. This seems fairly obvious. Consider the mother of the Umpqua shooter, who knowingly gave her mentally disturbed son firearms. She should have been charged with accessory to murder.

- Institute no-fly, no buy. If you're on the FBI's Terrorist Screening Center's no-fly list, then you can't buy a gun. This is what Republican Senators Susan Collins and Pat Toomey, as part of a bipartisan group that also included Republican Senator Jeff Flake, tried and failed to get passed. Opponents claimed the bill was flawed because of the inaccuracies on the no-fly list, which meant a handful of undeserving people might be briefly inconvenienced. The failure to pass this legislation is one of the most galling failures by Congress I've ever seen. Meanwhile, ISIS tells its followers to go to America because it's easy to buy guns.

- Repeal the Protection of Lawful Commerce in Arms Act. Guns are the only product in this country immune from liability. Yes, we live in a litigious society, but giving gun manufacturers immunity thanks to this law is just plain wrong.

- Repeal the Firearm Owners Protection Act. This law eases some gun sale restrictions, and has also barred the government from creating a database of gun dealer records. A bellwether of the National Rifle Association's powerful influence that arose during the strongly progun Reagan administration, it also authorizes sales of guns between private owners.

- Loosen the Family Educational Rights and Privacy Act (FERPA) and the Health Insurance Portability and Accountability Act (HIPAA). FERPA and HIPAA are designed to protect privacy; FERPA applies to educational records, while HIPAA applies to medical records. This one is obviously a slippery slope, since no one wants a situation where someone who made a mistake as a child or has a medical problem is denied a job. However, there is room to loosen regulations without harming an individual's right to privacy. FERPA laws must be relaxed so that employers can talk to one another about potential hires, to prevent the hiring of ticking time bombs like Alison's killer. HIPAA must be changed to allow doctors to warn law enforcement and mental health providers of potentially dangerous individuals so they can intervene before a tragedy occurs. These regulations should be loosened only to address individuals who present a real, credible threat to others. Astonishingly, Goodlatte at one time had a bill addressing FERPA in Congress, but it predictably died.

- Limit ammunition sales to individuals and require safe storage. There are gun owners who have literally hundreds of thousands of rounds stored in their homes. If a house fire were to occur, the entire neighborhood would be in jeopardy.

- Ban the sale of assault-style weapons—with one exception. Over and over again, we have seen that the AR15 is the mass shooter's weapon of choice. It is worlds away from a simple hunting rifle. Fans of the AR15 say it's fun to shoot. I'm sure it is. I wouldn't mind shooting one myself. Hell, for that matter, I'd like to fire a .50 caliber machine gun. Why not have them both available to check out at the gun range, so long as they don't leave the premises? They have no business on the streets.

- Limit magazines to ten rounds. This would at least slow down shooters using the thirty-round magazines legally allowed in most states.

- Implement Extreme Risk Protection Orders. These are in place and working in California and making their way across the country. These orders especially picked up steam after Parkland. I firmly believe this same legislation—for which Barbara and I testified in 2018, and which was rejected along party lines— will be passed. I believe that of all the measures I've outlined, this one has the best chance of becoming a law nationwide.

These are measures that most normal people and most responsible gun owners find reasonable. Other than the assault weapons ban, these measures don't take away a single gun from any law-abiding citizen. In a perfect world, I would also love to see the following measures taken:

- Institute a gun buyback program like Australia has. Australia implemented a gun buyback program after a particularly grievous mass shooting. In the years since, gun violence has plummeted and no similar attack has occurred.

- Outlaw open carry, which is allowed in forty-five states. The only people we should see carrying guns are law enforcement officers. If you go to a restaurant, a grocery store, or a movie theater and you see someone with a gun hanging off their hip, if they're not wearing a badge, you have absolutely no way of knowing whether they're a die-hard Second Amendment supporter "exercising their rights" or an unhinged lunatic about to make the national news.

- Dismantle the NRA as a lobbying organization. Enact laws that forbid the NRA from accepting money from gun manufacturers and force the organization to return to its original mission of promoting gun safety, a worthy cause it has turned its back on.

I've often thought that the NRA might implode from within, that responsible gun owners would get so fed up with the organization's cravenness that they would stage a coup. I've since learned from those who were once on the inside that an internal revolt would be about as successful as the plot against Hitler. I've been told that Wayne LaPierre rules the organization with terror and intimidation tactics. His enforcers worship at the church of the NRA.

That leaves responsible gun owners forced to brave intimidation and threats. Again I liken it to Hitler's Germany, where many members of the population recognized a problem but felt powerless to do anything about it. A group of gun owners, however small, are going to have to be the first to speak out. With any luck, it would embolden many more.

Unfortunately, the notion of implosion is a pipe dream. If anything, the immediate threat to the NRA structure comes not from reasonable gun owners, but from the most unreasonable. The threat comes from people like Adam Kraut, a gun rights lawyer, who narrowly lost a bid for a seat on the NRA's board of directors. Following his loss, Kraut told Reuters, "Some members feel it [the NRA] doesn't go far enough to defend what we believe to be the core of the Second Amendment." I can't even imagine how the organization could go any further.

The Republican Party is now the NRA party. Democrats and those on the left must offer something to truly energize voters. The November 2018 "blue wave" that took back the House showed promise, but they need to do a better job of reaching out to those one-time Trump supporters who now feel buyer's remorse. Of course, there's little point in even attempting to reach out to the Trump-or-bust wing nuts. Their minds will never be changed.

As the NRA continues to hone their message, I often think back to what Governor Terry McAuliffe told me: The only way we're going to get anything done on the gun issue is to get the NRA politicians out of office. The only way to do that is to undo the gerrymandered districts that have given Republicans artificial majorities in state houses across the country. Giffords, Brady, and Everytown have been stuck playing defense for too long. It's important to have people show up at town halls and marches on Washington, but the only way we're going to really change the equation is to vote and redistrict.

I've been saying it for a long time, and now the message has been taken up and amplified by the Parkland kids. Scorning, ridiculing, and voting out the NRA Republicans is the only path forward if we want to feel safe in public again.

20

CHRIS AND THE BLUE WAVE

Just days after Alison was murdered, Chris Hurst and I were walking across the WDBJ parking lot following a late-night interview for *Good Morning Britain* when he told me that he knew his path going forward: He was going to run for office.

Chris made good on that promise.

Already minor celebrities in Southern Virginia, Chris and Alison had become household names throughout the state. Alison's story received even wider coverage beginning in mid-February of 2017 when Chris announced he was resigning as the evening anchor at WDBJ to seek a seat in the Virginia House of Delegates. The announcement received coverage from every major news outlet in the United States, and a heavy chunk of the minor ones. It even made the rounds internationally.

When Chris told me he was going to run for office on that bleary, exhausting night in 2015, I immediately knew he was going to follow through, but it was too early to know the when, where, for what, and how of it. Chris knew he would be walking away from a great job and the adoration of viewers across the New River Valley and walking toward no income and less admiration once he put a "D" in front of his name.

Chris stayed at WDBJ for a year and half after Alison's murder. He had to walk by her desk every day and do the lead-ins for the inevitable stories of lives lost to gun violence in Roanoke. He handled it much better than I could have, but we knew it was taking its toll. Additionally, the station's sale to Gray Television was announced less than three months after Alison's murder. WDBJ went from being a privately owned, family-run company to a corporation, and as inevitably happens, the culture immediately changed. Cost cutting was immediate. Reporters who used to have a cameraman accompany them in the field soon became "one-man bands." Unlike many of the people who were laid off, including many camera operators, Chris wasn't affected since he was under contract. However, the high morale and esprit de corps that once existed at the station faded quickly. Even though he knew that he wouldn't be at WDBJ much longer, it was difficult for him.

In early spring of 2016, I connected Chris to a political consultant I'd met through the Giffords organization. She knew the lay of the land, and I was hoping that Chris would run against Bob Goodlatte that year.

The consultant's take was that if all the planets aligned, he just might pull it off. There was little question he would raise a lot of money for the campaign based on his exposure, his character, and his message, but if the votes weren't there it wouldn't matter. We were particularly concerned because initial numbers estimated that 60 percent of constituents were likely to favor a Republican candidate.

"Chris, if you are able to only lose by 52 percent to 48 percent, you'd be a hero in the Democratic party," she told him.

"Yeah," he said. "That's great, but a loss is a loss. And I want to win."

I couldn't disagree.

Like any good investigative journalist, Chris did his homework. He knew he wouldn't stand a chance against Goodlatte, so he decided the best option was to run for the Virginia House of Delegates, representing a district within the WDBJ viewing area.

By the end of 2016, Chris had his game plan in place. He saved every dime he could and decided to move to Blacksburg, Virginia, about an hour west of Roanoke, for a desperately needed change of scenery. Somehow he had continued to live in the apartment that he and Alison had moved into a month before she was killed. I don't know how he managed to stay there as long as he did, but I know it was extremely difficult for him.

Moving to Blacksburg put him out of Roanoke, but he wasn't going to leave the New River Valley and the people who had given him so much emotional support. He had briefly considered moving to Los Angeles to work with friends in the film industry, but he set that idea aside. Chris grew up in Philadelphia, but the New River Valley had become his home, and he wanted to stay close to it.

Chris set his sights on winning the 12th district, running against a three-term Republican incumbent, Joseph Yost, the same amiable young man we'd met at the Tech-JMU State game. Because he had a professional relationship with Yost, Chris told me, "I'm going to tell him face to face that I'm running against him. He might just drop out. He's got a young child, and I've heard his wife really wants him to be home instead of in Richmond."

"I wouldn't plan on it, Chris," I said. "His heart may not be in it, but I'll bet you the party tells him, 'Don't worry, Joseph. You don't have to do anything. We'll buy the seat for you.' And they're going to call you a carpetbagger right out of the gate."

And that's exactly what happened. Yost, who had never campaigned much in the past, sat back and let the party do the work for him. They threw a metric ton of money at him, and they likely crafted his campaign slogan: "Joseph Yost: From Here. For Us."

The district knew Chris from television, but they probably didn't expect to see him show up at their doorstep, and that's exactly what he did. From the time he announced in February until the November election, Chris knocked on ten thousand doors. Some of those doors were in Giles County, Yost's backyard, where he'd grown up. Even people who said they couldn't vote for Chris were impressed by his effort and his charm.

And man, can he charm. Barbara and I attended many events for him and hosted his first fundraiser at our home. We live far outside his district, but close to fifty people attended. I think Chris cleared three thousand dollars in campaign donations that night, which we thought was a great start. Chris's eloquence and ability to work a crowd and fire up an audience is something to see. Most people in politics can't even come close to matching it. A journalist from Philadelphia, Chris's hometown, trailed him for several days to write a story. As Chris addressed a group of Radford University student volunteers, I whispered to the journalist, "He was born to do this."

His connection with students at Radford and Virginia Tech was particularly striking. While Yost probably reminded them of their study hall teacher in high school, Chris was like the cool older brother they wanted to emulate. They flocked to him, and Chris, his campaign staff, and his volunteers managed to get thousands of students registered to vote. It was such a huge number that the Montgomery County registrar initially thought a mistake had been made.

Chris also demonstrated the ability to raise funds, an area where a lot of candidates get squeamish. They'll knock on doors and make appearances, but smiling and dialing takes work and a thick skin. It doesn't come naturally to most people, but unfortunately, in order to be a successful politician, it's a must. By the time all was said and done, Chris raised close to one million dollars, and he did it without taking a dime from big PACs. By contrast, Yost received close to 90 percent of his one million dollars from the Republican party and big PACs—including, of course, the NRA. It ended up being the second most expensive House race in the history of the Commonwealth of Virginia.

Barbara and I attended several fundraisers for Chris and we knocked on a few doors ourselves. One time, we met Chris in front of a pet shop on Main Street in Radford to get our marching orders. We were going over the walk list when some guy with a Trump bumper sticker on his pickup drove by and yelled, "This is Yost country!" He then made a U-turn, came back, and yelled, "Go home, Chris!" followed by an unintelligible expletive. We just shook our heads and laughed. Chris took it all in stride.

The weekend before the election, Barbara and I spent some time phone banking for Chris from his campaign office. He had been so thorough that most of the people we spoke with had already been contacted by him. In a few cases, people said, "Damn, I'm gonna vote for the guy, but just leave me alone already." That's covering your bases.

The last day that we were phone banking, I was impressed by all the young people who were sitting on every spare inch of the floor, putting together literature for the eleventh hour "Get Out the Vote" effort that would take place the following day. As we were leaving, I thanked them for their hard work.

"When Chris wins on Tuesday," I said, "it'll be because of you."

A couple of weeks before the election, Chris had confided in me that his polling showed he was up by four points.

"I hope you're using a different group than I had when I ran," I told him. "They told me I was within the margin of error to win, and you know how that turned out. I got my butt kicked. I hope they're right, but I just don't trust them. Look at what happened to Hillary."

"No, these guys are some of the best," Chris said. "They're pretty reliable." All we could do was hope.

Finally, the day arrived. For Chris, it was the culmination of incredibly hard work and relentless effort. For me, it felt like waiting for the outcome of an audition. It's down to you and the other guy for a role on Broadway. It's going to be elation or despair, nothing in between. It was a feeling I hadn't had in a long time. It wasn't my audition, but Chris had become my second son, and it sure felt like it.

At 7 p.m. on Tuesday, November 7, 2017, Barbara and I were in the ballroom at the Blacksburg Hyatt for the victory party. There were about a hundred people, and a palpable sense of anxious enthusiasm permeated the air as we awaited the results. The polls had just closed and there was no sign of Chris, but that didn't seem unusual. We figured that he was out canvassing until the polls closed—he was.

Around 7:45, I was chatting with some of the local television reporters who were setting up to film Chris when he arrived. I was still wondering where he was, and then my phone buzzed.

"Come to the Marriott," Chris said.

"What are you doing over there? I thought everything was taking place here."

"We're in the war room," he said. "They'll show you where it is when you get here."

I grabbed Barbara and we made the ten-minute drive to the Marriott. I didn't know why the war room had to be at a different hotel, but I supposed that was protocol.

We walked into a conference room. At a long table on one side of the room, Andrew Whitley, Chris's campaign manager, stared intently at his laptop, his phone at the ready. He was flanked by two other staffers doing the same. On the other side of the room, real-time results were being projected onto the wall, surrounded by white flip charts representing each precinct. Chris's parents, Harry and Marsha Hurst, were also there, along with other key backers. It was his brain trust and his family.

Chris spotted me and gave me a big hug. "I wanted you to be here when we got the results," he said.

The results started coming in, first a trickle, then a flood. Andrew jumped from his seat. "Yes!" he shouted, "We took Radford!" They viewed the city of Radford as a barometer for how Chris was going to fare. He took Radford by nearly 60 percent. Other results started coming in with nearly identical ratios.

One staffer who was following the other House races yelled, "Danica won!" Danica Roem made history as the first openly transgender person in state legislature anywhere in the country, beating a thirteen-term, self-proclaimed homophobe who had refused to refer to her as a woman during the campaign.

As the minutes ticked by, other races were being called for Democrats. What started as a modest expectation to pick up a half dozen seats became a rout. Candidates who had been given long shot odds had won.

At one point, Chris had 66 percent of the vote, but Yost's home, Giles County, still hadn't reported. Andrew was confidant, but I told him, "I remember being in the same frame of mind with the Gecker race. He was comfortably up until the Chesterfield County result came in, and it did him in."

"It won't happen here," Andrew said. "There's no way Yost can make up this much ground."

OK, I thought. *That's why you're the campaign manager.*

Even though we felt we were right on the cusp, the wait for Giles County was excruciating, as if someone were saying, "Yeah, we know you're gonna win, but we're just going to screw with you as long as we can to keep you in suspense."

And then the results flashed on the wall. Andrew hoped Chris would get 30 percent of Giles County and Chris only got 27 percent—but it didn't matter. Chris had 54.3 percent of the total vote. It was a decisive victory.

Every campaign at this level includes opposition research, not only what you have on your opponent, but what your opponent could potentially have on you. Chris told me early on that the local operatives were worried that I could be a negative factor in his campaign. They had a couple of pages devoted just to me. I felt a bit wounded, but given my visibility (and, shall we say, candor), I understood.

"Chris, I'll do as much or as little as you want me to do," I said.

"I told these guys you could say whatever the hell you want," he replied.

After Chris embraced his parents, he gave Barbara and me a hug. With tears of joy streaming down my cheeks, I said, "Well, I guess I wasn't such a drag on the campaign after all."

"Yeah, but had you not participated, I'd have won by a much bigger margin," Chris said with a grin.

"Oh, go fuck yourself," I said with a laugh. "I'm so proud of you. And you know Alison is, too."

That's a pretty typical example of our repartee.

The gun issue was number two in importance to voters in the Virginia election, yet Chris never emphasized it. People knew where he stood, and he didn't want to be a one-issue candidate. The *Roanoke Times* asked me what I thought about that. I told them that Chris didn't have to beat that particular drum. It was more important for him to talk about other issues they cared about, not just guns. He didn't need to overstate the obvious.

During his time in office so far, Chris has distinguished himself with his hard work, selflessness, and leadership. He has gained the respect of his colleagues, even those across the aisle. One day, as we were driving up to the kayak launch at Kibler Valley to do a run, Chris was ruminating on the future.

"People ask me all the time, 'What's next? Are you going to run for governor? Congress?' I've just decided to tell them I'm going to run for president."

"Well," I told him, "that's what I've been telling people for a long time. Except I tell them you *will* be president one day."

If he chooses to run, there isn't a doubt in my mind that he'll come out on top.

21

ALISON'S LEGACY

There are some who bring a light so great to the world that even
after they have gone, the light remains. —Unknown

Sixty thousand people woke up to Alison's smile each morning as they drank their coffee and started their day. She'd been in their homes, and when she died, many felt like they had lost a family member.

In the days and weeks following Alison's death, we received thousands of cards, letters, emails, and packages. A man in Texas spent hours upon hours fashioning a huge piece of oak into a rough-hewn cross with Alison's name etched into it, and then spent fifty dollars shipping it to Virginia. We received so many letters that it took us months to respond to them all. WDBJ had reams of printed emails.

Amy Whitaker, a former middle school teacher from our area, posted a message on my Facebook page that provided a real "wow" moment:

> What a gift to the world Alison is. When Tracy and I used to watch her
> as we drank our coffee in the morning, we often discussed that we knew
> she was going to make it big. No way she couldn't—the glow around

her, her professionalism, the way she made you feel like you'd known her forever, and the laughter just assured it. At the time, we thought that Alison would make it big in the news industry as the anchor for a major news organization. But look at her changing the world instead of reporting on it. Alison is changing the world by changing hearts, and there is no greater gift than that. Thank you doesn't even begin to cover it, Chris Hurst. And Andy Parker and Barbara Parker, thank you for gifting the world with Alison. May the inspiration and happiness Alison continues to bring the world be some balm for your unimaginable loss. Glow on, Alison, and while I would give anything to have you here reporting the news for a major news outlet, somehow it never seemed quite big enough for you.

Dylan Garner was one of Alison's journalism classmates at JMU. She encouraged him to join JMU's newspaper, the *Breeze,* and he has since gone on to work for the *Richmond Times-Dispatch*, where he wrote of his friendship with Alison. She was a mentor to him, he said, someone wise beyond her years who always offered him guidance even after she graduated.

She had been my true entry into this profession, and it always seemed like she had the right thing to say," Dylan wrote. "This was certainly the case when I had reached my breaking point as a member of the Breeze, and she spoke to me on the phone for upward of 20 minutes. I felt lost and misunderstood. She added clarity in that moment, and many others. . . . I owe Alison Parker so much that I can't describe it. I wish I could tell her that face to face. I simply would not be in the position I am today—much less sharing this story—without learning from the most driven, passionate person I've ever met.

But there was one letter, from a woman in Georgia named Rachel Franco, that particularly touched me. Rachel said that when she saw me being interviewed by Chris Cuomo on CNN's *New Day*, it broke her heart. She felt my pain, she said, not because she is a parent, but because in me, she saw her own father.

> I know you loved (and love) Alison as much as my dad loves me—more than life itself. And I can tell you, it's mutual. I love my dad more than life itself—and I know Alison loved you like this also. Trust me, daughters who have great dads just know this about each other. So, while I don't know Alison or you personally, please know how much I empathize with your loss.

My fight to end gun violence is far from over, and Alison's legacy is so much more than the way she died. It is the lasting recognition and eternal inspiration fueled by her spirit. Earlier I wrote about Alison and her cameraman Adam Ward receiving the Ted Yates Award. Since then, she has received many more tributes and awards, honors that serve to cement her legacy.

DePaul Community Resources in Roanoke created the "Alison Parker Young Professional Award," as one of their Women of Achievement Awards given at their yearly banquet.

WDBJ named their main studio "Studio A" in recognition of Alison and Adam.

The Salem Red Sox, a minor league baseball team in Virginia, named their press box for Alison and Adam.

Two songs were written for Alison, and two renowned watercolor artists have presented us with beautiful portraits of her.

The historic Grandin Theatre, a splendid old movie house in Roanoke, put a star with Alison and Adam's names on the sidewalk in front of their box office.

James Madison University honored Alison by dedicating their television studio to her. During the dedication, Dr. Marilou Johnson, who taught Alison, remembered her in a way that made us very proud.

> The media business is tough, and we can learn a valuable lesson from Alison in the manner in which she conducted herself personally. Her drive to achieve was never at the expense of others. She was probably the most unselfish student in class that year. She was a cheerleader for anyone sitting in the anchor seat or doing a live shot because she recognized that our success as a team meant we had to rely on each other.

One of the coolest tributes was made by a well-known Los Angeles street artist named "Teachr." Known for his stenciled portraits on traffic light cabinets around Hollywood, he has a following of art lovers and mainstream fans alike. His mantra "Teach Peace" usually accompanies his famous portraits. Sometimes his work stays up for weeks, sometimes just days. Teachr took the iconic picture of Alison in her red dress at the anchor desk and rendered that image in Los Angeles. His artwork stayed up for weeks, and as of this writing, a piece of art that he made on a box near city hall is still there. Barbara's sister Bailey is a friend of his, and Teachr gave her several copies on paper to send to us. One hangs in my office, one belongs to a close friend of Alison's, and one hangs in the Alison B. Parker Studio at JMU.

The scholarship that Barbara and I established in Alison's memory at the School of Media Arts and Design (SMAD) at JMU is the fastest-endowed scholarship in the history of the school. Each year, a merit scholarship is given to a rising senior SMAD major with an outstanding record in journalism who follows Alison's example by working for the student newspaper, the TV station, or internships outside the classroom. In addition, a renewable scholarship will be awarded each fall to an incoming freshman who shares Alison's deep passion for journalism and her commitment to academic excellence.

In February 2016, Barbara came up with the idea to start a foundation. The goal is to offer unique opportunities to experience the arts for kids in the Martinsville, Henry County, and Roanoke areas, kids who normally wouldn't have access or exposure to the arts. Chris, Barbara, our good friend Lynn Ward, and I created the nonprofit For Alison Foundation with seed money from donations by the National Association of Broadcasters and the Virginia Association of Broadcasters. So far the foundation is run by volunteers and we haven't been able to underwrite any huge programs, but we have found creative ways to fund unique projects.

We gave scholarships to kids who couldn't afford the Roanoke Symphony Orchestra summer camp. Chris arranged for production equipment to be donated to some Martinsville High School kids who wanted to start a daily television program at their school. The sixth graders at Martinsville Middle School received a grant to see a professional performance of the stories of Edgar Allan Poe. For the past two years, we have helped sponsor the Grandin Theatre Film Lab after-school program in Roanoke.

My favorite thing we've done is take Henry County high school kids to the American Shakespeare Center's Blackfriars Playhouse in Staunton, Virginia. Barbara took Alison to see a performance there when she was in middle school, and Scooter was hooked from then on. In fact, she took Chris there on his birthday in 2015.

Before I ever saw a production there, I was afraid it might be torture, and I'm sure those kids thought that too. But once I watched the professional actors play and sing songs from the stage balcony, I knew this was going to be a different experience than the one I expected. Reading Shakespeare is part of most educational curricula, and some think it's torture. When you read, you don't see the nuance. You don't see the bawdy humor jumping from the page. Shakespeare's plays were meant to be performed, not read.

I accompanied one of the groups to the playhouse, and I got to watch as bored teenagers were transformed into engaged patrons of the arts. I had as much fun watching their reactions as I did watching the show.

The For Alison Foundation has received a lot of bang for its buck. It has already touched lives. In the first year, the Martinsville High School TV kids graduated and went on to work in local television or seek degrees in broadcast journalism. Their equipment is being used by the next generation of on-air talent. Kids who went to the Grandin Theatre Film Lab's after-school program have gone on to win special Emmy awards for two of their short films, *Burden* and *When the Lights Come on Again*. We're bringing the Grandin Theatre Film Lab to Martinsville as a two-week summer program for young people.

Many of the kids who received Roanoke Symphony Orchestra summer camp scholarships are continuing their music education, and who knows, they might perform professionally someday. And I suspect the kids who saw Shakespeare—for some, the first play they had ever seen—might want to see another play or musical, or better yet, be in one. Thanks to the generosity of people in Southern Virginia and across the country, the For Alison Foundation continues to look for ways to make a difference. Alison was lucky to be involved in the arts when she was growing up, and it made an indelible impact on her life.

The For Alison Foundation is completely separate from our advocacy. I know Alison would have liked to be remembered for the way she lived rather than the way she died, and I know she would be happy that she is still touching people in ways she never would have imagined.

Alison was the major contributor to a WDBJ documentary called *Childhood Lost*, about a little girl, Hope, who had bounced around the foster care system. They became close and Alison gained her trust, allowing her to open up. The story had a happy ending for Hope when she was finally adopted by a foster parent.

Chris made sure that Alison's work on *Childhood Lost* was recognized, as well as her work on *The Long Goodbye*, a documentary about hospice, on which she had been working when she was murdered. Chris finished the documentary and it was featured on the station as *Alison's Stories on Hospice*. Both documentaries were submitted for consideration for the Radio Television Digital News Association's Edward R. Murrow Awards.

After Alison completed post-production on *Childhood*, she told me, "Dad, I think this is going to be really special. They're [the news directors] even saying they're going to present it for an Emmy."

Of course, being the insanely proud dad I was, I posted about her potential "Emmy Award–winning work" on my Facebook wall. As soon as she saw it, she called me, furious.

"Dad, you can't put that out there!" she fumed. "It makes it look like I'm bragging, and I just can't have that."

She was right, and, dutifully chastised, I removed the post. I'd made a mistake, but she knew her biggest fan's heart was in the right place. She didn't win the Emmy for that one, but she won an Edward R. Murrow Award for both *Childhood Lost* and her work on *The Long Goodbye*.

I wasn't aware of just how prestigious the Murrow Award was until Chris schooled me.

"The Emmys are great, but for a journalist, the Murrow Award is like an Oscar," he explained. "And they don't give them out of sympathy. You have to deserve it."

Chris was having dinner at our house when he received the email saying that Alison had won two Murrow Awards, one for each documentary. I was bursting with pride, but it was a bittersweet moment. She should have been celebrating with us.

The Virginia Association of Broadcasters hosted a ceremony in

Virginia Beach on June 24, 2016. There was no suspense at that one. Alison was named a "Distinguished Virginian" and we were presented with an enormous plaque with four silver plates attached.

Of course, I thought it ironic that one of the past winners of this award was Bob Goodlatte. I know Alison would have rolled her eyes at that.

The day after accepting the Distinguished Virginian Award, we had to fight traffic from Virginia Beach to Baltimore, where the Capital Emmy Awards ceremony was taking place that evening. We made it to the hotel just in time to change into formal wear and race to the ballroom across the street.

We soon spotted Chris, and the three of us walked together into the huge ballroom. There must have been more than five hundred people in attendance, including the regional television station nominees and guests. This was a big deal. We found the WDBJ table, where Chris's coanchor, Jean Jadhon, was already seated, along with some of Alison's favorites: reporters Tim Saunders and Joe Dashiell and weatherman Brent Watts. Each of them was up for an award, and Tim was up for two.

The program started with a directive to the winners: everyone gets one minute to speak, and then the band will play you off. When I looked at the novella-length program, I could see why they limited speeches to a minute. There was an award for just about every conceivable category remotely connected to television news. It appeared this was going to be a long slog, but even though there were so many awards to go through, the process moved quickly. Giant screens flanking the podium showed short clips of the nominees. There was suspense for every nominee, but those in charge of the production knew the outcomes beforehand and made sure that the emcee quickly announced the winner. I wish all awards ceremonies were so efficient.

After the first few winners gave their thank-you speeches, it seemed like the only people paying attention were the folks seated at the winners' station table. They whooped and hollered, but there was only a polite smattering of applause from the rest of the audience. The acceptance speeches could barely be heard over the din of the conversations going on around us.

Our table's opportunity to hoot and holler came when Joe won an Emmy for a documentary piece he had made. Joe is a rare breed in TV news, a fifty-something bespectacled beat reporter with a dry sense of humor that Alison loved.

Tim was probably in his mid-thirties, with sharp features that made him resemble a younger version of the farmer from *American Gothic*. He was the one who pitched Alison to station management for the morning reporter job, and her death hit him particularly hard. He won the next Emmy. And then won another a little later. It was amazing, but he's one solid journalist. Two months before Alison was killed, she and Tim were vying for the weekend anchor position. Two years later, Tim got it, and he deserved it.

Up next was Brent, a handsome meteorologist with a shock of white in the middle of a full head of black hair. Even though she rarely worked with him, Alison considered him a friend, too. Brent also picked up an Emmy for his work.

Jean was waiting her turn. Jean is a fixture at WDBJ; she looks great on camera, and Alison and I used to share an admiring laugh about the way she can flirt with an audience. Jean has been waiting for an Emmy for years, but like Susan Lucci from *All My Children,* she was often nominated, but went home empty-handed. This year, unfortunately, was no exception, but she remained cheerful and never showed a hint of disappointment. One day, just like Susan Lucci, she's going to pick up that statue.

Finally, Alison's nomination for Outstanding Live Reporter was on the big screens, and the din in the room instantly dropped a notch.

Alison had stiff competition from reporters in Baltimore and DC. We held our breath as the emcee announced a tie for the award. There had been several cowinners during the course of the evening, and up to that point every cowinner had been announced in the order they appeared in the program. Alison's was the first name listed.

When the emcee announced the name of the reporter from Baltimore, who was farther down the list, our hearts sank.

"Hey, at least she was nominated," Barbara said to me.

"Yeah," I said. "Damn." The Baltimore table cheered and the reporter gave her acceptance speech as the audience resumed their idle chatter, mostly oblivious to her remarks.

She left the podium and we sat there dejected, patiently awaiting the name of the next reporter on the list. The emcee stepped up to the mike.

"And the second winner for Outstanding Live Reporter is Alison Parker."

She did it. They broke protocol just to make it special.

Everyone at our table jumped up and embraced and then Chris, Barbara, and I made our way to the stage.

Then something wonderful happened. The evening-long chatter stopped cold, and then everyone in the room rose to their feet in a standing ovation, cheering wildly.

When we got to the podium, there was total silence. Chris offered a few eloquent remarks, and as the band began to play, I leaned over to the mike.

"I'm going to keep fighting for you, Scooter," I said.

It was an incredible moment, if a poignant one. Alison had triumphed, but she wasn't there to experience the joy of her accomplishment, to see my uncontainable pride.

Yet somehow her soul was there with us, and I know she could feel the outpouring of love from every person in the packed ballroom.

There is one more honor that certainly deserves mention. Hope, the young lady from *Childhood Lost*, is now in middle school, and she wants to follow in Alison's footsteps and become a journalist. Alison continues to inspire and change lives.

Every day is a struggle; it just varies by degree. What keeps me going is the fight to set things right. It's the strangers on the street or the grocery store cashiers who tell me to keep on fighting, because they're right there with me. It's receiving a personal note from President Barack Obama, who wrote us three days before leaving the White House to commend us on our courage. It's the little winks from Alison that let me know we're still connected and always will be.

EPILOGUE

I have a recurring daydream. I imagine that I'm sitting at the kitchen island and Scooter comes bounding through the kitchen door as though nothing ever happened. She's wearing her favorite running shorts and sneakers, and her Nantahala Outdoor Center cap, her hair in a ponytail. Jack jumps up to greet her, and she calls out "Doggggggg!" in her high-pitched "dog voice." She plops her big silver catchall bag on the counter, then comes over and gives me a big hug. It's a vision I have frequently. It brings me a brief moment of joy before I return to reality.

I rarely dream of Alison, but when I do, it is beyond painful. In the dream, she is back with us, but we all know that she doesn't have long to live. We hold each other and cry. It is a cruel and devastating dream, but even so, I still want her to visit me in my dreams. It lets me know we're still connected.

Chris told me that the night before Alison was killed, they had a conversation about death, related to the hospice story she was working on at the time. She told Chris that if she was ever in that state, she would want him to pull the plug, move on, and be happy.

Easier said than done.

A while back, I told Chris that one day he's going to meet someone special. He's going to fall in love again. There is nothing wrong with that, no betrayal in that, because Alison will always remain a part of his life.

It was incredibly hard to say those words because in the brief time they were together, I could see the profound love they shared.

"Yeah, I know," Chris said. "But whoever it is better be pretty damn special. She set a high bar, and she'd be pissed if I ended up with a girl that didn't meet her standards."

Barbara, Chris, and I are aware that when Alison died, something essential inside us died too. For me, life now is like being in the process of drowning, treading water just enough to pop up for a quick breath of air before going back under. Time has not healed us, but it has allowed us to snatch bigger breaths of air. Mike Bell told us that Alison would want us to live, and I know that's true, but we live in a new reality where joy is rare and fleeting.

I've been a Type 1 diabetic for more than thirty years. Dealing with Alison's loss is like managing diabetes. It's chronic and malingering. At least once each day, no matter what you do, you feel the vitality-sapping effect. I can mitigate the melancholy, but it's never going to go away. It is like an incurable disease, and the best I can do is physically and emotionally survive another day.

Andrea McCarren's question still haunts me: "How does the coolest dad in the world lose the coolest daughter?" That's the way I remember it being asked, but maybe what she meant to say was, "How does the coolest dad cope with losing the coolest daughter?"

The only way I can begin to cope is knowing that Barbara (the coolest mom in the world) and I guided her so she could become the exceptional person she was. We raised her older brother, Drew, in the same way. In their own ways, they were and are successful by any measure.

We took Alison and Drew everywhere with us, and we exposed them to art, theater, travel, and adventure. We were a tight-knit family that enjoyed being together.

Alison's luminescence was obvious in both her professional and personal life. She was competitive but compassionate, and she had all the tools to become a superstar. Everything came naturally for her.

Drew was diagnosed with Asperger's syndrome when he was almost four years old. He had to contend with the occasional bullies in school, and he didn't have close friends. Barbara and I pushed him to succeed without being overbearing, and we always tried to strike the right balance of being either cajoling or demanding when the situation called for it. We did it with love and respect, and we made sure that he had opportunities to prove himself to others.

After Drew's high school graduation, he went on to earn a degree at East Tennessee State University. When he can take time away from his job, he loves to travel by train to Washington, DC, spend time in the funky little city of Asheville, North Carolina, or go visit family across the country. As of this writing, he's saving his money for a trip to Japan.

Drew never resented the fact that things came so easily for Alison, and he was proud of everything she accomplished. She was equally proud of him, especially when she grew older and fully understood how much he had struggled to accomplish goals that she took for granted.

Some people choose not to make the same mistakes that their parents did and instead make creative new mistakes, like becoming "helicopter moms," or attempting to be their kid's best friend. Barbara and I both had the *Mad Men*-era childhood, with parents who seemed to care as much about appearance as they cared for us, so Barbara and I tried to be parents first, with rules and expectations. Thankfully, Drew and Alison respected those rules. Maybe we just got lucky, but I like to think that our parenting skills and engagement had something to do with the outcome

There is a wonderful, possibly apocryphal credo, often attributed to Hunter S. Thompson, that I have always tried to follow: "Life should not be a journey to the grave with the intention of arriving safely in a pretty and well-preserved body, but rather to skid in broadside in a cloud of smoke, thoroughly used up, totally worn out, and loudly proclaiming, 'Wow! What a Ride!"

Barbara and I tried to instill that same credo in Drew and Alison, and in their own ways, they adopted it. They were always curious and never shied away from an adventure. It's what made them who they were and are.

The simplified version of this credo is to live each day like it's your last on earth. Alison certainly did, and in Drew's own unique way, he is doing the same.

My "wild ride" continues, although the path is different from the one I would have chosen. It is steeped in melancholy. There's no avoiding it, and it will be a part of the ride until the ride one day stops.

Barbara and I can take some solace in knowing that with Alison, there are no regrets. We do not think to ourselves, *If only I'd said this or done that*. We talked to Alison every day. We shared setbacks and triumphs. And in the end, she and Drew were and are living their best possible lives.

What few laments I have are selfish. I'll never see Alison on the anchor desk at *CBS Evening News*. I'll never see her happily married. I'll never see her children. Yet even though I won't see these things come to pass, I know she lived a life far richer than many who live to a ripe old age. We will always remember her as young, beautiful, and in love with a life that was exactly how she wanted it to be. In the last moment of her life, I have to think she knew that.

I'm in this fight for the long run. It may take a while, but I'm going to outlast the people who allow guns to flood the market, who have the blood of innocents on their hands. I said I'd do whatever it takes, and I wake up every day with that mission.

I think back to the question the ABC journalist asked me in front of the Beacon Theatre in New York: "Why do you do this?" It was the first time I'd heard that question. My instinctive response was to tell her it has to stop because the next victim could be you, or a family member, or someone close to you.

If I could shoulder the load and stop it by myself, I would do it in a heartbeat. But I can't. I need help. The people already in the fight need help, voices, and action from those who are still on the sidelines saying, "It could never happen to me."

It absolutely could.

Telemachus "Tel" Orfanos, who survived the Las Vegas mass shooting, might have thought the odds of being caught in another mass shooting were slim to none. He was killed one year later at the Borderline Bar and Grill mass shooting in Thousand Oaks, California. That's how insane, how absurd this problem is.

For those of you reading this book who are still on the sidelines, it's time to get in the game. Join a Moms or a Brady chapter. Make your voices heard and your votes count, just like in November 2018. We all deserve to live in a country without fear of gun violence. Fight with me.

Until we end this scourge, your life and the lives of your loved ones depend on it.

When I met with the Parkland kids before their town hall meeting in Blacksburg on August 2, 2018, *VICE* was following them for a documentary. At one point the journalist turned to me and asked, "What does it take to keep going?"

In that moment, my answer was "hope." I think it was the right answer. The "Blue Wave" in the 2018 midterms provided another dose of hope, and I believe hope goes hand in hand with action.

I have also been asked, countless times, if I think I'm making a difference. If I have inspired others through my action, then the answer is "yes." That is enough to move the needle.

In October 2018, Barbara, Chris, and I attended a reception following the release of a documentary called *Virginia 12*, which chronicled Chris's campaign victory. As we ate our fried chicken, Chris pointed out the surreal circumstances we had found ourselves in.

"You know," he said, "the three of us have done some of the hardest things anyone can do. Barbara started a foundation, I ran for elected office and won, and you wrote a book."

"Yeah, I guess so," I said. "I think she'd be proud of us."

That's the hope I cling to, and it's why I will never stop trying to honor Alison through action. It's why I still talk to her every day. And because love is eternal, in her own mysterious way, she talks back:

"Yeah, Dad you're still pretty cool. I'm proud of you. Keep paddling with me."

ACKNOWLEDGMENTS

I have several people to thank for making this book a reality. A giant salute goes to Ben R. Williams. He gave me the roadmap, I drove, and he made my story much richer thanks to his immeasurable talent. As John Adams said of Thomas Jefferson, Ben has a "happy talent for composition and singular felicity of expression."

I never even considered this book a possibility, or even an aspiration, until best-selling author Beth Macy reached out and said, "Andy, I think you've got a book in you." Beth reached out only a couple of months after Alison's death, and while I was flattered, I dismissed the idea. I didn't think there was enough of a story. People knew what had happened, and that was it.

As the months went by, I realized I did have a story to tell about my journey. So thank you, Beth, for seeing it before I did. And for the same reason, thanks go to my publisher at Apollo, Julia Abramoff, who reached out to me two years before I started writing. When other publishers were afraid of the subject matter, she, along with my agent, Laurie Liss, believed this story needed to be told. There's a reason you don't see any books out there like this one.

To another best-selling author, Ellis Henican, thank you for patiently listening while I bitched about how long it takes to get a book published. You were right.

Thank you to Frank Tavares and Jay Kernis for doing a deep dive on the first manuscript. Thank you to Bill McCarren for being a great friend and making me feel like I legitimately belong to the National Press Club. Thanks also to every journalist who crossed my path and made me feel like part of the family; there are far too many of you to name each one.

I couldn't fight the Google fight without you, Lenny Pozner. You were willing to watch and report video cruelty that I absolutely couldn't. Thank you.

Thank you to Senator Tim Kaine for your moving foreword. I'm grateful to have two steadfast senators, Senator Kaine and Senator Mark Warner, I can call friends, as well as the best chief of staff on the hill, Mike Henry.

Thanks go to Lori Haas, who found me wandering in the media whirlwind and provided me the means to get down in the weeds on policy. She has been a great friend and gracious host, providing base camp when Barbara and I and/or Chris stay in Richmond.

Thank you, Drew Parker, a.k.a. "Buddy," for always being there and always taking care of the house and Jack while Mom and Dad were traveling.

Thank you to Chris Hurst for being an inspiration. I lost my daughter, but I gained a second son (who is never bashful about giving his "stepdad" shit when appropriate).

Finally, to my wife and life partner, Barbara, I know there would be no book were it not for you. You were the first to read and edit any of it, and you kept the narrative from sliding into the ditch. And thank you most of all for putting up with my bullshit for all these years. I don't say it enough: I love you.

Barbara and me in the anchor seats with Alison during her time as an intern at WDBJ.

Alison as a WDBJ anchor.

Alison and Chris on TV together at the St. Patrick's Day Parade.

One of our many paddling trips.

Alison and me after our hike to the top of the Mayan pyramid of Coba in Quintana Roo, Mexico.

Alison and Chris on his birthday.

The celebration of life held in Alison's honor.

The WDBJ memorial for Alison and Adam.

Barbara and me with Michael Bloomberg and John Feinblatt.

Barbara, Chris, and me with Anderson Cooper.

Barbara and me with Spike Lee.

Accepting the Emmy Award on Alison's behalf.

Barbara and me meeting President Barack Obama at the CNN town hall, Guns in America, on January 7, 2016.

The March for Our Lives event on March 24, 2018, in Washington, DC.

Protesting the NRA.

Speaking at the Whatever It Takes rally on Capitol Hill on September 10, 2015.